마이갓 5 Step 모의고사 공부!

1 ●**Vocabulary** 필수 단어 암기 & Test
① 단원별 필수 단어 암기 ② 영어 → 한글 Test ③ 한글 → 영어 Test

2 ●**Text** 지문과 해설
① 전체 지문 해석 ② 페이지별 필기 공간 확보 ③ N회독을 통한 지문 습득

3 ●**Practice 1** 빈칸 시험 (w/ 문법 힌트)
① 해석 없는 반복 빈칸 시험 ② 문법 힌트를 통한 어법 숙지
③ 주요 문법과 암기 내용 최종 확인

4 ●**Practice 2** 빈칸 시험 (w/ 해석)
① 주요 내용/어법/어휘 빈칸 ② 한글을 통한 내용 숙지
③ 반복 시험을 통한 빈칸 암기

5 ●**Quiz** 객관식 예상문제를 콕콕!
① 수능형 객관식 변형문제 ② 100% 자체 제작 변형문제 ③ 빈출 내신 문제 유형 연습

영어 내신의 끝
마이갓 모의고사 고1, 2

1 등급을 위한 5단계 노하우
2 모의고사 연도 및 시행월 별 완전정복
3 내신변형 완전정복

영어 내신의 끝
마이갓 교과서 고1, 2

1 등급을 위한 10단계 노하우
2 교과서 레슨별 완전정복
3 영어 영역 마스터를 위한 지름길

마이갓 교재
보듬책방 온라인 스토어 (https://smartstore.naver.com/bdbooks)

마이갓 10 Step 영어 내신 공부법

Vocabulary

필수 단어 암기 & Test
① 단원별 필수 단어 암기
② 영어 → 한글 Test
③ 한글 → 영어 Test

Grammar

단원별 중요 문법과 연습 문제
① 기초 문법 설명
② 교과서 적용 예시 소개
③ 기초/ Advanced Test

Text

지문과 해설
① 전체 지문 해석
② 페이지별 필기 공간 확보
③ N회독을 통한 지문 습득

Practice 3

빈칸 시험 (w/ 해석)
① 주요 내용/어법/어휘 빈칸
② 한글을 통한 내용 숙지
③ 반복 시험을 통한 빈칸 암기

Practice 2

빈칸 시험 (w/ 해석)
① 주요 내용/어법/어휘 빈칸
② 한글을 통한 내용 숙지
③ 반복 시험을 통한 빈칸 암기

Practice 1

어휘 & 어법 선택 시험
① 시험에 나오는 어법 어휘 공략
② 중요 어법/어휘 선택형 시험
③ 반복 시험을 통한 포인트 숙지

Quiz

객관식 예상문제를 콕콕!
① 수능형 객관식 변형문제
② 100% 자체 제작 변형문제
③ 빈출 내신 문제 유형 연습

Final Test

주관식 서술형 예상문제
① 어순/영작/어법 등
   주관식 서술형 문제 대비!
② 100% 자체 제작 변형문제

전체 영작 연습

직접 영작 해보기
① 주어진 단어를 활용한
   전체 서술형 영작 훈련
② 쓰기를 통한 내용 암기

학교 기출 문제

지문과 해설
① 단원별 실제 학교 기출
   문제 모음
② 객관식부터 서술형까지
   완벽 커버!

23년 고1
3월 모의고사

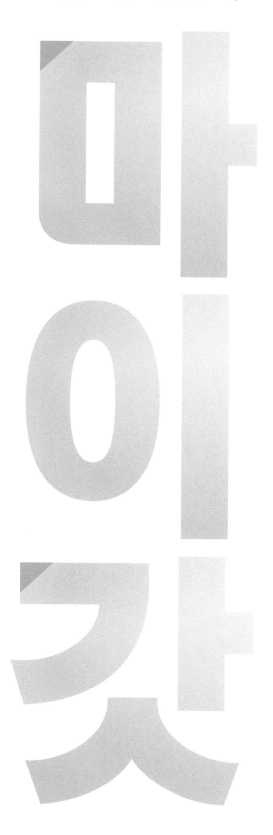

마이갓

연습과 실전 모두 잡는 내신대비 완벽
| workbook |

CONTENTS

2023 고1 3월 WORK BOOK

보듬영어

2023 고1

3
월
WORK BOOK

———

2023년 고1 3월 모의고사 내신대비용 WorkBook & 변형문제

Voca

❶ voca	❷ text	❸ [/]	❹ _____	❺ quiz 1	❻ quiz 2	❼ quiz 3	❽ quiz 4	❾ quiz 5

18	resident	거주자		every once in a while	이따금
	apartment	아파트		sniff	코를 킁킁거리다
	recently	최근에		deeply	깊게
	observe	알다, 목격하다		realize	깨닫다
	kid	아이, 어린이		giant	거대한
	repair	수리; 수리하다		freeze	얼어붙다, 등골이 오싹하다
	pay attention to	~에 주의를[관심을] 기울이다		no longer	더는 ~이 아닌
	condition	상태		wonderful	멋진
	playground	놀이터		experience	경험
	equipment	설비		issue	문제
	swing	그네		survival	생존
	damage	손상하다		motivation	동기
	fall off	떨어져 나가다		meat	고기
	slide	미끄럼틀		clearly	분명히
	facility	시설		menu	메뉴, 식단, 차림표
	terrible	형편없는	20	difficult	어려운
	move	이사하다		maintain	유지하다
	appreciate	감사하다		constant	일정한
	immediate	즉각적인		level	수준
	solve	해결하다		attention	주의 (집중)
	matter	문제		throughout	내내
19	trip	여행		rhythm	리듬
	grizzly bear	회색곰		characterise	특징짓다
	native	자연의, 태어난		peak	정점, 최고조
	habitat	서식지		valley	저점, 골짜기

Voca

| ❶ voca | ❷ text | ❸ [/] | ❹ ____ | ❺ quiz 1 | ❻ quiz 2 | ❼ quiz 3 | ❽ quiz 4 | ❾ quiz 5 |

	energy	에너지		disease	질환, 질병
	achieve	이루다, 성취하다		dangerous	위험한
	confident	자신감이 있는		mass	대중(의)
	benefit	이익, 혜택		education	교육
	schedule	(~을 하기로) 계획을 잡다		train	훈련시키다
	demanding	힘든, 부담이 큰		avoid	피하다
	task	작업, 과업		seek	찾다, 구하다
	cope with	~을 처리하다		divorce	단절, 이혼
	observe	관찰하다		stress	부담, 긴장
	note	알아차리다, 주의하다		indeed	실제로, 참으로
	take a while	얼마간의 시간이 걸리다		risk	위험 (요소)
	warm up	준비되다	22	approach	접근하다
21	adopt	받아들이다, 채택하다		course	과목, 과정
	technology	기술		task	과제, 과업
	cost	비용		rubber-stamp	고무도장
	livelihood	생계 수단		tuxedo	턱시도
	push aside	~을 밀쳐 놓다		colorful	화려한, 다채로운
	progress	발전, 전진		funeral	장례식
	lifestyle	생활 방식		bathing suit	수영복
	remove	없애다		religious	종교적인
	hate	싫어하다		service	예식
	produce	생산하다, 제작하다		probably	아마
	physical	육체의, 신체의		appropriate	적합한, 알맞은
	pain	고통, 통증		occasion	행사
	disability	장애		setting	상황, 장소

Voca

❶ voca	❷ text	❸ [/]	❹ ___	❺ quiz 1	❻ quiz 2	❼ quiz 3	❽ quiz 4	❾ quiz 5

	skillful	숙련된, 능숙한		lead	이끌다	
	flexible	유연한		intend	의도하다	
	strategy	전략		path	길	
	multiple-choice test	선다형 시험		comfortable	편안한	
23	social	사회의		be good at	~을 잘하다	
	economic	경제의		reward	보상을 주다; 보상	
	situation	상황		realize	깨닫다	
	wage	임금, 급료		deep	깊은	
	level	수준		breathe	호흡하다, 숨쉬다	
	condition	여건, 조건		slippery	미끄러운	
	improve	개선되다, 향상되다		superhuman	초인적인	
	gradually	점차		effort	노력	
	form	형태		effectively	사실상, 실제로	
	transport	운송, 수송		situation	상황	
	cheap	저렴한, 싼		employment	고용	
	industrial	산업의		secure	안정적인	
	revolution	혁명		ultimately	궁극적으로	
	railway	철도		unsatisfying	만족스럽지 못한	
	seaside	해안가, 바닷가	25	decrease	감소하다	
	resort	리조트, 휴양지		period	기간	
	coast-to-coast	대륙 횡단의		gap	차이	
	arrival	출현, 도래		slightly	약간	
	tourism	관광 산업		increase	증가하다	
	growth	성장, 발전		steadily	꾸준히	
24	success	성공		except	~을 제외하고	

Voca

| ❶ voca | ❷ text | ❸ [/] | ❹ ____ | ❺ quiz 1 | ❻ quiz 2 | ❼ quiz 3 | ❽ quiz 4 | ❾ quiz 5 |

	for the first time	처음으로, 최초로		reservation	예약
26	trousers	바지		accompany	동행하다
	adventurous	모험적인		lend	빌려주다
	career	경력		contact	연락하다
	wildlife	야생 동물		information	정보
	photographer	사진작가	29	noticeable	눈에 띄는
	design	설계하다		characteristic	특징, 특성
	airplane	비행기		project	투영하다
	persuade	설득하다		physically	신체적으로
	slightly	약간		cartoon	만화
	end up -ing	결국 ~하게 되다		character	캐릭터, 등장인물
	car dealer	자동차 판매원		resemble	닮다
	exciting	흥미진진한, 신나는		achieve	달성하다, 이루다
	nonetheless	그렇더라도		facial	얼굴의
27	article	기사		feature	특징, 특색
	publish	출간하다		front	앞의
	look for	~을 찾다		animated	만화 영화의
	writing	원고, 글		appropriate	적절한, 적당한
	include	포함하다		strategy	전략
	high-quality	고화질의		emotionally	감정적으로
	send	보내다		appealing	매력적인
28	chance	기회		enlarge	확대하다
	fee	요금		childlike	어린이 같은
	admission	입장	30	major	주요한, 중요한
	first-come, first-served	선착순의		philosophical	철학적인

Voca

| ❶ voca | ❷ text | ❸ [/] | ❹ _____ | ❺ quiz 1 | ❻ quiz 2 | ❼ quiz 3 | ❽ quiz 4 | ❾ quiz 5 |

	shift	변화		recovery	회복
	industrial	산업의		westward	서쪽으로
	competitive	경쟁적인		lengthen	연장하다
	geographically	지리적으로		eastward	동쪽으로
	spread out	~을 퍼뜨리다		shorten	단축하다
	relation	관계		sizable	큰
	buyer	구매자		impact	영향
	client	고객		performance	경기력, 성과
	realize	깨닫다		perform	행하다, 수행하다
	quality	양질의, 질 좋은		significantly	상당히
	reasonable	합리적인		professional	프로의, 전문적인
	equally	마찬가지로		recent	최근의
	essential	매우 중요한		additional	추가적인
	customer	고객		evidence	증거
	modernization	현대화		tough	힘든
	marketing	마케팅	32	confidence	자신감, 확신
	revolution	혁명		achieve	성취하다
	demand	수요		set out	~에 착수하다
	meet	충족시키다		over-optimism	지나친 낙관주의
	diverse	다양한		certain	특정한
	complex	복잡한		time frame	기간
31	differ	다르다		estimate	추산하다, 어림잡다
	reset	재설정하다		amount	양
	biological clock	체내 시계		alongside	~와 함께
	overcome	극복하다		item	항목

Voca

	task	과제, 과업		clothing	옷
	expect	기대하다		perfect	완성하다
	attention	주의		nail	못
	fit	맞추다		drive	(못·말뚝 등을) 박다
	available	이용 가능한		cloth	천, 직물
	significant	상당한		physical	물리적인
	there is no point -ing	~하는 것은 무의미하다		reality	실체
	period	시간, 기간		picture	그리다
33	race	경주, 달리기		product	제품
	countryside	시골		design	설계하다
	discover	발견하다		process	과정
	still	여전히		period	기간
	biologist	생물학자		vision	비전
	sometimes	때때로		decision	결정
	effect	효과, 영향, 결과		activity	활동
	evolutionary	진화의		in harmony	조화롭게, 한마음이 되어
	principle	원리		bring ~ into existence	~을 생겨나게 하다
	evolve	진화하다	35	affect	영향을 미치다
	generation	세대		main character	주인공
	bunny	토끼		focus	초점
	case	경우		character	등장인물
	pass on	~을 물려주다, ~을 전달하다		interpret	해석하다
	gene	유전자		conflict	갈등
	species	종		arise	발생하다
34	creator	만들어 낸 사람, 창조자		pray for	~을 간절히 바라다

Voca

	outcome	결과		community	공동체
	consider	생각해 보다		allow	~하게 하다, 허용하다
	tale	이야기		organize	조직하다
	shift	바꾸다		efficiently	효율적으로
	viewpoint	관점		produce	생산하다
	evil	사악한	37	natural	자연의
	stepsister	의붓자매		form	형성하다, 형성되다
	kingdom	왕국		mineral	광물
	exist	존재하다		melt	녹이다, 녹다
	willingly	기꺼이		material	물질
	viewpoint	관점		magma	마그마
36	Old Stone Age	구석기 시대		surface	표면
	band	무리		trap	가두다
	wander	(걸어서) 돌아다니다		atom	원자
	in search of	~을 찾아		heat energy	열에너지
	farming	농사		combine	결합하다
	settle down	정착하다		crystal	결정, 결정체
	farm	농경지		depend on	~에 달려있다
	grow	재배하다		partly	부분적으로
	crop	농작물		rapidly	빨리
	tool	도구		generally	일반적으로
	task	일		unaided eye	육안, 맨눈
	toolmaker	도구 제작자		arrange	배열하다
	share	함께 하다, 공유하다		orderly	질서있는
	ax	도끼		element	원소

Voca

| ❶ voca | ❷ text | ❸ [/] | ❹ ___ | ❺ quiz 1 | ❻ quiz 2 | ❼ quiz 3 | ❽ quiz 4 | ❾ quiz 5 |

	determine	결정하다		expectation	기대
	individual	개별의		affect	영향을 미치다
38	complex	복합의, 복잡한	40	trustworthy	신뢰할 수 있는
	break down	~을 분해하다, 분해되다		look for	~을 찾다
	nutrient	영양소		evidence	증거
	release	방출하다		evolutionary	진화의
	provide	제공하다		positive	긍정적인
	fuel	연료		prospect	전망
	a number of	많은		psychologist	심리학자
	structure	구조		product review	상품 평
	hold	가지고 있다		cue	신호
	other than	~외에		signal	나타내다
	rather	상당히		consider	생각하다
	store	저장하다		local	지역의, 현지의
	commonly	흔히		tasty	맛있는
	tend to	~하는 경향이 있다		in demand	수요가 많은
	mistaken	잘못된		more often than not	대개, 자주
	assumption	가정		adopt	따르다, 채택하다
	characteristic	특성		practice	행동, 관행
	description	설명, 묘사	41-42	master	달인
	contain	포함하다		piece	(장기, 체스의) 말, 조각
	impression	인상		reproduce	재현하다
	depending upon	~에 따라		position	위치
	original	최초의, 원래의		memory	기억
	lecturer	강사, 강연자		beginner	초보자

Voca

| ❶ voca | ❷ text | ❸ [/] | ❹ _____ | ❺ quiz 1 | ❻ quiz 2 | ❼ quiz 3 | ❽ quiz 4 | ❾ quiz 5 |

place	기억해 내다, 놓다		ballet	발레
randomly	무작위로		step	스텝, 걸음(걸이)
difference	차이		make up	~을 이루다, ~을 구성하다
reduce	줄어들다, 줄이다		routine	정해진 춤 동작
expert	전문가		range	범위
advantage	유리함		recognize	인식하다
familiar	익숙한	43-45	palace	궁전
pattern	패턴, 모형, 방식		approach	접근하다
previously	이전에		gate	문
face	직면하다		smelly	냄새가 나는
involve	~와 관련 있다		guard	경비병
domain	분야		freeze	얼어붙다, 얼다
disappear	사라지다		shock	충격
beneficial	유익한		come to one's sense	정신을 차리다, 의식을 되찾다
effect	효과		shout	소리치다
structure	구조		demand	요구하다
observe	관찰하다		get off	~에서 내려오다
including	~을 포함하여		return	돌아오다
training	훈련		wise	현명한
accurately	정확하게		offer	제안하다
note	음표		take-out	테이크아웃의, 사 가지고 가는
unusual	특이한		fries	감자튀김
order	배열하다		immediately	즉시
movement	동작		call for	~을 시키다, ~을 요구하다
experienced	숙련된		continue	계속하다

Voca

영 ○ 한

❶ voca	❷ text	❸ [/]	❹ ____	❺ quiz 1	❻ quiz 2	❼ quiz 3	❽ quiz 4	❾ quiz 5
gesture	행동							
massage	마사지, 안마							
relaxing	편안한							
tiny	매우 작은							
kindness	친절, 친절한 행위							
disappear	사라지다							
sword	칼							
scare ~ away	~을 겁주어 쫓아내다							
eventually	결국, 마침내							
take up	~을 차지하다							
whole	전체(의)							

Voca Test

영 ◇ 한

❶ voca	❷ text	❸ [/]	❹ ____	❺ quiz 1	❻ quiz 2	❼ quiz 3	❽ quiz 4	❾ quiz 5
18	resident							
	apartment							
	recently							
	observe							
	kid							
	repair							
	pay attention to							
	condition							
	playground							
	equipment							
	swing							
	damage							
	fall off							
	slide							
	facility							
	terrible							
	move							
	appreciate							
	immediate							
	solve							
	matter							
19	trip							
	grizzly bear							
	native							
	habitat							

❶ voca	❷ text	❸ [/]	❹ ____	❺ quiz 1	❻ quiz 2	❼ quiz 3	❽ quiz 4	❾ quiz 5
	every once in a while							
	sniff							
	deeply							
	realize							
	giant							
	freeze							
	no longer							
	wonderful							
	experience							
	issue							
	survival							
	motivation							
	meat							
	clearly							
	menu							
20	difficult							
	maintain							
	constant							
	level							
	attention							
	throughout							
	rhythm							
	characterise							
	peak							
	valley							

Voca Test

영▶한

	❶ voca	❷ text	❸ [/]	❹ ____	❺ quiz 1	❻ quiz 2	❼ quiz 3	❽ quiz 4	❾ quiz 5

	energy		disease	
	achieve		dangerous	
	confident		mass	
	benefit		education	
	schedule		train	
	demanding		avoid	
	task		seek	
	cope with		divorce	
	observe		stress	
	note		indeed	
	take a while		risk	
	warm up	22	approach	
21	adopt		course	
	technology		task	
	cost		rubber-stamp	
	livelihood		tuxedo	
	push aside		colorful	
	progress		funeral	
	lifestyle		bathing suit	
	remove		religious	
	hate		service	
	produce		probably	
	physical		appropriate	
	pain		occasion	
	disability		setting	

Voca Test

영 〉 한

❶ voca	❷ text	❸ [/]	❹ ___	❺ quiz 1	❻ quiz 2	❼ quiz 3	❽ quiz 4	❾ quiz 5
	skillful			lead				
	flexible			intend				
	strategy			path				
	multiple-choice test			comfortable				
23	social			be good at				
	economic			reward				
	situation			realize				
	wage			deep				
	level			breathe				
	condition			slippery				
	improve			superhuman				
	gradually			effort				
	form			effectively				
	transport			situation				
	cheap			employment				
	industrial			secure				
	revolution			ultimately				
	railway			unsatisfying				
	seaside		25	decrease				
	resort			period				
	coast-to-coast			gap				
	arrival			slightly				
	tourism			increase				
	growth			steadily				
24	success			except				

oca Tes

❶ voca	❷ text	❸ [/]	❹ ____	❺ quiz 1	❻ quiz 2	❼ quiz 3	❽ quiz 4	❾ quiz 5
	for the first time				reservation			
26	trousers				accompany			
	adventurous				lend			
	career				contact			
	wildlife				information			
	photographer			29	noticeable			
	design				characteristic			
	airplane				project			
	persuade				physically			
	slightly				cartoon			
	end up -ing				character			
	car dealer				resemble			
	exciting				achieve			
	nonetheless				facial			
27	article				feature			
	publish				front			
	look for				animated			
	writing				appropriate			
	include				strategy			
	high-quality				emotionally			
	send				appealing			
28	chance				enlarge			
	fee				childlike			
	admission			30	major			
	first-come, first-served				philosophical			

Voca Test

❶ voca	❷ text	❸ [/]	❹ _____	❺ quiz 1	❻ quiz 2	❼ quiz 3	❽ quiz 4	❾ quiz 5
	shift				recovery			
	industrial				westward			
	competitive				lengthen			
	geographically				eastward			
	spread out				shorten			
	relation				sizable			
	buyer				impact			
	client				performance			
	realize				perform			
	quality				significantly			
	reasonable				professional			
	equally				recent			
	essential				additional			
	customer				evidence			
	modernization				tough			
	marketing			32	confidence			
	revolution				achieve			
	demand				set out			
	meet				over-optimism			
	diverse				certain			
	complex				time frame			
31	differ				estimate			
	reset				amount			
	biological clock				alongside			
	overcome				item			

 oca Test

❶ voca	❷ text	❸ [/]	❹ ＿＿	❺ quiz 1	❻ quiz 2	❼ quiz 3	❽ quiz 4	❾ quiz 5
	task			clothing				
	expect			perfect				
	attention			nail				
	fit			drive				
	available			cloth				
	significant			physical				
	there is no point -ing			reality				
	period			picture				
33	race			product				
	countryside			design				
	discover			process				
	still			period				
	biologist			vision				
	sometimes			decision				
	effect			activity				
	evolutionary			in harmony				
	principle			bring ~ into existence				
	evolve		35	affect				
	generation			main character				
	bunny			focus				
	case			character				
	pass on			interpret				
	gene			conflict				
	species			arise				
34	creator			pray for				

Voca Test

영 ▶ 한

❶ voca	❷ text	❸ [/]	❹ ____	❺ quiz 1	❻ quiz 2	❼ quiz 3	❽ quiz 4	❾ quiz 5
	outcome			community				
	consider			allow				
	tale			organize				
	shift			efficiently				
	viewpoint			produce				
	evil		37	natural				
	stepsister			form				
	kingdom			mineral				
	exist			melt				
	willingly			material				
	viewpoint			magma				
36	Old Stone Age			surface				
	band			trap				
	wander			atom				
	in search of			heat energy				
	farming			combine				
	settle down			crystal				
	farm			depend on				
	grow			partly				
	crop			rapidly				
	tool			generally				
	task			unaided eye				
	toolmaker			arrange				
	share			orderly				
	ax			element				

oca Test

영▶한

	❶ voca	❷ text	❸ [/]	❹ _____	❺ quiz 1	❻ quiz 2	❼ quiz 3	❽ quiz 4	❾ quiz 5

	❶ voca	❷ text	❸ [/]	❹	❺ quiz 1		❻ quiz 2	❼ quiz 3	❽ quiz 4	❾ quiz 5
38	determine					expectation				
	individual					affect				
	complex				**40**	trustworthy				
	break down					look for				
	nutrient					evidence				
	release					evolutionary				
	provide					positive				
	fuel					prospect				
	a number of					psychologist				
	structure					product review				
	hold					cue				
	other than					signal				
	rather					consider				
	store					local				
	commonly					tasty				
	tend to					in demand				
	mistaken					more often than not				
	assumption					adopt				
	characteristic					practice				
	description				**41-42**	master				
	contain					piece				
	impression					reproduce				
	depending upon					position				
	original					memory				
	lecturer					beginner				

Voca Test

영 ▶ 한

❶ voca	❷ text	❸ [/]	❹ _____	❺ quiz 1	❻ quiz 2	❼ quiz 3	❽ quiz 4	❾ quiz 5
place					ballet			
randomly					step			
difference					make up			
reduce					routine			
expert					range			
advantage					recognize			
familiar			43-45		palace			
pattern					approach			
previously					gate			
face					smelly			
involve					guard			
domain					freeze			
disappear					shock			
beneficial					come to one's sense			
effect					shout			
structure					demand			
observe					get off			
including					return			
training					wise			
accurately					offer			
note					take-out			
unusual					fries			
order					immediately			
movement					call for			
experienced					continue			

Voca Test

❶ voca	❷ text	❸ [/]	❹ ____	❺ quiz 1	❻ quiz 2	❼ quiz 3	❽ quiz 4	❾ quiz 5
gesture								
massage								
relaxing								
tiny								
kindness								
disappear								
sword								
scare ~ away								
eventually								
take up								
whole								

Voca Test

❶ voca	❷ text	❸ [/]	❹ ____	❺ quiz 1	❻ quiz 2	❼ quiz 3	❽ quiz 4	❾ quiz 5
18		거주자					이따금	
		아파트					코를 킁킁거리다	
		최근에					깊게	
		알다, 목격하다					깨닫다	
		아이, 어린이					거대한	
		수리; 수리하다					얼어붙다, 등골이 오싹하다	
		~에 주의를[관심을] 기울이다					더는 ~이 아닌	
		상태					멋진	
		놀이터					경험	
		설비					문제	
		그네					생존	
		손상하다					동기	
		떨어져 나가다					고기	
		미끄럼틀					분명히	
		시설					메뉴, 식단, 차림표	
		형편없는	20				어려운	
		이사하다					유지하다	
		감사하다					일정한	
		즉각적인					수준	
		해결하다					주의 (집중)	
		문제					내내	
19		여행					리듬	
		회색곰					특징짓다	
		자연의, 태어난					정점, 최고조	
		서식지					저점, 골짜기	

Voca Test

❶ voca	❷ text	❸ [/]	❹ ＿＿	❺ quiz 1	❻ quiz 2	❼ quiz 3	❽ quiz 4	❾ quiz 5
			에너지			질환, 질병		
			이루다, 성취하다			위험한		
			자신감이 있는			대중(의)		
			이익, 혜택			교육		
			(~을 하기로) 계획을 잡다			훈련시키다		
			힘든, 부담이 큰			피하다		
			작업, 과업			찾다, 구하다		
			~을 처리하다			단절, 이혼		
			관찰하다			부담, 긴장		
			알아차리다, 주의하다			실제로, 참으로		
			얼마간의 시간이 걸리다			위험 (요소)		
21			준비되다	22		접근하다		
			받아들이다, 채택하다			과목, 과정		
			기술			과제, 과업		
			비용			고무도장		
			생계 수단			턱시도		
			~을 밀쳐 놓다			화려한, 다채로운		
			발전, 전진			장례식		
			생활 방식			수영복		
			없애다			종교적인		
			싫어하다			예식		
			생산하다, 제작하다			아마		
			육체의, 신체의			적합한, 알맞은		
			고통, 통증			행사		
			장애			상황, 장소		

Voca Test

❶ voca	❷ text	❸ [/]	❹ ____	❺ quiz 1	❻ quiz 2	❼ quiz 3	❽ quiz 4	❾ quiz 5
		숙련된, 능숙한					이끌다	
		유연한					의도하다	
		전략					길	
		선다형 시험					편안한	
23		사회의					~을 잘하다	
		경제의					보상을 주다; 보상	
		상황					깨닫다	
		임금, 급료					깊은	
		수준					호흡하다, 숨쉬다	
		여건, 조건					미끄러운	
		개선되다, 향상되다					초인적인	
		점차					노력	
		형태					사실상, 실제로	
		운송, 수송					상황	
		저렴한, 싼					고용	
		산업의					안정적인	
		혁명					궁극적으로	
		철도					만족스럽지 못한	
		해안가, 바닷가		25			감소하다	
		리조트, 휴양지					기간	
		대륙 횡단의					차이	
		출현, 도래					약간	
		관광 산업					증가하다	
		성장, 발전					꾸준히	
24		성공					~을 제외하고	

Voca Test

❶ voca	❷ text	❸ [/]	❹ ____	❺ quiz 1	❻ quiz 2	❼ quiz 3	❽ quiz 4	❾ quiz 5

		처음으로, 최초로			예약
26		바지			동행하다
		모험적인			빌려주다
		경력			연락하다
		야생 동물			정보
		사진작가	29		눈에 띄는
		설계하다			특징, 특성
		비행기			투영하다
		설득하다			신체적으로
		약간			만화
		결국 ~하게 되다			캐릭터, 등장인물
		자동차 판매원			닮다
		흥미진진한, 신나는			달성하다, 이루다
		그렇더라도			얼굴의
27		기사			특징, 특색
		출간하다			앞의
		~을 찾다			만화 영화의
		원고, 글			적절한, 적당한
		포함하다			전략
		고화질의			감정적으로
		보내다			매력적인
28		기회			확대하다
		요금			어린이 같은
		입장	30		주요한, 중요한
		선착순의			철학적인

Voca Test

❶ voca	❷ text	❸ [/]	❹ ____	❺ quiz 1	❻ quiz 2	❼ quiz 3	❽ quiz 4	❾ quiz 5
		변화			회복			
		산업의			서쪽으로			
		경쟁적인			연장하다			
		지리적으로			동쪽으로			
		~을 퍼뜨리다			단축하다			
		관계			큰			
		구매자			영향			
		고객			경기력, 성과			
		깨닫다			행하다, 수행하다			
		양질의, 질 좋은			상당히			
		합리적인			프로의, 전문적인			
		마찬가지로			최근의			
		매우 중요한			추가적인			
		고객			증거			
		현대화			힘든			
		마케팅	32		자신감, 확신			
		혁명			성취하다			
		수요			~에 착수하다			
		충족시키다			지나친 낙관주의			
		다양한			특정한			
		복잡한			기간			
31		다르다			추산하다, 어림잡다			
		재설정하다			양			
		체내 시계			~와 함께			
		극복하다			항목			

Voca Test

❶ voca	❷ text	❸ [/]	❹ ____	❺ quiz 1	❻ quiz 2	❼ quiz 3	❽ quiz 4	❾ quiz 5
		과제, 과업				옷		
		기대하다				완성하다		
		주의				못		
		맞추다				(못·말뚝 등을) 박다		
		이용 가능한				천, 직물		
		상당한				물리적인		
		~하는 것은 무의미하다				실체		
		시간, 기간				그리다		
33		경주, 달리기				제품		
		시골				설계하다		
		발견하다				과정		
		여전히				기간		
		생물학자				비전		
		때때로				결정		
		효과, 영향, 결과				활동		
		진화의				조화롭게, 한마음이 되어		
		원리				~을 생겨나게 하다		
		진화하다	35			영향을 미치다		
		세대				주인공		
		토끼				초점		
		경우				등장인물		
		~을 물려주다, ~을 전달하다				해석하다		
		유전자				갈등		
		종				발생하다		
34		만들어 낸 사람, 창조자				~을 간절히 바라다		

Voca Test

❶ voca	❷ text	❸ [/]	❹ _____	❺ quiz 1	❻ quiz 2	❼ quiz 3	❽ quiz 4	❾ quiz 5
		결과			공동체			
		생각해 보다			~하게 하다, 허용하다			
		이야기			조직하다			
		바꾸다			효율적으로			
		관점			생산하다			
		사악한	37		자연의			
		의붓자매			형성하다, 형성되다			
		왕국			광물			
		존재하다			녹이다, 녹다			
		기꺼이			물질			
		관점			마그마			
36		구석기 시대			표면			
		무리			가두다			
		(걸어서) 돌아다니다			원자			
		~을 찾아			열에너지			
		농사			결합하다			
		정착하다			결정, 결정체			
		농경지			~에 달려있다			
		재배하다			부분적으로			
		농작물			빨리			
		도구			일반적으로			
		일			육안, 맨눈			
		도구 제작자			배열하다			
		함께 하다, 공유하다			질서있는			
		도끼			원소			

Voca Test

❶ voca	❷ text	❸ [/]	❹ ____	❺ quiz 1	❻ quiz 2	❼ quiz 3	❽ quiz 4	❾ quiz 5
		결정하다					기대	
		개별의					영향을 미치다	
38		복합의, 복잡한		40			신뢰할 수 있는	
		~을 분해하다, 분해되다					~을 찾다	
		영양소					증거	
		방출하다					진화의	
		제공하다					긍정적인	
		연료					전망	
		많은					심리학자	
		구조					상품 평	
		가지고 있다					신호	
		~외에					나타내다	
		상당히					생각하다	
		저장하다					지역의, 현지의	
		흔히					맛있는	
		~하는 경향이 있다					수요가 많은	
		잘못된					대개, 자주	
		가정					따르다, 채택하다	
		특성					행동, 관행	
		설명, 묘사		41-42			달인	
		포함하다					(장기, 체스의) 말, 조각	
		인상					재현하다	
		~에 따라					위치	
		최초의, 원래의					기억	
		강사, 강연자					초보자	

Voca Test

		❸	❹	❺ quiz 1	❻ quiz 2	❼ quiz 3	❽ quiz 4	❾ quiz 5
		기억해 내다, 놓다					발레	
		무작위로					스텝, 걸음(걸이)	
		차이					~을 이루다, ~을 구성하다	
		줄어들다, 줄이다					정해진 춤 동작	
		전문가					범위	
		유리함					인식하다	
		익숙한	43-45				궁전	
		패턴, 모형, 방식					접근하다	
		이전에					문	
		직면하다					냄새가 나는	
		~와 관련 있다					경비병	
		분야					얼어붙다, 얼다	
		사라지다					충격	
		유익한					정신을 차리다, 의식을 되찾다	
		효과					소리치다	
		구조					요구하다	
		관찰하다					~에서 내려오다	
		~을 포함하여					돌아오다	
		훈련					현명한	
		정확하게					제안하다	
		음표					테이크아웃의, 사 가지고 가는	
		특이한					감자튀김	
		배열하다					즉시	
		동작					~을 시키다, ~을 요구하다	
		숙련된					계속하다	

Voca Test

❶ voca	❷ text	❸ [/]	❹ ____	❺ quiz 1	❻ quiz 2	❼ quiz 3	❽ quiz 4	❾ quiz 5
		행동						
		마사지, 안마						
		편안한						
		매우 작은						
		친절, 친절한 행위						
		사라지다						
		칼						
		~을 겁주어 쫓아내다						
		결국, 마침내						
		~을 차지하다						
		전체(의)						

2021 고1 3월 모의고사

❶ voca　　❷ text　　❸ [/]　　❹ ____　　❺ quiz 1　　❻ quiz 2　　❼ quiz 3　　❽ quiz 4　　❾ quiz 5

18 목적

❶ To whom it may concern, I am a resident of the Blue Sky Apartment.

저는 Blue Sky 아파트의 거주자입니다.

❷ Recently I observed that the kid zone is in need of repairs.

최근에 저는 아이들을 위한 구역이 수리가 필요하다는 것을 알게 되었습니다.

❸ I want you to pay attention to the poor condition of the playground equipment in the zone.

저는 귀하께서 그 구역 놀이터 설비의 열악한 상태에 관심을 기울여 주시기를 바랍니다.

❹ The swings are damaged, the paint is falling off, and some of the bolts on the slide are missing.

그네가 손상되었고, 페인트가 떨어져 나가고 있고, 미끄럼틀의 볼트 몇 개가 빠져 있습니다.

❺ The facilities have been in this terrible condition since we moved here.

(놀이터) 시설은 우리가 이곳으로 이사 온 이후로 이렇게 형편없는 상태였습니다.

❻ They are dangerous to the children playing there. Would you please have them repaired?

그것은 거기서 노는 아이들에게 위험합니다. 그것을 수리해 주시겠습니까?

❼ I would appreciate your immediate attention to solve this matter.

이 문제를 해결하기 위해 즉각적인 관심을 두시면 감사하겠습니다.

❽ Yours sincerely,

Nina Davis

Nina Davis 드림

19 심경

❶ On a two-week trip in the Rocky Mountains, I saw a grizzly bear in its native habitat.

로키산맥에서 2주간의 여행 중, 나는 자연 서식지에서 회색곰 한 마리를 보았다.

❷ At first, I felt joy as I watched the bear walk across the land.

처음에 나는 그 곰이 땅을 가로질러 걸어가는 모습을 보았을 때 기분이 좋았다.

❸ He stopped every once in a while to turn his head about, sniffing deeply.

그것은 이따금 멈춰 서서 고개를 돌려 깊게 코를 킁킁거렸다.

❹ He was following the scent of something, and slowly I began to realize that this giant animal was smelling me! I froze.

그것은 무언가의 냄새를 따라가고 있었고, 나는 서서히 거대한 이 동물이 내 냄새를 맡고 있다는 것을 깨닫기 시작했다! 나는 얼어붙었다.

❺ This was no longer a wonderful experience; it was now an issue of survival.

이것은 더는 멋진 경험이 아니었고, 이제 생존의 문제였다.

❻ The bear's motivation was to find meat to eat, and I was clearly on his menu.

그 곰의 동기는 먹을 고기를 찾는 것이었고, 나는 분명히 그의 메뉴에 올라 있었다.

20 요지

❶ It is difficult for any of us to maintain a constant level of attention throughout our working day.

우리 중 누구라도 근무일 내내 일정한 수준의 주의집중을 유지하기는 어렵다.

❷ We all have body rhythms characterised by peaks and valleys of energy and alertness.

우리 모두 에너지와 기민함의 정점과 저점을 특징으로 하는 신체 리듬을 가지고 있다.

❸ You will achieve more, and feel confident as a benefit, if you schedule your most demanding tasks at times when you are best able to cope with them.

가장 힘든 작업을 그것을 가장 잘 처리할 수 있는 시간에 하도록 계획을 잡으면, 더 많은 것을 이루고 이익으로 자신감을 느낄 것이다.

❹ If you haven't thought about energy peaks before, take a few days to observe yourself.

만약 전에 에너지 정점에 관해 생각해 본 적이 없다면, 며칠 동안 자신을 관찰하라.

❺ Try to note the times when you are at your best. We are all different.

자신이 가장 좋은 상태일 때를 알아차리도록 노력하라. 우리는 모두 다르다.

❻ For some, the peak will come first thing in the morning, but for others it may take a while to warm up.

어떤 사람에게는 정점이 아침에 제일 먼저 오지만, 다른 사람에게는 준비되는 데 얼마간의 시간이 걸릴 수도 있다.

21 주장

❶ If we adopt technology, we need to pay its costs.

만약 우리가 기술을 받아들이면, 우리는 그것의 비용을 치러야 한다.

❷ Thousands of traditional livelihoods have been pushed aside by progress, and the lifestyles around those jobs removed.

수천 개의 전통적인 생계 수단이 발전에 의해 밀려났으며, 그 직업과 관련된 생활 방식이 없어졌다.

❸ Hundreds of millions of humans today work at jobs they hate, producing things they have no love for.

오늘날 수억 명의 사람들이 자기가 싫어하는 일자리에서 일하면서, 자신이 아무런 애정을 느끼지 못하는 것들을 생산한다.

❹ Sometimes these jobs cause physical pain, disability, or chronic disease.

때때로 이러한 일자리는 육체적 고통, 장애 또는 만성 질환을 유발한다.

❺ Technology creates many new jobs that are certainly dangerous.

기술은 확실히 위험한 많은 새로운 일자리를 창출한다.

❻ At the same time, mass education and media train humans to avoid low-tech physical work, to seek jobs working in the digital world.

동시에, 대중 교육과 대중 매체는 낮은 기술의 육체노동을 피하고 디지털 세계에서 일하는 직업을 찾도록 인간을 훈련시킨다.

❼ The divorce of the hands from the head puts a stress on the human mind.

머리로부터 손이 단절되는 것은 인간의 정신에 부담을 준다.

❽ Indeed, the sedentary nature of the best-paying jobs is a health risk — for body and mind.

실제로, 가장 보수가 좋은 직업의 주로 앉아서 하는 특성은 신체와 정신에 건강 위험 요소이다.

22 의미

❶ When students are starting their college life, they may approach every course, test, or learning task the same way, using what we like to call "the rubber-stamp approach."

대학 생활을 시작할 때 학생들은 우리가 '고무도장 방식'이라고 부르고 싶은 방법을 이용하여, 모든 과목이나, 시험, 학습 과제를 똑같은 방식으로 접근할지도 모른다.

❷ Think about it this way: Would you wear a tuxedo to a baseball game?

그것을 이런 식으로 생각해 보라. 여러분은 야구 경기에 턱시도를 입고 가겠는가?

❸ A colorful dress to a funeral? A bathing suit to religious services? Probably not.

장례식에 화려한 드레스를 입고 가겠는가? 종교적인 예식에 수영복을 입고 가겠는가? 아마 아닐 것이다.

❹ You know there's appropriate dress for different occasions and settings.

다양한 행사와 상황마다 적합한 옷이 있음을 여러분은 알고 있다.

❺ Skillful learners know that "putting on the same clothes" won't work for every class.

숙련된 학습자는 '같은 옷을 입는 것'이 모든 수업에 효과가 있지는 않을 것임을 알고 있다.

❻ They are flexible learners. They have different strategies and know when to use them.

그들은 유연한 학습자이다. 그들은 다양한 전략을 갖고 있으며 그것을 언제 사용해야 하는지 안다.

❼ They know that you study for multiple-choice tests differently than you study for essay tests.

그들은 선다형 시험은 논술 시험을 위해 학습하는 것과는 다르게 학습한다는 것을 안다.

❽ And they not only know what to do, but they also know how to do it.

그리고 그들은 무엇을 해야 하는지 알고 있을 뿐만 아니라, 그것을 어떻게 해야 하는지도 알고 있다.

23 주제

❶ As the social and economic situation of countries got better, wage levels and working conditions improved.

국가들의 사회적, 경제적 상황이 더 나아지면서, 임금 수준과 근로 여건이 개선되었다.

❷ Gradually people were given more time off.

점차 사람들은 더 많은 휴가를 받게 되었다.

❸ At the same time, forms of transport improved and it became faster and cheaper to get to places.

동시에, 운송 형태가 개선되었고 장소를 이동하는 것이 더 빠르고 더 저렴해졌다.

❹ England's industrial revolution led to many of these changes.

영국의 산업 혁명이 이러한 변화 중 많은 것을 일으켰다.

❺ Railways, in the nineteenth century, opened up now famous seaside resorts such as Blackpool and Brighton.

19세기에, 철도로 인해 Blackpool과 Brighton 같은 현재 유명한 해안가 리조트가 들어서게 되었다.

❻ With the railways came many large hotels.

철도가 생기면서 많은 대형 호텔이 생겨났다.

❼ In Canada, for example, the new coast-to-coast railway system made possible the building of such famous hotels as Banff Springs and Chateau Lake Louise in the Rockies.

예를 들어, 캐나다에서는 새로운 대륙 횡단 철도 시스템이 로키산맥의 Banff Springs와 Chateau Lake Louise 같은 유명한 호텔의 건설을 가능하게 했다.

❽ Later, the arrival of air transport opened up more of the world and led to tourism growth.

이후에 항공 운송의 출현은 세계의 더 많은 곳으로 가는 길을 열어 주었고 관광 산업의 성장을 이끌었다.

24 제목

❶ Success can lead you off your intended path and into a comfortable rut.

성공은 여러분을 의도한 길에서 벗어나 틀에 박힌 편안한 생활로 이끌 수 있다.

❷ If you are good at something and are well rewarded for doing it, you may want to keep doing it even if you stop enjoying it.

여러분이 어떤 일을 잘하고 그것을 하는 것에 대한 보상을 잘 받는다면, 그것을 즐기지 않게 되더라도 계속 그것을 하고 싶을 수도 있다.

❸ The danger is that one day you look around and realize you're so deep in this comfortable rut that you can no longer see the sun or breathe fresh air;

위험한 점은 어느 날 여러분이 주변을 둘러보고, 자신이 틀에 박힌 이 편안한 생활에 너무나 깊이 빠져 있어서 더는 태양을 보거나 신선한 공기를 호흡할 수 없으며,

❹ the sides of the rut have become so slippery that it would take a superhuman effort to climb out; and, effectively, you're stuck.

그 틀에 박힌 생활의 양쪽 면이 너무나 미끄럽게 되어 기어올라 나오려면 초인적인 노력이 필요할 것이고, 사실상 자신이 꼼짝할 수 없다는 것을 깨닫게 된다는 것이다.

❺ And it's a situation that many working people worry they're in now.

그리고 그것은 많은 근로자가 현재 자신이 처해 있다고 걱정하는 상황이다.

❻ The poor employment market has left them feeling locked in what may be a secure, or even well-paying — but ultimately unsatisfying — job.

열악한 고용 시장이 그들을 안정적이거나 심지어 보수가 좋을 수도 있지만, 궁극적으로는 만족스럽지 못한 일자리에 갇혀 있다고 느끼게 해 놓았다.

26 일치

❶ Lilian Bland was born in Kent, England in 1878. Unlike most other girls at the time she wore trousers and spent her time enjoying adventurous activities like horse riding and hunting.

Lilian Bland는 1878년 잉글랜드 Kent에서 태어났다. 그 당시 대부분의 다른 여자아이와 달리 그녀는 바지를 입었고, 승마와 사냥 같은 모험적인 활동을 즐기며 시간을 보냈다.

❷ Lilian began her career as a sports and wildlife photographer for British newspapers.

Lilian은 영국 신문사의 스포츠와 야생 동물 사진작가로 자신의 경력을 시작했다.

❸ In 1910 she became the first woman to design, build, and fly her own airplane.

1910년에 그녀는 자신의 비행기를 설계하고, 제작하고, 비행한 최초의 여성이 되었다.

❹ In order to persuade her to try a slightly safer activity, Lilian's dad bought her a car.

약간 더 안전한 활동을 하도록 그녀를 설득하기 위해, Lilian의 아버지는 그녀에게 자동차를 사주었다.

❺ Soon Lilian was a master driver and ended up working as a car dealer.

곧 Lilian은 뛰어난 운전자가 되었고 결국 자동차 판매원으로 일하게 되었다.

❻ She never went back to flying but lived a long and exciting life nonetheless.

그녀는 결코 비행을 다시 시작하지 않았지만, 그렇더라도 오랫동안 흥미진진한 삶을 살았다.

❼ She married, moved to Canada, and had a kid.

그녀는 결혼하여 캐나다로 이주했고, 아이를 낳았다.

❽ Eventually, she moved back to England, and lived there for the rest of her life.

결국 잉글랜드로 돌아와 거기서 생의 마지막 기간을 보냈다.

29 어법

❶ The most noticeable human characteristic projected onto animals is that they can talk in human language.

동물에게 투영된 가장 눈에 띄는 인간의 특징은 동물이 인간의 언어로 대화할 수 있다는 점이다.

❷ Physically, animal cartoon characters and toys made after animals are also most often deformed in such a way as to resemble humans.

신체적으로도, 동물 만화 캐릭터와 동물을 본떠 만든 장난감은 또한 인간을 닮게 하는 방식으로 변형되는 경우가 아주 많다.

❸ This is achieved by showing them with humanlike facial features and deformed front legs to resemble human hands.

이것은 인간과 같은 얼굴 특징과 사람의 손을 닮게 변형된 앞다리를 가지고 있는 것으로 그것들을 보여줌으로써 달성된다.

❹ In more recent animated movies the trend has been to show the animals in a more "natural" way.

더 최근의 만화 영화에서 추세는 동물을 더 '자연스러운' 방식으로 묘사하는 것이었다.

❺ However, they still use their front legs like human hands (for example, lions can pick up and lift small objects with one paw), and they still talk with an appropriate facial expression.

그러나 그것들은 여전히 사람의 손처럼 앞다리를 사용하고, 여전히 적절한 표정을 지으며 이야기한다.

❻ A general strategy that is used to make the animal characters more emotionally appealing, both to children and adults, is to give them enlarged and deformed childlike features.

동물 캐릭터를 아이와 어른 모두에게 더 감정적으로 매력적이게 만들기 위해 이용하는 일반적인 전략은 그것들에 확대되고 변형된 어린이 같은 특징을 부여하는 것이다.

30 어휘

❶ The major philosophical shift in the idea of selling came when industrial societies became more affluent, more competitive, and more geographically spread out during the 1940s and 1950s.

산업 사회가 1940년대와 1950년대 동안 더 부유하고, 더 경쟁적이고, 더 지리적으로 퍼져 나가게 되면서 판매 개념에 주요한 철학적 변화가 일어났다.

❷ This forced business to develop closer relations with buyers and clients, which in turn made business realize that it was not enough to produce a quality product at a reasonable price.

이로 인해 기업은 구매자 및 고객과 더 긴밀한 관계를 발전시켜야 했고, 이것은 결과적으로 기업이 합리적인 가격에 양질의 제품을 생산하는 것으로는 충분하지 않다는 것을 깨닫게 했다.

❸ In fact, it was equally essential to deliver products that customers actually wanted. Henry Ford produced his best-selling T-model Ford in one color only (black) in 1908, but in modern societies this was no longer possible.

사실, 고객이 실제로 원하는 제품을 내놓는 것이 마찬가지로 매우 중요했다. 1908년에 Henry Ford는 자신의 가장 많이 팔렸던 T-모델 Ford를 단 하나의 색상(검은색)으로만 생산했지만, 현대사회에서는 이것이 더 이상 가능하지 않았다.

❹ The modernization of society led to a marketing revolution that destroyed the view that production would create its own demand. Customers, and the desire to meet their diverse and often complex needs, became the focus of business.

사회의 현대화는 생산이 그 자체의 수요를 창출할 것이라는 견해를 강화하는 마케팅 혁명으로 이어졌다. 고객과 그들의 다양하고 흔히 복잡한 욕구를 충족하고자 하는 욕망이 기업의 초점이 되었다.

31 빈칸

❶ People differ in how quickly they can reset their biological clocks to overcome jet lag, and the speed of recovery depends on the direction of travel.

시차로 인한 피로감을 극복하기 위해서 자신의 체내 시계를 얼마나 빨리 재설정할 수 있는지는 사람마다 서로 다르며, 그 회복 속도는 이동 방향에 달려있다.

❷ Generally, it's easier to fly westward and lengthen your day than it is to fly eastward and shorten it.

일반적으로 동쪽으로 비행하여 여러분의 하루를 단축하는 것보다 서쪽으로 비행하여 여러분의 하루를 연장하는 것이 더 쉽다.

❸ This east-west difference in jet lag is sizable enough to have an impact on the performance of sports teams.

시차로 인한 피로감에서 이러한 동서의 차이는 스포츠 팀의 경기력에 영향을 미칠 만큼 충분히 크다.

❹ Studies have found that teams flying westward perform significantly better than teams flying eastward in professional baseball and college football.

연구에 따르면 서쪽으로 비행하는 팀이 동쪽으로 비행하는 팀보다 프로 야구와 대학 미식 축구에서 상당히 더 잘한다.

❺ A more recent study of more than 46,000 Major League Baseball games found additional evidence that eastward travel is tougher than westward travel.

46,000 경기가 넘는 메이저 리그 야구 경기에 대한 더 최근의 연구에 의해 동쪽으로 이동하는 것이 서쪽으로 이동하는 것보다 더 힘들다는 추가적인 증거가 발견되었다.

32 빈칸

❶ If you want the confidence that comes from achieving what you set out to do each day, then it's important to understand how long things are going to take.

만약 매일 하고자 착수하는 일을 성취함으로써 얻게 되는 자신감을 원한다면 일이 얼마나 시간이 걸릴지 아는 것이 중요하다.

❷ Over-optimism about what can be achieved within a certain time frame is a problem.

어떤 특정 기간 내에 성취될 수 있는 것에 대한 지나친 낙관주의는 문제다.

❸ So work on it.

그러므로 그것을 개선하려고 노력하라.

❹ Make a practice of estimating the amount of time needed alongside items on your 'things to do' list, and learn by experience when tasks take a greater or lesser time than expected.

'해야 할 일' 목록에 있는 항목과 함께, 필요한 시간의 양을 추산하는 것을 습관화하고, 과제가 언제 예상보다 더 많은 시간 또는 더 적은 시간이 걸리는지 경험을 통해 배우라.

❺ Give attention also to fitting the task to the available time.

그 이용 가능한 시간에 과제를 맞추는 것에도 또한 주의를 기울이라.

❻ There are some tasks that you can only set about if you have a significant amount of time available.

이용할 수 있는 시간의 양이 상당히 있어야만 시작할 수 있는 몇몇 과제가 있다.

❼ There is no point in trying to gear up for such a task when you only have a short period available.

이용할 수 있는 시간이 짧은 시간밖에 없을 때 그런 과제를 위해 준비를 갖추려고 애쓰는 것은 무의미하다.

❽ So schedule the time you need for the longer tasks and put the short tasks into the spare moments in between.

그러므로 시간이 더 오래 걸리는 과제를 위해 필요한 시간을 계획하고, 그 사이의 남는 시간에 시간이 짧게 걸리는 과제를 배치하라.

33 빈칸

❶ In Lewis Carroll's *Through the Looking-Glass*, the Red Queen takes Alice on a race through the countryside.

Lewis Carroll의 Through the Looking-Glass에서 붉은 여왕은 Alice를 시골을 통과하는 한 경주에 데리고 간다.

❷ They run and they run, but then Alice discovers that they're still under the same tree that they started from.

그들은 달리고 또 달리지만, 그러다가 Alice는 자신들이 출발했던 나무 아래에 여전히 있음을 발견한다.

❸ The Red Queen explains to Alice: "*here*, you see, it takes all the running you can do, to keep in the same place."

붉은 여왕은 Alice에게 "'여기서는' 보다시피 같은 장소에 머물러 있으려면 네가 할 수 있는 모든 뜀박질을 해야 한단다."라고 설명한다.

❹ Biologists sometimes use this Red Queen Effect to explain an evolutionary principle.

생물학자들은 때때로 이 '붉은 여왕 효과'를 사용해 진화 원리를 설명한다.

❺ If foxes evolve to run faster so they can catch more rabbits, then only the fastest rabbits will live long enough to make a new generation of bunnies that run even faster — in which case, of course, only the fastest foxes will catch enough rabbits to thrive and pass on their genes.

만약 여우가 더 많은 토끼를 잡기 위해 더 빨리 달리도록 진화한다면, 그러면 오직 가장 빠른 토끼만이 충분히 오래 살아 훨씬 더 빨리 달리는 새로운 세대의 토끼를 낳을 텐데, 물론 이 경우 가장 빠른 여우만이 충분한 토끼를 잡아 번성하여 자신들의 유전자를 물려줄 것이다.

❻ Even though they might run, the two species just stay in place.

그 두 종이 달린다 해도 그것들은 제자리에 머무를 뿐이다.

34 빈칸

❶ Everything in the world around us was finished in the mind of its creator before it was started.

우리 주변 세상의 모든 것은 시작되기 전에 그것을 만들어 낸 사람의 마음속에서 완성되었다.

❷ The houses we live in, the cars we drive, and our clothing — all of these began with an idea.

우리가 사는 집, 우리가 운전하는 자동차, 우리의 옷, 이 모든 것이 아이디어에서 시작했다.

❸ Each idea was then studied, refined and perfected before the first nail was driven or the first piece of cloth was cut.

각각의 아이디어는 그런 다음, 첫 번째 못이 박히거나 첫 번째 천 조각이 재단되기 전에, 연구되고, 다듬어지고, 완성되었다.

❹ Long before the idea was turned into a physical reality, the mind had clearly pictured the finished product.

그 아이디어가 물리적 실체로 바뀌기 훨씬 전에 마음은 완제품을 분명하게 그렸다.

❺ The human being designs his or her own future through much the same process.

인간은 거의 같은 과정을 통해 자신의 미래를 설계한다.

❻ We begin with an idea about how the future will be.

우리는 미래가 어떨지에 대한 아이디어로 시작한다.

❼ Over a period of time we refine and perfect the vision.

일정 기간에 걸쳐서 우리는 그 비전을 다듬어 완성한다.

❽ Before long, our every thought, decision and activity are all working in harmony to bring into existence what we have mentally concluded about the future.

머지않아, 우리의 모든 생각, 결정, 활동은 우리가 미래에 대해 머릿속에서 완성한 것을 생겨나게 하려고 모두 조화롭게 작용하게 된다.

35 무관

❶ *Whose* story it is affects what the story is.

'누구의' 이야기인지가 '무슨' 이야기인지에 영향을 미친다.

❷ Change the main character, and the focus of the story must also change.

주인공을 바꾸면, 이야기의 초점도 틀림없이 바뀐다.

❸ If we look at the events through another character's eyes, we will interpret them differently.

만약 우리가 다른 등장인물의 눈을 통해 사건을 본다면, 우리는 그것을 다르게 해석할 것이다.

❹ We'll place our sympathies with someone new.

우리는 새로운 누군가에게 공감할 것이다.

❺ When the conflict arises that is the heart of the story, we will be praying for a different outcome.

이야기의 핵심인 갈등이 발생할 때, 우리는 다른 결과를 간절히 바랄 것이다.

❻ Consider, for example, how the tale of Cinderella would shift if told from the viewpoint of an evil stepsister.

예를 들어, 신데렐라 이야기가 사악한 의붓자매의 관점에서 이야기된다면 어떻게 바뀔지 생각해 보라.

❼ *Gone with the Wind* is Scarlett O'Hara's story, but what if we were shown the same events from the viewpoint of Rhett Butler or Melanie Wilkes?

Gone with the Wind는 Scarlett O'Hara의 이야기이지만, 만약 같은 사건이 Rhett Butler나 Melanie Wilkes의 관점에서 우리에게 제시된다면 어떠할 것인가?

36 순서

❶ In the Old Stone Age, small bands of 20 to 60 people wandered from place to place in search of food.

구석기 시대에는 20~60명의 작은 무리가 식량을 찾아 이곳저곳을 돌아다녔다.

❷ Once people began farming, they could settle down near their farms.

일단 농사를 짓기 시작하면서, 사람들은 자신들의 농경지 근처에 정착할 수 있었다.

❸ As a result, towns and villages grew larger.

그 결과, 도시와 마을이 더 커졌다.

❹ Living in communities allowed people to organize themselves more efficiently.

공동체 생활을 통해 사람들은 자신들을 더 효율적으로 조직할 수 있었다.

❺ They could divide up the work of producing food and other things they needed.

그들은 식량과 자신들에게 필요한 다른 것들을 생산하는 일을 나눌 수 있었다.

❻ While some workers grew crops, others built new houses and made tools.

어떤 노동자들은 농작물을 재배한 반면, 다른 노동자들은 새로운 집을 짓고 도구를 만들었다.

❼ Village dwellers also learned to work together to do a task faster.

마을 거주자들은 또한 일을 더 빨리 하기 위해 함께 일하는 것도 배웠다.

❽ For example, toolmakers could share the work of making stone axes and knives.

예를 들어, 도구 제작자들은 돌도끼와 돌칼을 만드는 작업을 함께 할 수 있었다.

❾ By working together, they could make more tools in the same amount of time.

함께 일함으로써, 그들은 같은 시간 안에 더 많은 도구를 만들 수 있었다.

37 순서

❶ Natural processes form minerals in many ways.

자연 과정은 많은 방법으로 광물을 형성한다.

❷ For example, hot melted rock material, called magma, cools when it reaches the Earth's surface, or even if it's trapped below the surface.

예를 들어, 마그마라고 불리는 뜨거운 용암 물질은 지구의 표면에 도달할 때, 또는 심지어 표면 아래에 갇혔을 때도 식는다.

❸ As magma cools, its atoms lose heat energy, move closer together, and begin to combine into compounds.

마그마가 식으면서, 마그마의 원자는 열에너지를 잃고, 서로 더 가까이 이동해, 화합물로 결합하기 시작한다.

❹ During this process, atoms of the different compounds arrange themselves into orderly, repeating patterns.

이 과정 동안, 서로 다른 화합물의 원자가 질서 있고 반복적인 패턴으로 배열된다.

❺ The type and amount of elements present in a magma partly determine which minerals will form.

마그마에 존재하는 원소의 종류와 양이 어떤 광물이 형성될지를 부분적으로 결정한다.

❻ Also, the size of the crystals that form depends partly on how rapidly the magma cools.

또한, 형성되는 결정의 크기는 부분적으로는 마그마가 얼마나 빨리 식느냐에 달려있다.

❼ When magma cools slowly, the crystals that form are generally large enough to see with the unaided eye.

마그마가 천천히 식으면, 형성되는 결정은 일반적으로 육안으로 볼 수 있을 만큼 충분히 크다.

❽ This is because the atoms have enough time to move together and form into larger crystals.

이것은 원자가 함께 이동해 더 큰 결정을 형성할 충분한 시간을 가지기 때문이다.

❾ When magma cools rapidly, the crystals that form will be small.

마그마가 빠르게 식으면, 형성되는 결정은 작을 것이다.

❿ In such cases, you can't easily see individual mineral crystals.

그런 경우에는 개별 광물 결정을 쉽게 볼 수 없다.

38 삽입

❶ All carbohydrates are basically sugars. Complex carbohydrates are the good carbohydrates for your body.

모든 탄수화물은 기본적으로 당이다. 복합 탄수화물은 몸에 좋은 탄수화물이다.

❷ These complex sugar compounds are very difficult to break down and can trap other nutrients like vitamins and minerals in their chains.

이러한 복당류 화합물은 분해하기 매우 어렵고 비타민과 미네랄 같은 다른 영양소를 그것의 사슬 안에 가두어 둘 수 있다.

❸ As they slowly break down, the other nutrients are also released into your body, and can provide you with fuel for a number of hours.

그것들이 천천히 분해되면서, 다른 영양소도 여러분의 몸으로 방출되고, 많은 시간 동안 여러분에게 연료를 공급할 수 있다.

❹ Bad carbohydrates, on the other hand, are simple sugars. Because their structure is not complex, they are easy to break down and hold few nutrients for your body other than the sugars from which they are made.

반면에 나쁜 탄수화물은 단당류이다. 그것의 구조는 복잡하지 않기 때문에, 그것은 분해되기 쉽고 그것이 만들어지는 당 외에 몸을 위한 영양소를 거의 가지고 있지 않다.

❺ Your body breaks down these carbohydrates rather quickly and what it cannot use is converted to fat and stored in the body.

여러분의 몸은 이러한 탄수화물을 상당히 빨리 분해하고 그것(몸)이 사용할 수 없는 것은 지방으로 바뀌어 몸에 저장된다.

39 삽입

❶ People commonly make the mistaken assumption that because a person has one type of characteristic, then they automatically have other characteristics which go with it.

흔히 사람들은 어떤 사람이 한 가지 유형의 특성을 가지고 있기 때문에, 그러면 자동적으로 그것과 어울리는 다른 특성을 가지고 있다는 잘못된 가정을 한다.

❷ In one study, university students were given descriptions of a guest lecturer before he spoke to the group.

한 연구에서, 대학생들은 초청 강사가 그 (대학생) 집단에게 강연을 하기 전에 그 강사에 대한 설명을 들었다.

❸ Half the students received a description containing the word 'warm', the other half were told the speaker was 'cold'.

학생들의 절반은 '따뜻하다'라는 단어가 포함된 설명을 들었고 나머지 절반은 그 강사가 '차갑다'는 말을 들었다.

❹ The guest lecturer then led a discussion, after which the students were asked to give their impressions of him.

그러고 나서 그 초청 강사가 토론을 이끌었고, 그 후에 학생들은 그(강사)에 대한 그들의 인상을 말해 달라고 요청받았다.

❺ As expected, there were large differences between the impressions formed by the students, depending upon their original information of the lecturer.

예상한 대로, 학생들에 의해 형성된 인상 간에는 그 강사에 대한 학생들의 최초 정보에 따라 큰 차이가 있었다.

❻ It was also found that those students who expected the lecturer to be warm tended to interact with him more.

또한, 그 강사가 따뜻할 것이라 기대한 학생들은 그와 더 많이 소통하는 경향이 있다는 것이 밝혀졌다.

❼ This shows that different expectations not only affect the impressions we form but also our behaviour and the relationship which is formed.

이것은 서로 다른 기대가 우리가 형성하는 인상뿐만 아니라 우리의 행동 및 형성되는 관계에도 영향을 미친다는 것을 보여 준다.

40 요약

❶ To help decide what's risky and what's safe, who's trustworthy and who's not, we look for *social evidence*.

무엇이 위험하고 무엇이 안전한지, 누구를 신뢰할 수 있고 누구를 신뢰할 수 없는지를 결정하는 것을 돕기 위해, 우리는 '사회적 증거'를 찾는다.

❷ From an evolutionary view, following the group is almost always positive for our prospects of survival.

진화의 관점에서 볼 때, 집단을 따르는 것이 거의 항상 우리의 생존 전망에 긍정적이다.

❸ "If everyone's doing it, it must be a sensible thing to do," explains famous psychologist and best selling writer of *Influence*, Robert Cialdini.

"모든 사람이 그것을 하고 있다면, 그것은 해야 할 분별 있는 일인 것이 틀림없다."라고 유명한 심리학자이자 Influence 를 쓴 베스트셀러 작가인 Robert Cialdini는 설명한다.

❹ While we can frequently see this today in product reviews, even subtler cues within the environment can signal trustworthiness. Consider this: when you visit a local restaurant, are they busy?

오늘날 상품 평에서 이것을 자주 볼 수 있지만, 환경 내의 훨씬 더 미묘한 신호가 신뢰성을 나타낼 수 있다. 이것을 생각해 보라. 여러분이 어떤 지역의 음식점을 방문할 때, 그들이 바쁜가?

❺ Is there a line outside or is it easy to find a seat?

밖에 줄이 있는가, 아니면 자리를 찾기가 쉬운가?

❻ It is a hassle to wait, but a line can be a powerful cue that the food's tasty, and these seats are in demand.

기다리는 것은 성가신 일이지만, 줄은 음식이 맛있고 이곳의 좌석은 수요가 많다는 강력한 신호일 수 있다.

❼ More often than not, it's good to adopt the practices of those around you.

대개는 주변에 있는 사람들의 행동을 따르는 것이 좋다.

41~42 제목, 어휘

❶ Chess masters shown a chess board in the middle of a game for 5 seconds with 20 to 30 pieces still in play can immediately reproduce the position of the pieces from memory.

체스판을 게임 중간에 20~30개의 말들이 아직 놓여있는 상태로 5초 동안 본 체스의 달인들은 그 말들의 위치를 기억으로부터 즉시 재현할 수 있다.

❷ Beginners, of course, are able to place only a few.

물론 초보자들은 겨우 몇 개(의 위치)만 기억해 낼 수 있다.

❸ Now take the same pieces and place them on the board randomly and the difference is much reduced.

이제 같은 말들을 가져다가 체스판에 무작위로 놓으면 그 차이는 크게 줄어든다.

❹ The expert's advantage is only for familiar patterns — those previously stored in memory.

전문가의 유리함은 익숙한 패턴, 즉 이전에 기억에 저장된 패턴에 대해서만 있다.

❺ Faced with unfamiliar patterns, even when it involves the same familiar domain, the expert's advantage disappears.

익숙하지 않은 패턴에 직면하면, 같은 익숙한 분야와 관련 있는 경우라도 전문가의 유리함은 사라진다.

❻ The beneficial effects of familiar structure on memory have been observed for many types of expertise, including music.

익숙한 구조가 기억에 미치는 유익한 효과는 음악을 포함하여 많은 유형의 전문 지식에서 관찰되어왔다.

❼ People with musical training can reproduce short sequences of musical notation more accurately than those with no musical training when notes follow conventional sequences, but the advantage is much reduced when the notes are ordered randomly.

음표가 전형적인 순서를 따를 때는 음악 훈련을 받은 사람이 음악 훈련을 받지 않은 사람보다 짧은 연속된 악보를 더 정확하게 재현할 수 있지만, 음표가 무작위로 배열되면 그 유리함이 훨씬 줄어든다.

❽ Expertise also improves memory for sequences of movements. Experienced ballet dancers are able to repeat longer sequences of steps than less experienced dancers, and they can repeat a sequence of steps making up a routine better than steps ordered randomly.

전문 지식은 또한 연속 동작에 대한 기억을 향상시킨다. 숙련된 발레 무용수가 경험이 적은 무용수보다 더 긴 연속 스텝을 반복할 수 있고, 무작위로 배열된 스텝보다 정해진 춤 동작을 이루는 연속 스텝을 더 잘 반복할 수 있다.

❾ In each case, memory range is increased by the ability to recognize familiar sequences and patterns.

각각의 경우, 기억의 범위는 익숙한 순서와 패턴을 인식하는 능력에 의해 늘어난다.

43~45 순서, 지칭, 세부 내용

❶ Once upon a time, there was a king who lived in a beautiful palace. While the king was away, a monster approached the gates of the palace.

옛날 옛적에, 아름다운 궁전에 사는 한 왕이 있었다. 왕이 없는 동안, 한 괴물이 궁전 문으로 접근했다.

❷ The monster was so ugly and smelly that the guards froze in shock. He passed the guards and sat on the king's throne.

그 괴물이 너무 추하고 냄새가 나서 경비병들은 충격으로 얼어붙었다. 그(괴물)는 경비병들을 지나 왕의 왕좌에 앉았다.

❸ The guards soon came to their senses, went in, and shouted at the monster, demanding that he get off the throne. With each bad word the guards used, the monster grew more ugly and smelly.

경비병들은 곧 정신을 차리고 안으로 들어가 그 괴물을 향해 소리치며 그에게 왕좌에서 내려올 것을 요구했다. 경비병들이 나쁜 말을 사용할 때마다, 그 괴물은 더 추해졌고, 더 냄새가 났다.

❹ The guards got even angrier — they began to brandish their swords to scare the monster away from the palace. But he just grew bigger and bigger, eventually taking up the whole room.

경비병들은 한층 더 화가 났다. 그들은 그 괴물을 겁주어 궁전에서 쫓아내려고 칼을 휘두르기 시작했다. 하지만 그는 그저 점점 더 커져서 결국 방 전체를 차지했다.

❺ He grew more ugly and smelly than ever. Eventually the king returned. He was wise and kind and saw what was happening. He knew what to do.

그는 그 어느 때 보다 더 추해졌고, 더 냄새가 났다. 마침내 왕이 돌아왔다. 그는 현명하고 친절했으며 무슨 일이 일어나고 있는지 알아차렸다. 그는 무엇을 해야 할지 알았다.

❻ He smiled and said to the monster, "Welcome to my palace!" He asked the monster if he wanted a cup of coffee. The monster began to grow smaller as he drank the coffee. The king offered him some take-out pizza and fries.

그는 미소를 지으며 그 괴물에게 "나의 궁전에 온 것을 환영하오!"라고 말했다. 왕은 그 괴물에게 그가 커피 한 잔을 원하는 지 물었다. 괴물은 그 커피를 마시면서 더 작아지기 시작했다. 왕은 그에게 약간의 테이크아웃 피자와 감자튀김을 제안했다.

❼ The guards immediately called for pizza. The monster continued to get smaller with the king's kind gestures.

경비병들은 즉시 피자를 시켰다. 그 괴물은 왕의 친절한 행동에 몸이 계속 더 작아졌다.

❽ He then offered the monster a full body massage. As the guards helped with the relaxing massage, the monster became tiny. With another act of kindness to the monster, he just disappeared.

그러고 나서 그는 그 괴물에게 전신 마사지를 제안했다. 경비병들이 편안한 마사지를 도와주자 그 괴물은 매우 작아졌다. 그 괴물에게 또 한 번의 친절한 행동을 베풀자, 그는 바로 사라졌다.

2021 고1 3월 모의고사 ❶ 회차 : 점 / 200점

❶ voca ❷ text ❸ [/] ❹ ____ ❺ quiz 1 ❻ quiz 2 ❼ quiz 3 ❽ quiz 4 ❾ quiz 5

18

To [who / whom]¹⁾ it may concern,

I am a resident of the Blue Sky Apartment. Recently I observed [that / which]²⁾ the kid zone is in need of repairs. I want you to pay attention [to / at]³⁾ the poor condition of the playground e_____⁴⁾ in the zone. The swings are damaged, the paint is [fallen / falling]⁵⁾ off, and some of the bolts on the slide are missing. The facilities have been in this terrible condition since we moved here. They are dangerous to the children [played / playing]⁶⁾ there. Would you please have them [repaired / to repair]⁷⁾ ? I would appreciate your immediate attention to solve this matter.

Yours sincerely,

Nina Davis

관계자분께
저는 Blue Sky 아파트의 거주자입니다. 최근에 저는 아이들을 위한 구역이 수리가 필요하다는 것을 알게 되었습니다. 저는 귀하께서 그 구역 놀이터 설비의 열악한 상태에 관심을 기울여 주시기를 바랍니다. 그네가 손상되었고, 페인트가 떨어져 나가고 있고, 미끄럼틀의 볼트 몇 개가 빠져 있습니다. (놀이터) 시설은 우리가 이곳으로 이사 온 이후로 이렇게 형편없는 상태였습니다. 그것은 거기서 노는 아이들에게 위험합니다. 그것을 수리해 주시겠습니까? 이 문제를 해결하기 위해 즉각적인 관심을 두시면 감사하겠습니다. Nina Davis 드림

19

On a two-week trip in the Rocky Mountains, I saw a grizzly bear in its [native / naive]⁸⁾ habitat. At first, I felt joy as I [watched / watching]⁹⁾ the bear [walk / to walk]¹⁰⁾ across the land. He stopped every once in a while [turning / to turn]¹¹⁾ his head about, [sniffed / sniffing]¹²⁾ deeply. He was [followed / following]¹³⁾ the scent of something, and slowly I began to realize [that / what]¹⁴⁾ this giant animal (가리키는 것은? _____)¹⁵⁾ was smelling me! I froze. This was no longer a wonderful experience; it was now an issue of survival. The bear's [motivation / inspiration]¹⁶⁾ was to find meat to eat, and I was clearly on his menu.

로키산맥에서 2주간의 여행 중, 나는 자연 서식지에서 회색곰 한 마리를 보았다. 처음에 나는 그 곰이 땅을 가로질러 걸어가는 모습을 보았을 때 기분이 좋았다. 그것은 이따금 멈춰 서서 고개를 돌려 깊게 코를 킁킁거렸다. 그것은 무언가의 냄새를 따라가고 있었고, 나는 서서히 거대한 이 동물이 내 냄새를 맡고 있다는 것을 깨닫기 시작했다! 나는 얼어붙었다. 이것은 더는 멋진 경험이 아니었고, 이제 생존의 문제였다. 그 곰의 동기는 먹을 고기를 찾는 것이었고, 나는 분명히 그의 메뉴에 올라 있었다.

20

It is difficult for [any / none]¹⁷⁾ of us to [maintain / containing]¹⁸⁾ a constant level of attention throughout our working day. We all have body rhythms [characterise / characterised]¹⁹⁾ by peaks and valleys of energy and alertness. You will achieve more, and feel [confident / confidently]²⁰⁾ as a benefit, if you schedule your most [demanded / demanding]²¹⁾ tasks at times when you are best able to [cope / catch up]²²⁾ with <u>them</u> (가리키는 것은? _____)²³⁾ . If you haven't [thought / been thought]²⁴⁾ about energy peaks before, [take / taking]²⁵⁾ a few days to observe yourself. Try to note the times when you are at your best. We are all different. For some, the peak will come first thing in the morning, but for others it may take a while to warm up.

우리 중 누구라도 근무일 내내 일정한 수준의 주의집중을 유지하기는 어렵다. 우리 모두 에너지와 기민함의 정점과 저점을 특징으로 하는 신체 리듬을 가지고 있다. 가장 힘든 작업을 그것을 가장 잘 처리할 수 있는 시간에 하도록 계획을 잡으면, 더 많은 것을 이루고 이익으로 자신감을 느낄 것이다. 만약 전에 에너지 정점에 관해 생각해 본 적이 없다면, 며칠 동안 자신을 관찰하라. 자신이 가장 좋은 상태일 때를 알아차리도록 노력하라. 우리는 모두 다르다. 어떤 사람에게는 정점이 아침에 제일 먼저 오지만, 다른 사람에게는 준비되는 데 얼마간의 시간이 걸릴 수도 있다.

21

If we [adopt / adapt]²⁶⁾ technology, we need to pay [its / their]²⁷⁾ costs. Thousands of traditional livelihoods have been [pushed / pushing]²⁸⁾ aside by progress, and the lifestyles around those jobs [removed / removing]²⁹⁾. Hundreds of millions of humans today [work / works]³⁰⁾ at jobs they hate, [produce / producing]³¹⁾ things (생략된 것은? _____)³²⁾ they have no love for. Sometimes these jobs cause [physical / psychological]³³⁾ pain, disability, or chronic disease. Technology creates many new jobs that are certainly dangerous. At the same time, mass education and media train humans to [avoid / face]³⁴⁾ low-tech physical work, to seek jobs [worked / working]³⁵⁾ in the digital world. The divorce of the hands from the head [put / puts]³⁶⁾ a stress on the human mind. Indeed, the [sedentary / lively]³⁷⁾ nature of the best-paying jobs is a health risk — for body and mind.

만약 우리가 기술을 받아들이면, 우리는 그것의 비용을 치러야 한다. 수천 개의 전통적인 생계 수단이 발전에 의해 밀려났으며, 그 직업과 관련된 생활 방식이 없어졌다. 오늘날 수억 명의 사람들이 자기가 싫어하는 일자리에서 일하면서, 자신이 아무런 애정을 느끼지 못하는 것들을 생산한다. 때때로 이러한 일자리는 육체적 고통, 장애 또는 만성 질환을 유발한다. 기술은 확실히 위험한 많은 새로운 일자리를 창출한다. 동시에, 대중 교육과 대중 매체는 낮은 기술의 육체노동을 피하고 디지털 세계에서 일하는 직업을 찾도록 인간을 훈련시킨다. 머리로부터 손이 단절되는 것은 인간의 정신에 부담을 준다. 실제로, 가장 보수가 좋은 직업의 주로 앉아서 하는 특성은 신체와 정신에 건강 위험 요소이다.

22

When students are starting their college life, they may [**approach** / **approach to**]³⁸⁾ every course, test, or learning task the [**same** / **different**]³⁹⁾ way, using what we like to call "the rubber-stamp approach." Think about <u>it</u> (가리키는 것은? ＿＿＿＿＿＿)⁴⁰⁾ this way: Would you wear a tuxedo to a baseball game? A colorful dress to a funeral? A bathing suit to religious services? Probably not. You know there's appropriate dress for different occasions and settings. Skillful learners know [**that** / **what**]⁴¹⁾ "putting on the same clothes" won't work for every class. They are [**rigid** / **flexible**]⁴²⁾ learners. They have [**difficult** / **different**]⁴³⁾ strategies and know when to use [**it** / **them**]⁴⁴⁾. They know [**what** / **that**]⁴⁵⁾ you study for multiple-choice tests [**different** / **differently**]⁴⁶⁾ than you study for essay tests. And they not only know [**what** / **how**]⁴⁷⁾ to do, but they also know [**what** / **how**]⁴⁸⁾ to do it.

대학 생활을 시작할 때 학생들은 우리가 '고무도장 방식'이라고 부르고 싶은 방법을 이용하여, 모든 과목이나, 시험, 학습 과제를 똑같은 방식으로 접근할지도 모른다. 그것을 이런 식으로 생각해 보라. 여러분은 야구 경기에 턱시도를 입고 가겠는가? 장례식에 화려한 드레스를 입고 가겠는가? 종교적인 예식에 수영복을 입고 가겠는가? 아마 아닐 것이다. 다양한 행사와 상황마다 적합한 옷이 있음을 여러분은 알고 있다. 숙련된 학습자는 '같은 옷을 입는 것'이 모든 수업에 효과가 있지는 않을 것임을 알고 있다. 그들은 유연한 학습자이다. 그들은 다양한 전략을 갖고 있으며 그것을 언제 사용해야 하는지 안다. 그들은 선다형 시험은 논술 시험을 위해 학습하는 것과는 다르게 학습한다는 것을 안다. 그리고 그들은 무엇을 해야 하는지 알고 있을 뿐만 아니라, 그것을 어떻게 해야 하는지도 알고 있다.

23

As the social and economic situation of countries got better, wage levels and working conditions [**improved** / **disproved**]⁴⁹⁾. Gradually people were [**given** / **giving**]⁵⁰⁾ more time off. At the same time, forms of [**transport** / **transmit**]⁵¹⁾ improved and [**it** / **they**]⁵²⁾ became faster and cheaper to get to places. England's industrial revolution led to many of these changes. Railways, in the nineteenth century, [**opened** / **opening**]⁵³⁾ up now famous seaside resorts such as Blackpool and Brighton. With the railways [**came** / **coming**]⁵⁴⁾ many large hotels. In Canada, for example, the new coast-to-coast railway system made [**possible** / **possibly**]⁵⁵⁾ the building of such famous hotels as Banff Springs and Chateau Lake Louise in the Rockies. Later, the arrival of air transport opened up more of the world and led to tourism growth.

국가들의 사회적, 경제적 상황이 더 나아지면서, 임금 수준과 근로 여건이 개선되었다. 점차 사람들은 더 많은 휴가를 받게 되었다. 동시에, 운송 형태가 개선되었고 장소를 이동하는 것이 더 빠르고 더 저렴해졌다. 영국의 산업 혁명이 이러한 변화 중 많은 것을 일으켰다. 19세기에, 철도로 인해 Blackpool과 Brighton 같은 현재 유명한 해안가 리조트가 들어서게 되었다. 철도가 생기면서 많은 대형 호텔이 생겨났다. 예를 들어, 캐나다에서는 새로운 대륙 횡단 철도 시스템이 로키산맥의 Banff Springs와 Chateau Lake Louise 같은 유명한 호텔의 건설을 가능하게 했다. 이후에 항공 운송의 출현은 세계의 더 많은 곳으로 가는 길을 열어 주었고 관광 산업의 성장을 이끌었다.

24

[Success / Succession]⁵⁶⁾ can lead you off your [intended / pretended]⁵⁷⁾ path and into a comfortable rut. If you are good at something and are well [rewarded / rewarding]⁵⁸⁾ for doing <u>it</u> (의미하는 바를 한글로 쓰시오.   )⁵⁹⁾, you may want to keep [doing / from doing]⁶⁰⁾ it even if you stop [enjoying / to enjoy]⁶¹⁾ it. The danger is [that / what]⁶²⁾ one day you look around and realize you're so deep in this comfortable rut [that / when]⁶³⁾ you can no longer see the sun or [breath / breathe]⁶⁴⁾ fresh air; the sides of the rut have become so slippery [that / when]⁶⁵⁾ it would take a superhuman effort to climb out; and, effectively, you're stuck. And it's a situation that many working people worry they're in now. The poor employment market has [left / left for]⁶⁶⁾ them feeling locked in [what / that]⁶⁷⁾ may be a secure, or even well-paying — but ultimately unsatisfying — job.

성공은 여러분을 의도한 길에서 벗어나 틀에 박힌 편안한 생활로 이끌 수 있다. 여러분이 어떤 일을 잘하고 그것을 하는 것에 대한 보상을 잘 받는다면, 그것을 즐기지 않게 되더라도 계속 그것을 하고 싶을 수도 있다. 위험한 점은 어느 날 여러분이 주변을 둘러보고, 자신이 틀에 박힌 이 편안한 생활에 너무나 깊이 빠져 있어서 더는 태양을 보거나 신선한 공기를 호흡할 수 없으며, 그 틀에 박힌 생활의 양쪽 면이 너무나 미끄럽게 되어 기어올라 나오려면 초인적인 노력이 필요할 것이고, 사실상 자신이 꼼짝할 수 없다는 것을 깨닫게 된다는 것이다. 그리고 그것은 많은 근로자가 현재 자신이 처해 있다고 걱정하는 상황이다. 열악한 고용 시장이 그들을 안정적이거나 심지어 보수가 좋을 수도 있지만, 궁극적으로는 만족스럽지 못한 일자리에 갇혀 있다고 느끼게 해 놓았다.

25

The above graph shows [a / the]⁶⁸⁾ number of births and deaths in Korea from 2016 to 2021. The number of births [continued / is continued]⁶⁹⁾ to decrease throughout the whole period. The gap between the number of births and deaths [was / were]⁷⁰⁾ the largest in 2016. In 2019, the gap between the number of births and deaths [was / were]⁷¹⁾ the smallest, with the number of births slightly larger than [that / those]⁷²⁾ of deaths. The number of deaths increased steadily during the whole period, except the period from 2018 to 2019. In 2021, the number of deaths was larger than that of births.

위 그래프는 2016년부터 2023년까지 한국에서의 출생자 수와 사망자 수를 보여 준다. 출생자 수는 전체 기간 내내 계속 감소했다. 출생자 수와 사망자 수 사이의 차이는 2016년에 가장 컸다. 2019년에는 출생자 수와 사망자 수 사이의 차이가 가장 작았는데, 출생자 수가 사망자 수보다 약간 더 컸다. 사망자 수는 2018년과 2019년까지의 기간을 제외하고 전체 기간 동안 꾸준히 증가했다. 2023년에는 사망자 수가 출생자 수보다 더 컸다.

26

Lilian Bland was born in Kent, England in 1878. [Like / Unlike]73) most other girls at the time she wore trousers and spent her time [enjoying / to enjoy]74) adventurous activities like horse riding and hunting. Lilian began her career as a sports and wildlife photographer for British newspapers. In 1910 she became the first woman to design, build, and fly her own airplane. In order to [persuade / permit]75) her [trying / to try]76) a slightly safer activity, Lilian's dad bought her a car. Soon Lilian was a master driver and ended up [working / to work]77) as a car dealer. She never went back to flying but lived a long and exciting life [likewise / nonetheless]78). She married, moved to Canada, and had a kid. Eventually, she moved back to England, and lived there for the rest of her life.

Lilian Bland는 1878년 잉글랜드 Kent에서 태어났다. 그 당시 대부분의 다른 여자아이와 달리 그녀는 바지를 입었고, 승마와 사냥 같은 모험적인 활동을 즐기며 시간을 보냈다. Lilian은 영국 신문사의 스포츠와 야생 동물 사진작가로 자신의 경력을 시작했다. 1910년에 그녀는 자신의 비행기를 설계하고, 제작하고, 비행한 최초의 여성이 되었다. 약간 더 안전한 활동을 하도록 그녀를 설득하기 위해, Lilian의 아버지는 그녀에게 자동차를 사주었다. 곧 Lilian은 뛰어난 운전자가 되었고 결국 자동차 판매원으로 일하게 되었다. 그녀는 결코 비행을 다시 시작하지 않았지만, 그렇더라도 오랫동안 흥미진진한 삶을 살았다. 그녀는 결혼하여 캐나다로 이주했고, 아이를 낳았다. 결국 잉글랜드로 돌아와 거기서 생의 마지막 기간을 보냈다.

29

The most noticeable human characteristic projected onto animals [is / are]79) that they can talk in human language. [Physically / Psychologically]80), animal cartoon characters and toys [made / are made]81) after animals are also most often [deformed / deforming]82) in such a way as to [resemble / resemble with]83) humans. This is achieved by showing [it / them]84) with humanlike facial features and deformed front legs to resemble human hands. In more recent [animated / animating]85) movies the trend has been to show the animals in a more "natural" way. However, they still use their front legs like human hands (for example, lions can pick up and lift small objects with one paw), and they still talk [to / with]86) an appropriate facial expression. A general strategy that is used to [make / making]87) the animal characters more emotionally [appealed / appealing]88), both to children and adults, is to give them [enlarged / enlarging]89) and [deformed / deforming]90) childlike features.

동물에게 투영된 가장 눈에 띄는 인간의 특징은 동물이 인간의 언어로 대화할 수 있다는 점이다. 신체적으로도, 동물 만화 캐릭터와 동물을 본떠 만든 장난감은 또한 인간을 닮게 하는 방식으로 변형되는 경우가 아주 많다. 이것은 인간과 같은 얼굴 특징과 사람의 손을 닮게 변형된 앞다리를 가지고 있는 것으로 그것들을 보여줌으로써 달성된다. 더 최근의 만화 영화에서 추세는 동물을 더 '자연스러운' 방식으로 묘사하는 것이었다. 그러나 그것들은 여전히 사람의 손처럼 앞다리를 사용하고, 여전히 적절한 표정을 지으며 이야기한다. 동물 캐릭터를 아이와 어른 모두에게 더 감정적으로 매력적이게 만들기 위해 이용하는 일반적인 전략은 그것들에 확대되고 변형된 어린이 같은 특징을 부여하는 것이다.

30

The major philosophical shift in the idea of selling came when industrial societies became more [fluent / affluent]⁹¹⁾, more competitive, and more geographically [spread / spreading]⁹²⁾ out during the 1940s and 1950s. This forced business to develop closer relations with buyers and clients, [that / which]⁹³⁾ in turn made business realize [that / what]⁹⁴⁾ it was not enough to produce a quality product at a reasonable price. In fact, it was equally essential to [deliver / delivering]⁹⁵⁾ products that customers actually wanted. Henry Ford produced his best-selling T-model Ford in one color only (black) in 1908, but in modern societies this was no longer possible. The modernization of society led to a marketing revolution that [destroyed / was destroyed]⁹⁶⁾ the view <u>that</u> (주관대?목적절 접속사? 동격의 접속사?)⁹⁷⁾ [product / production]⁹⁸⁾ would create [its / their]⁹⁹⁾ own demand. Customers, and the desire to meet their diverse and often complex needs, became the focus of business.

산업 사회가 1940년대와 1950년대 동안 더 부유하고, 더 경쟁적이고, 더 지리적으로 퍼져 나가게 되면서 판매 개념에 주요한 철학적 변화가 일어났다. 이로 인해 기업은 구매자 및 고객과 더 긴밀한 관계를 발전시켜야 했고, 이것은 결과적으로 기업이 합리적인 가격에 양질의 제품을 생산하는 것으로는 충분하지 않다는 것을 깨닫게 했다. 사실, 고객이 실제로 원하는 제품을 내놓는 것이 마찬가지로 매우 중요했다. 1908년에 Henry Ford는 자신의 가장 많이 팔렸던 T-모델 Ford를 단 하나의 색상(검은색)으로만 생산했지만, 현대사회에서는 이것이 더 이상 가능하지 않았다. 사회의 현대화는 생산이 그 자체의 수요를 창출할 것이라는 견해를 강화하는 마케팅 혁명으로 이어졌다. 고객과 그들의 다양하고 흔히 복잡한 욕구를 충족하고자 하는 욕망이 기업의 초점이 되었다.

31

People [differ / are differed]¹⁰⁰⁾ in how [quick / quickly]¹⁰¹⁾ they can reset their biological clocks to overcome jet lag, and the speed of recovery [depends / depending]¹⁰²⁾ on the direction of travel. Generally, it's easier to fly westward and lengthen your day than it is to fly eastward and shorten [it / them]¹⁰³⁾. This east-west difference in jet lag is [sizable enough / enough sizable]¹⁰⁴⁾ to have an impact on the performance of sports teams. Studies have [found / been found]¹⁰⁵⁾ that teams [flew / flying]¹⁰⁶⁾ westward perform significantly better than teams flying eastward in professional baseball and college football. A more recent study of more than 46,000 Major League Baseball games found additional evidence [which / that]¹⁰⁷⁾ eastward travel is tougher than westward travel.

시차로 인한 피로감을 극복하기 위해서 자신의 체내 시계를 얼마나 빨리 재설정할 수 있는지는 사람마다 서로 다르며, 그 회복 속도는 이동 방향에 달려 있다. 일반적으로 동쪽으로 비행하여 여러분의 하루를 단축하는 것보다 서쪽으로 비행하여 여러분의 하루를 연장하는 것이 더 쉽다. 시차로 인한 피로감에서 이러한 동서의 차이는 스포츠 팀의 경기력에 영향을 미칠 만큼 충분히 크다. 연구에 따르면 서쪽으로 비행하는 팀이 동쪽으로 비행하는 팀보다 프로 야구와 대학 미식 축구에서 상당히 더 잘한다. 46,000 경기가 넘는 메이저 리그 야구 경기에 대한 더 최근의 연구에 의해 동쪽으로 이동하는 것이 서쪽으로 이동하는 것보다 더 힘들다는 추가적인 증거가 발견되었다.

32

If you want the confidence that [comes / coming]108) from achieving [that / what]109) you set out to do each day, then it's important to understand [how / what]110) long things are going to take. Over-optimism about what can be achieved within a certain time frame is a problem. So work on it. Make a practice of [estimating / estimation]111) the amount of time [needed / needing]112) alongside items on your 'things to do' list, and learn by experience when tasks take a greater or lesser time than expected. [Give / Giving]113) attention also to [fit / fitting]114) the task to the available time. There are some tasks that you can only set about [if / whether]115) you have a significant amount of time available. There is no point [in / by]116) trying to gear up for such a task when you only have a short period available. So schedule the time you need for the longer tasks and put the short tasks into the spare moments in between.

만약 매일 하고자 착수하는 일을 성취함으로써 얻게 되는 자신감을 원한다면 일이 얼마나 시간이 걸릴지 아는 것이 중요하다. 어떤 특정 기간 내에 성취될 수 있는 것에 대한 지나친 낙관주의는 문제다. 그러므로 그것을 개선하려고 노력하라. '해야 할 일' 목록에 있는 항목과 함께, 필요한 시간의 양을 추산하는 것을 습관화하고, 과제가 언제 예상보다 더 많은 시간 또는 더 적은 시간이 걸리는지 경험을 통해 배우라. 그 이용 가능한 시간에 과제를 맞추는 것에도 또한 주의를 기울이라. 이용할 수 있는 시간의 양이 상당히 있어야만 시작할 수 있는 몇몇 과제가 있다. 이용할 수 있는 시간이 짧은 시간밖에 없을 때 그런 과제를 위해 준비를 갖추려고 애쓰는 것은 무의미하다. 그러므로 시간이 더 오래 걸리는 과제를 위해 필요한 시간을 계획하고, 그 사이의 남는 시간에 시간이 짧게 걸리는 과제를 배치하라.

33

In Lewis Carroll's *Through the Looking-Glass*, the Red Queen takes Alice on a race through the countryside. They run and they run, but then Alice discovers [that / what]117) they're still under the same tree from [which / that]118) they started. The Red Queen explains to Alice: "*here*, you see, it takes all the running you can do, to keep in the same place." Biologists sometimes use this Red Queen Effect to [explain / explain about]119) an evolutionary [principle / principal]120). If foxes [evolve / are evolved]121) to run faster so they can catch more rabbits, then only the fastest rabbits will live [enough long / long enough]122) to make a new generation of bunnies that run even faster — in which case, of course, only the fastest foxes will catch enough rabbits to thrive and pass on their genes. Even though they might run, the two species just stay in place.

Lewis Carroll의 Through the Looking-Glass에서 붉은 여왕은 Alice를 시골을 통과하는 한 경주에 데리고 간다. 그들은 달리고 또 달리지만, 그러다가 Alice는 자신들이 출발했던 나무 아래에 여전히 있음을 발견한다. 붉은 여왕은 Alice에게 "'여기서는' 보다시피 같은 장소에 머물러 있으려면 네가 할 수 있는 모든 뜀박질을 해야 한단다."라고 설명한다. 생물학자들은 때때로 이 '붉은 여왕 효과'를 사용해 진화 원리를 설명한다. 만약 여우가 더 많은 토끼를 잡기 위해 더 빨리 달리도록 진화한다면, 그러면 오직 가장 빠른 토끼만이 충분히 오래 살아 훨씬 더 빨리 달리는 새로운 세대의 토끼를 낳을 텐데, 물론 이 경우 가장 빠른 여우만이 충분한 토끼를 잡아 번성하여 자신들의 유전자를 물려줄 것이다. 그 두 종이 달린다 해도 그것들은 제자리에 머무를 뿐이다.

34

Everything in the world around us [was / were]123) finished in the mind of its creator before it was started. The houses we live in, the cars we drive, and our clothing — all of these began with an idea. Each idea was then studied, [refined / refining]124) and perfected before the first nail was driven or the first piece of cloth was cut. Long before the idea [turned / was turned]125) into a physical reality, the mind had clearly pictured the finished product. The human being designs his or her own future through [much / many]126) the same process. We begin with an idea about [how / what]127) the future will be. Over a period of time we [refine / confine]128) and perfect the vision. Before long, our every thought, decision and activity are all working in harmony to [bring / be brought]129) into existence what we have mentally [concluded / been concluded]130) about the future.

우리 주변 세상의 모든 것은 시작되기 전에 그것을 만들어 낸 사람의 마음속에서 완성되었다. 우리가 사는 집, 우리가 운전하는 자동차, 우리의 옷, 이 모든 것이 아이디어에서 시작했다. 각각의 아이디어는 그런 다음, 첫 번째 못이 박히거나 첫 번째 천 조각이 재단되기 전에, 연구되고, 다듬어지고, 완성되었다. 그 아이디어가 물리적 실체로 바뀌기 훨씬 전에 마음은 완제품을 분명하게 그렸다. 인간은 거의 같은 과정을 통해 자신의 미래를 설계한다. 우리는 미래가 어떨지에 대한 아이디어로 시작한다. 일정 기간에 걸쳐서 우리는 그 비전을 다듬어 완성한다. 머지않아, 우리의 모든 생각, 결정, 활동은 우리가 미래에 대해 머릿속에서 완성한 것을 생겨나게 하려고 모두 조화롭게 작용하게 된다.

35

Whose story it is [affects / is affected]131) [how / what]132) the story is. Change the main character, [or / and]133) the focus of the story must also change. If we look at the events through another character's eyes, we will interpret [it / them]134) differently. We'll place our sympathies with someone new. When the conflict [arises / arouses]135) that is the heart of the story, we will be [prayed / praying]136) for a different outcome. Consider, for example, how the tale of Cinderella would shift if [told / telling]137) from the viewpoint of an evil stepsister. *Gone with the Wind* is Scarlett O'Hara's story, but what if we were [shown / showing]138) the same events from the viewpoint of Rhett Butler or Melanie Wilkes?

'누구의' 이야기인지가 '무슨' 이야기인지에 영향을 미친다. 주인공을 바꾸면, 이야기의 초점도 틀림없이 바뀐다. 만약 우리가 다른 등장인물의 눈을 통해 사건을 본다면, 우리는 그것을 다르게 해석할 것이다. 우리는 새로운 누군가에게 공감할 것이다. 이야기의 핵심인 갈등이 발생할 때, 우리는 다른 결과를 간절히 바랄 것이다. 예를 들어, 신데렐라 이야기가 사악한 의붓자매의 관점에서 이야기된다면 어떻게 바뀔지 생각해 보라. Gone with the Wind는 Scarlett O'Hara의 이야기이지만, 만약 같은 사건이 Rhett Butler나 Melanie Wilkes의 관점에서 우리에게 제시된다면 어떠할 것인가?

36

In the Old Stone Age, small bands of 20 to 60 people [wandered / wondered]139) from place to place in search of food. Once people began farming, they could [settle / be settled]140) down near their farms. As a result, towns and villages grew larger. Living in communities allowed people [organizing / to organize]141) [them / themselves]142) more efficiently. They could divide up the work of producing food and other things (생략된 것은? _____)143) they needed. While some workers grew crops, others built new houses and made tools. Village dwellers also learned [working / to work]144) together to do a task faster. For example, toolmakers could share the work of making stone axes and knives. [By / In]145) working together, they could make more tools in the same amount of time.

구석기 시대에는 20~60명의 작은 무리가 식량을 찾아 이곳저곳을 돌아다녔다. 일단 농사를 짓기 시작하면서, 사람들은 자신들의 농경지 근처에 정착할 수 있었다. 그 결과, 도시와 마을이 더 커졌다. 공동체 생활을 통해 사람들은 자신들을 더 효율적으로 조직할 수 있었다. 그들은 식량과 자신들에게 필요한 다른 것들을 생산하는 일을 나눌 수 있었다. 어떤 노동자들은 농작물을 재배한 반면, 다른 노동자들은 새로운 집을 짓고 도구를 만들었다. 마을 거주자들은 또한 일을 더 빨리 하기 위해 함께 일하는 것도 배웠다. 예를 들어, 도구 제작자들은 돌도끼와 돌칼을 만드는 작업을 함께 할 수 있었다. 함께 일함으로써, 그들은 같은 시간 안에 더 많은 도구를 만들 수 있었다.

37

Natural processes form minerals in many ways. For example, hot melted rock material, [called / is called]146) magma, cools when it [arrives / reaches]147) the Earth's surface, or even if it's trapped below the surface. As magma cools, [its / their]148) atoms lose heat energy, move closer together, and begin to combine into compounds. [While / During]149) this process, atoms of the different compounds arrange [them / themselves]150) into orderly, repeating patterns. The type and amount of elements present in a magma partly determine [which / what]151) minerals will form. Also, the size of the crystals that form [depends / depending]152) partly on how [rapid / rapidly]153) the magma cools. When magma cools slowly, the crystals that form are generally large enough to see with the unaided eye. This is [why / because]154) the atoms have enough time to move together and form into larger crystals. When magma cools rapidly, the crystals that form will be small. In such cases, you can't easily see individual mineral crystals.

자연 과정은 많은 방법으로 광물을 형성한다. 예를 들어, 마그마라고 불리는 뜨거운 용암 물질은 지구의 표면에 도달할 때, 또는 심지어 표면 아래에 갇혔을 때도 식는다. 마그마가 식으면서, 마그마의 원자는 열에너지를 잃고, 서로 더 가까이 이동해, 화합물로 결합하기 시작한다. 이 과정 동안, 서로 다른 화합물의 원자가 질서 있고 반복적인 패턴으로 배열된다. 마그마에 존재하는 원소의 종류와 양이 어떤 광물이 형성될지를 부분적으로 결정한다. 또한, 형성되는 결정의 크기는 부분적으로는 마그마가 얼마나 빨리 식느냐에 달려있다. 마그마가 천천히 식으면, 형성되는 결정은 일반적으로 육안으로 볼 수 있을 만큼 충분히 크다. 이것은 원자가 함께 이동해 더 큰 결정을 형성할 충분한 시간을 가지기 때문이다. 마그마가 빠르게 식으면, 형성되는 결정은 작을 것이다. 그런 경우에는 개별 광물 결정을 쉽게 볼 수 없다.

38

All carbohydrates are basically sugars. Complex carbohydrates are the good carbohydrates for your body. These complex sugar compounds are very difficult to [**break** / be broken]155) down and can trap other nutrients like vitamins and minerals in their chains. As they slowly break down, [other / **the other**]156) nutrients are also [**released** / releasing]157) into your body, and can provide you [to / **with**]158) fuel for [**a** / the]159) number of hours. Bad carbohydrates, on the other hand, are simple sugars. Because their structure is not complex, they are easy to break down and hold few nutrients for your body other than the sugars from [what / **which**]160) they are made. Your body breaks down these carbohydrates rather quickly and what it cannot use [**converts** / is converted]161) to fat and stored in the body.

모든 탄수화물은 기본적으로 당이다. 복합 탄수화물은 몸에 좋은 탄수화물이다. 이러한 복당류 화합물은 분해하기 매우 어렵고 비타민과 미네랄 같은 다른 영양소를 그것의 사슬 안에 가두어 둘 수 있다. 그것들이 천천히 분해되면서, 다른 영양소도 여러분의 몸으로 방출되고, 많은 시간 동안 여러분에게 연료를 공급할 수 있다. 반면에 나쁜 탄수화물은 단당류이다. 그것의 구조는 복잡하지 않기 때문에, 그것은 분해되기 쉽고 그것이 만들어지는 당 외에 몸을 위한 영양소를 거의 가지고 있지 않다. 여러분의 몸은 이러한 탄수화물을 상당히 빨리 분해하고 그것(몸)이 사용할 수 없는 것은 지방으로 바뀌어 몸에 저장된다.

39

People commonly make the mistaken assumption [which / **that**]162) because a person has one type of characteristic, then they automatically have other characteristics [**which** / what]163) go with it. In one study, university students [gave / **were given**]164) descriptions of a guest lecturer before he spoke to the group. Half the students received a description [contained / **containing**]165) the word 'warm', [another / **the other**]166) half were told the speaker was 'cold'. The guest lecturer then led a discussion, after [what / **which**]167) the students [asked / **were asked**]168) to give their impressions of him. As [**expected** / expecting]169), there were large differences between the impressions formed by the students, depending upon their original information of the lecturer. It was also found that those students who expected the lecturer to be warm [**tended** / tending]170) to interact with him more. This shows [**that** / what]171) different expectations not only [**affect** / affect on]172) the impressions we form but also our behaviour and the relationship which is formed.

흔히 사람들은 어떤 사람이 한 가지 유형의 특성을 가지고 있기 때문에, 그러면 자동적으로 그것과 어울리는 다른 특성을 가지고 있다는 잘못된 가정을 한다. 한 연구에서, 대학생들은 초청 강사가 그 (대학생) 집단에게 강연을 하기 전에 그 강사에 대한 설명을 들었다. 학생들의 절반은 '따뜻하다'라는 단어가 포함된 설명을 들었고 나머지 절반은 그 강사가 '차갑다'는 말을 들었다. 그리고 나서 그 초청 강사가 토론을 이끌었고, 그 후에 학생들은 그(강사)에 대한 그들의 인상을 말해 달라고 요청받았다. 예상한 대로, 학생들에 의해 형성된 인상 간에는 그 강사에 대한 학생들의 최초 정보에 따라 큰 차이가 있었다. 또한, 그 강사가 따뜻할 것이라 기대한 학생들은 그와 더 많이 소통하는 경향이 있다는 것이 밝혀졌다. 이것은 서로 다른 기대가 우리가 형성하는 인상뿐만 아니라 우리의 행동 및 형성되는 관계에도 영향을 미친다는 것을 보여 준다.

40

To help decide what's risky and what's safe, who's trustworthy and who's not, we look for *social evidence*. From an evolutionary view, [followed / following]173) the group is almost always positive for our prospects of survival. "If everyone's doing it, it must be a [sensible / sensitive]174) thing to do," [explains / explains about]175) famous psychologist and best selling writer of *Influence*, Robert Cialdini. While we can frequently see this today in product reviews, even subtler cues within the environment can signal trustworthiness. Consider this: when you visit a local restaurant, are they busy? Is there a line outside or is [it / this]176) easy to find a seat? It is a hassle to wait, but a line can be a powerful cue that the food's tasty, and these seats are in demand. More often than not, it's good to [adopt / adapt]177) the practices of those around you.

무엇이 위험하고 무엇이 안전한지, 누구를 신뢰할 수 있고 누구를 신뢰할 수 없는지를 결정하는 것을 돕기 위해, 우리는 '사회적 증거'를 찾는다. 진화의 관점에서 볼 때, 집단을 따르는 것이 거의 항상 우리의 생존 전망에 긍정적이다. "모든 사람이 그것을 하고 있다면, 그것은 해야 할 분별 있는 일인 것이 틀림없다."라고 유명한 심리학자이자 Influence를 쓴 베스트셀러 작가인 Robert Cialdini는 설명한다. 오늘날 상품 평에서 이것을 자주 볼 수 있지만, 환경 내의 훨씬 더 미묘한 신호가 신뢰성을 나타낼 수 있다. 이것을 생각해 보라. 여러분이 어떤 지역의 음식점을 방문할 때, 그들이 바쁜가? 밖에 줄이 있는가, 아니면 자리를 찾기가 쉬운가? 기다리는 것은 성가신 일이지만, 줄은 음식이 맛있고 이곳의 좌석은 수요가 많다는 강력한 신호일 수 있다. 대개는 주변에 있는 사람들의 행동을 따르는 것이 좋다.

41,42

Chess masters [shown / showing]178) a chess board in the middle of a game for 5 seconds with 20 to 30 pieces still in play can immediately reproduce the position of the pieces from memory. Beginners, of course, are able to place only a [few / little]179). Now take the same pieces and place [it / them]180) on the board randomly and the difference is much reduced. The expert's advantage is only for familiar patterns — those previously stored in memory. [Faced / Facing]181) with unfamiliar patterns, even when it involves the same familiar domain, the expert's advantage [disappears / is disappeared]182).

The [beneficent / beneficial]183) effects of familiar structure on memory have [observed / been observed]184) for many types of expertise, including music. People with musical training can reproduce short sequences of musical notation more accurately than those with no musical training when notes follow unusual [sequences / consequences]185), but the advantage is much [reduced / reducing]186) when the notes are ordered randomly. Expertise also improves memory for sequences of movements. [Experienced / Experiencing]187) ballet dancers are able to repeat longer sequences of steps than less experienced dancers, and they can repeat a sequence of steps [made / making]188) up a routine better than steps ordered randomly. In each case, memory range [increases / is increased]189) by the ability to recognize familiar sequences and patterns.

체스판을 게임 중간에 20~30개의 말들이 아직 놓여있는 상태로 5초 동안 본 체스의 달인들은 그 말들의 위치를 기억으로부터 즉시 재현할 수 있다. 물론 초보자들은 겨우 몇 개(의 위치)만 기억해 낼 수 있다. 이제 같은 말들을 가져다가 체스판에 무작위로 놓으면 그 차이는 크게 줄어든다. 전문가의 유리함은 익숙한 패턴, 즉 이전에 기억에 저장된 패턴에 대해서만 있다. 익숙하지 않은 패턴에 직면하면, 같은 익숙한 분야와 관련 있는 경우라도 전문가의 유리함은 사라진다. 익숙한 구조가 기억에 미치는 유익한 효과는 음악을 포함하여 많은 유형의 전문 지식에서 관찰되어 왔다. 음표가 전형적인 순서를 따를 때는 음악 훈련을 받은 사람이 음악 훈련을 받지 않은 사람보다 짧은 연속된 악보를 더 정확하게 재현할 수 있지만, 음표가 무작위로 배열되면 그 유리함이 훨씬 줄어든다. 전문 지식은 또한 연속 동작에 대한 기억을 향상시킨다. 숙련된 발레 무용수가 경험이 적은 무용수보다 더 긴 연속 스텝을 반복할 수 있고, 무작위로 배열된 스텝보다 정해진 춤 동작을 이루는 연속 스텝을 더 잘 반복할 수 있다. 각각의 경우, 기억의 범위는 익숙한 순서와 패턴을 인식하는 능력에 의해 늘어난다.

43,44,45번

Once upon a time, there was a king who lived in a beautiful palace. [While / During]¹⁹⁰⁾ the king was away, a monster [approached / approached to]¹⁹¹⁾ the gates of the palace. The monster was so ugly and smelly [that / that]¹⁹²⁾ the guards froze in shock. He passed the guards and sat on the king's throne. The guards soon came to their senses, went in, and shouted at the monster, [demanded / demanding]¹⁹³⁾ that he get off the throne. With each bad word the guards [used / using]¹⁹⁴⁾, the monster grew more ugly and smelly. The guards got even angrier — they began to brandish their swords to scare the monster away from the palace. But he just grew bigger and bigger, eventually [took / taking]¹⁹⁵⁾ up the whole room. He grew more ugly and smelly than ever. Eventually the king returned. He was wise and kind and saw what was [happened / happening]¹⁹⁶⁾. He knew what to do. He smiled and said to the monster, "Welcome to my palace!" He asked the monster [if / that]¹⁹⁷⁾ he wanted a cup of coffee. The monster began to grow smaller as he drank the coffee. The king offered him some take-out pizza and fries. The guards immediately called for pizza. The monster [continued / was continued]¹⁹⁸⁾ to get smaller with the king's kind gestures. He then offered the monster a full body massage. As the guards helped with the [relaxed / relaxing]¹⁹⁹⁾ massage, the monster became tiny. With another act of kindness to the monster, he just [disappeared / was disappeared]²⁰⁰⁾.

옛날 옛적에, 아름다운 궁전에 사는 한 왕이 있었다. 왕이 없는 동안, 한 괴물이 궁전 문으로 접근했다. 그 괴물이 너무 추하고 냄새가 나서 경비병들은 충격으로 얼어붙었다. 그(괴물)는 경비병들을 지나 왕의 왕좌에 앉았다. 경비병들은 곧 정신을 차리고 안으로 들어가 그 괴물을 향해 소리치며 그에게 왕좌에서 내려올 것을 요구했다. 경비병들이 나쁜 말을 사용할 때마다, 그 괴물은 더 추해졌고, 더 냄새가 났다. 경비병들은 한층 더 화가 났다. 그들은 그 괴물을 겁주어 궁전에서 쫓아내려고 칼을 휘두르기 시작했다. 하지만 그는 그저 점점 더 커져서 결국 방 전체를 차지했다. 그는 그 어느 때 보다 더 추해졌고, 더 냄새가 났다. 마침내 왕이 돌아왔다. 그는 현명하고 친절했으며 무슨 일이 일어나고 있는지 알아차렸다. 그는 무엇을 해야 할지 알았다. 그는 미소를 지으며 그 괴물에게 "나의 궁전에 온 것을 환영하오!" 라고 말했다. 왕은 그 괴물에게 그가 커피 한 잔을 원하는지 물었다. 괴물은 그 커피를 마시면서 더 작아지기 시작했다. 왕은 그에게 약간의 테이크아웃 피자와 감자튀김을 제안했다. 경비병들은 즉시 피자를 시켰다. 그 괴물은 왕의 친절한 행동에 몸이 계속 더 작아졌다. 그러고 나서 그는 그 괴물에게 전신 마사지를 제안했다. 경비병들이 편안한 마사지를 도와주자 그 괴물은 매우 작아졌다. 그 괴물에게 또 한 번의 친절한 행동을 베풀자, 그는 바로 사라졌다.

18

To [who / whom]1) it may concern,

I am a resident of the Blue Sky Apartment. Recently I observed [that / which]2) the kid zone is in need of repairs. I want you to pay attention [to / at]3) the poor condition of the playground e_____4) in the zone. The swings are damaged, the paint is [fallen / falling]5) off, and some of the bolts on the slide are missing. The facilities have been in this terrible condition since we moved here. They are dangerous to the children [played / playing]6) there. Would you please have them [repaired / to repair]7) ? I would appreciate your immediate attention to solve this matter.

Yours sincerely, Nina Davis

19

On a two-week trip in the Rocky Mountains, I saw a grizzly bear in its [native / naive]8) habitat. At first, I felt joy as I [watched / watching]9) the bear [walk / to walk]10) across the land. He stopped every once in a while [turning / to turn]11) his head about, [sniffed / sniffing]12) deeply. He was [followed / following]13) the scent of something, and slowly I began to realize [that / what]14) this giant animal (가리키는 것은? _____)15) was smelling me! I froze. This was no longer a wonderful experience; it was now an issue of survival. The bear's [motivation / inspiration]16) was to find meat to eat, and I was clearly on his menu.

20

It is difficult for [any / none]17) of us to [maintain / containing]18) a constant level of attention throughout our working day. We all have body rhythms [characterise / characterised]19) by peaks and valleys of energy and alertness. You will achieve more, and feel [confident / confidently]20) as a benefit, if you schedule your most [demanded / demanding]21) tasks at times when you are best able to [cope / catch up]22) with them (가리키는 것은? _____)23) . If you haven't [thought / been thought]24) about energy peaks before, [take / taking]25) a few days to observe yourself. Try to note the times when you are at your best. We are all different. For some, the peak will come first thing in the morning, but for others it may take a while to warm up.

21

If we [adopt / adapt]²⁶⁾ technology, we need to pay [its / their]²⁷⁾ costs. Thousands of traditional livelihoods have been [pushed / pushing]²⁸⁾ aside by progress, and the lifestyles around those jobs [removed / removing]²⁹⁾. Hundreds of millions of humans today [work / works]³⁰⁾ at jobs they hate, [produce / producing]³¹⁾ things (생략된 것은? _____)³²⁾ they have no love for. Sometimes these jobs cause [physical / psychological]³³⁾ pain, disability, or chronic disease. Technology creates many new jobs that are certainly dangerous. At the same time, mass education and media train humans to [avoid / face]³⁴⁾ low-tech physical work, to seek jobs [worked / working]³⁵⁾ in the digital world. The divorce of the hands from the head [put / puts]³⁶⁾ a stress on the human mind. Indeed, the [sedentary / lively]³⁷⁾ nature of the best-paying jobs is a health risk — for body and mind.

22

When students are starting their college life, they may [approach / approach to]³⁸⁾ every course, test, or learning task the [same / different]³⁹⁾ way, using what we like to call "the rubber-stamp approach." Think about it (가리키는 것은? _____)⁴⁰⁾ this way: Would you wear a tuxedo to a baseball game? A colorful dress to a funeral? A bathing suit to religious services? Probably not. You know there's appropriate dress for different occasions and settings. Skillful learners know [that / what]⁴¹⁾ "putting on the same clothes" won't work for every class. They are [rigid / flexible]⁴²⁾ learners. They have [difficult / different]⁴³⁾ strategies and know when to use [it / them]⁴⁴⁾. They know [what / that]⁴⁵⁾ you study for multiple-choice tests [different / differently]⁴⁶⁾ than you study for essay tests. And they not only know [what / how]⁴⁷⁾ to do, but they also know [what / how]⁴⁸⁾ to do it.

23

As the social and economic situation of countries got better, wage levels and working conditions [improved / disproved]⁴⁹⁾. Gradually people were [given / giving]⁵⁰⁾ more time off. At the same time, forms of [transport / transmit]⁵¹⁾ improved and [it / they]⁵²⁾ became faster and cheaper to get to places. England's industrial revolution led to many of these changes. Railways, in the nineteenth century, [opened / opening]⁵³⁾ up now famous seaside resorts such as Blackpool and Brighton. With the railways [came / coming]⁵⁴⁾ many large hotels. In Canada, for example, the new coast-to-coast railway system made [possible / possibly]⁵⁵⁾ the building of such famous hotels as Banff Springs and Chateau Lake Louise in the Rockies. Later, the arrival of air transport opened up more of the world and led to tourism growth.

24

[Success / Succession]56) can lead you off your [intended / pretended]57) path and into a comfortable rut. If you are good at something and are well [rewarded / rewarding]58) for doing it (의미하는 바를 한글로 쓰시오.   )59), you may want to keep [doing / from doing]60) it even if you stop [enjoying / to enjoy]61) it. The danger is [that / what]62) one day you look around and realize you're so deep in this comfortable rut [that / when]63) you can no longer see the sun or [breath / breathe]64) fresh air; the sides of the rut have become so slippery [that / when]65) it would take a superhuman effort to climb out; and, effectively, you're stuck. And it's a situation that many working people worry they're in now. The poor employment market has [left / left for]66) them feeling locked in [what / that]67) may be a secure, or even well-paying — but ultimately unsatisfying — job.

25

The above graph shows [a / the]68) number of births and deaths in Korea from 2016 to 2021. The number of births [continued / is continued]69) to decrease throughout the whole period. The gap between the number of births and deaths [was / were]70) the largest in 2016. In 2019, the gap between the number of births and deaths [was / were]71) the smallest, with the number of births slightly larger than [that / those]72) of deaths. The number of deaths increased steadily during the whole period, except the period from 2018 to 2019. In 2021, the number of deaths was larger than that of births.

26

Lilian Bland was born in Kent, England in 1878. [Like / Unlike]73) most other girls at the time she wore trousers and spent her time [enjoying / to enjoy]74) adventurous activities like horse riding and hunting. Lilian began her career as a sports and wildlife photographer for British newspapers. In 1910 she became the first woman to design, build, and fly her own airplane. In order to [persuade / permit]75) her [trying / to try]76) a slightly safer activity, Lilian's dad bought her a car. Soon Lilian was a master driver and ended up [working / to work]77) as a car dealer. She never went back to flying but lived a long and exciting life [likewise / nonetheless]78). She married, moved to Canada, and had a kid. Eventually, she moved back to England, and lived there for the rest of her life.

29

The most noticeable human characteristic projected onto animals [is / are]79) that they can talk in human language. [Physically / Psychologically]80), animal cartoon characters and toys [made / are made]81) after animals are also most often [deformed / deforming]82) in such a way as to [resemble / resemble with]83) humans. This is achieved by showing [it / them]84) with humanlike facial features and deformed front legs to resemble human hands. In more recent [animated / animating]85) movies the trend has been to show the animals in a more "natural" way. However, they still use their front legs like human hands (for example, lions can pick up and lift small objects with one paw), and they still talk [to / with]86) an appropriate facial expression. A general strategy that is used to [make / making]87) the animal characters more emotionally [appealed / appealing]88), both to children and adults, is to give them [enlarged / enlarging]89) and [deformed / deforming]90) childlike features.

30

The major philosophical shift in the idea of selling came when industrial societies became more [fluent / affluent]91), more competitive, and more geographically [spread / spreading]92) out during the 1940s and 1950s. This forced business to develop closer relations with buyers and clients, [that / which]93) in turn made business realize [that / what]94) it was not enough to produce a quality product at a reasonable price. In fact, it was equally essential to [deliver / delivering]95) products that customers actually wanted. Henry Ford produced his best-selling T-model Ford in one color only (black) in 1908, but in modern societies this was no longer possible. The modernization of society led to a marketing revolution that [destroyed / was destroyed]96) the view that (주관대?목적절 접속사? 동격의 접속사?)97) [product / production]98) would create [its / their]99) own demand. Customers, and the desire to meet their diverse and often complex needs, became the focus of business.

31

People [differ / are differed]100) in how [quick / quickly]101) they can reset their biological clocks to overcome jet lag, and the speed of recovery [depends / depending]102) on the direction of travel. Generally, it's easier to fly westward and lengthen your day than it is to fly eastward and shorten [it / them]103). This east-west difference in jet lag is [sizable enough / enough sizable]104) to have an impact on the performance of sports teams. Studies have [found / been found]105) that teams [flew / flying]106) westward perform significantly better than teams flying eastward in professional baseball and college football. A more recent study of more than 46,000 Major League Baseball games found additional evidence [which / that]107) eastward travel is tougher than westward travel.

32

If you want the confidence that [comes / coming]108) from achieving [that / what]109) you set out to do each day, then it's important to understand [how / what]110) long things are going to take. Over-optimism about what can be achieved within a certain time frame is a problem. So work on it. Make a practice of [estimating / estimation]111) the amount of time [needed / needing]112) alongside items on your 'things to do' list, and learn by experience when tasks take a greater or lesser time than expected. [Give / Giving]113) attention also to [fit / fitting]114) the task to the available time. There are some tasks that you can only set about [if / whether]115) you have a significant amount of time available. There is no point [in / by]116) trying to gear up for such a task when you only have a short period available. So schedule the time you need for the longer tasks and put the short tasks into the spare moments in between.

33

In Lewis Carroll's *Through the Looking-Glass*, the Red Queen takes Alice on a race through the countryside. They run and they run, but then Alice discovers [that / what]117) they're still under the same tree from [which / that]118) they started. The Red Queen explains to Alice: "*here*, you see, it takes all the running you can do, to keep in the same place." Biologists sometimes use this Red Queen Effect to [explain / explain about]119) an evolutionary [principle / principal]120). If foxes [evolve / are evolved]121) to run faster so they can catch more rabbits, then only the fastest rabbits will live [enough long / long enough]122) to make a new generation of bunnies that run even faster — in which case, of course, only the fastest foxes will catch enough rabbits to thrive and pass on their genes. Even though they might run, the two species just stay in place.

34

Everything in the world around us [was / were]123) finished in the mind of its creator before it was started. The houses we live in, the cars we drive, and our clothing — all of these began with an idea. Each idea was then studied, [refined / refining]124) and perfected before the first nail was driven or the first piece of cloth was cut. Long before the idea [turned / was turned]125) into a physical reality, the mind had clearly pictured the finished product. The human being designs his or her own future through [much / many]126) the same process. We begin with an idea about [how / what]127) the future will be. Over a period of time we [refine / confine]128) and perfect the vision. Before long, our every thought, decision and activity are all working in harmony to [bring / be brought]129) into existence what we have mentally [concluded / been concluded]130) about the future.

35

Whose story it is [affects / is affected]131) [how / what]132) the story is. Change the main character, [or / and]133) the focus of the story must also change. If we look at the events through another character's eyes, we will interpret [it / them]134) differently. We'll place our sympathies with someone new. When the conflict [arises / arouses]135) that is the heart of the story, we will be [prayed / praying]136) for a different outcome. Consider, for example, how the tale of Cinderella would shift if [told / telling]137) from the viewpoint of an evil stepsister. *Gone with the Wind* is Scarlett O'Hara's story, but what if we were [shown / showing]138) the same events from the viewpoint of Rhett Butler or Melanie Wilkes?

36

In the Old Stone Age, small bands of 20 to 60 people [wandered / wondered]139) from place to place in search of food. Once people began farming, they could [settle / be settled]140) down near their farms. As a result, towns and villages grew larger. Living in communities allowed people [organizing / to organize]141) [them / themselves]142) more efficiently. They could divide up the work of producing food and other things (생략된 것은? _____)143) they needed. While some workers grew crops, others built new houses and made tools. Village dwellers also learned [working / to work]144) together to do a task faster. For example, toolmakers could share the work of making stone axes and knives. [By / In]145) working together, they could make more tools in the same amount of time.

37

Natural processes form minerals in many ways. For example, hot melted rock material, [called / is called]146) magma, cools when it [arrives / reaches]147) the Earth's surface, or even if it's trapped below the surface. As magma cools, [its / their]148) atoms lose heat energy, move closer together, and begin to combine into compounds. [While / During]149) this process, atoms of the different compounds arrange [them / themselves]150) into orderly, repeating patterns. The type and amount of elements present in a magma partly determine [which / what]151) minerals will form. Also, the size of the crystals that form [depends / depending]152) partly on how [rapid / rapidly]153) the magma cools. When magma cools slowly, the crystals that form are generally large enough to see with the unaided eye. This is [why / because]154) the atoms have enough time to move together and form into larger crystals. When magma cools rapidly, the crystals that form will be small. In such cases, you can't easily see individual mineral crystals.

38

All carbohydrates are basically sugars. Complex carbohydrates are the good carbohydrates for your body. These complex sugar compounds are very difficult to [break / be broken]155) down and can trap other nutrients like vitamins and minerals in their chains. As they slowly break down, [other / the other]156) nutrients are also [released / releasing]157) into your body, and can provide you [to / with]158) fuel for [a / the]159) number of hours. Bad carbohydrates, on the other hand, are simple sugars. Because their structure is not complex, they are easy to break down and hold few nutrients for your body other than the sugars from [what / which]160) they are made. Your body breaks down these carbohydrates rather quickly and what it cannot use [converts / is converted]161) to fat and stored in the body.

39

People commonly make the mistaken assumption [which / that]162) because a person has one type of characteristic, then they automatically have other characteristics [which / what]163) go with it. In one study, university students [gave / were given]164) descriptions of a guest lecturer before he spoke to the group. Half the students received a description [contained / containing]165) the word 'warm', [another / the other]166) half were told the speaker was 'cold'. The guest lecturer then led a discussion, after [what / which]167) the students [asked / were asked]168) to give their impressions of him. As [expected / expecting]169), there were large differences between the impressions formed by the students, depending upon their original information of the lecturer. It was also found that those students who expected the lecturer to be warm [tended / tending]170) to interact with him more. This shows [that / what]171) different expectations not only [affect / affect on]172) the impressions we form but also our behaviour and the relationship which is formed.

40

To help decide what's risky and what's safe, who's trustworthy and who's not, we look for *social evidence*. From an evolutionary view, [followed / following]173) the group is almost always positive for our prospects of survival. "If everyone's doing it, it must be a [sensible / sensitive]174) thing to do," [explains / explains about]175) famous psychologist and best selling writer of *Influence*, Robert Cialdini. While we can frequently see this today in product reviews, even subtler cues within the environment can signal trustworthiness. Consider this: when you visit a local restaurant, are they busy? Is there a line outside or is [it / this]176) easy to find a seat? It is a hassle to wait, but a line can be a powerful cue that the food's tasty, and these seats are in demand. More often than not, it's good to [adopt / adapt]177) the practices of those around you.

41,42

Chess masters [shown / showing]178) a chess board in the middle of a game for 5 seconds with 20 to 30 pieces still in play can immediately reproduce the position of the pieces from memory. Beginners, of course, are able to place only a [few / little]179). Now take the same pieces and place [it / them]180) on the board randomly and the difference is much reduced. The expert's advantage is only for familiar patterns — those previously stored in memory. [Faced / Facing]181) with unfamiliar patterns, even when it involves the same familiar domain, the expert's advantage [disappears / is disappeared]182).

The [beneficent / beneficial]183) effects of familiar structure on memory have [observed / been observed]184) for many types of expertise, including music. People with musical training can reproduce short sequences of musical notation more accurately than those with no musical training when notes follow unusual [sequences / consequences]185), but the advantage is much [reduced / reducing]186) when the notes are ordered randomly. Expertise also improves memory for sequences of movements. [Experienced / Experiencing]187) ballet dancers are able to repeat longer sequences of steps than less experienced dancers, and they can repeat a sequence of steps [made / making]188) up a routine better than steps ordered randomly. In each case, memory range [increases / is increased]189) by the ability to recognize familiar sequences and patterns.

43,44,45번

Once upon a time, there was a king who lived in a beautiful palace. [While / During]190) the king was away, a monster [approached / approached to]191) the gates of the palace. The monster was so ugly and smelly [that / that]192) the guards froze in shock. He passed the guards and sat on the king's throne. The guards soon came to their senses, went in, and shouted at the monster, [demanded / demanding]193) that he get off the throne. With each bad word the guards [used / using]194), the monster grew more ugly and smelly. The guards got even angrier — they began to brandish their swords to scare the monster away from the palace. But he just grew bigger and bigger, eventually [took / taking]195) up the whole room. He grew more ugly and smelly than ever. Eventually the king returned. He was wise and kind and saw what was [happened / happening]196). He knew what to do. He smiled and said to the monster, "Welcome to my palace!" He asked the monster [if / that]197) he wanted a cup of coffee. The monster began to grow smaller as he drank the coffee. The king offered him some take-out pizza and fries. The guards immediately called for pizza. The monster [continued / was continued]198) to get smaller with the king's kind gestures. He then offered the monster a full body massage. As the guards helped with the [relaxed / relaxing]199) massage, the monster became tiny. With another act of kindness to the monster, he just [disappeared / was disappeared]200).

18

To whom it may concern,

I am a r_____1) of the Blue Sky Apartment. Recently I observed that the kid zone is in need of repairs. I want you to pay a_____2) to the poor condition of the playground e_____3) in the zone. The swings are damaged, the paint is falling off, and some of the bolts on the slide are missing. The f_____4) have been in this terrible condition s_____5) we moved here. They are dangerous to the children playing there. Would you please have them r_____6) ? I would a_____7) your immediate attention to solve this matter.

Yours sincerely,

Nina Davis

관계자분께
저는 Blue Sky 아파트의 거주자입니다. 최근에 저는 아이들을 위한 구역이 수리가 필요하다는 것을 알게 되었습니다. 저는 귀하께서 그 구역 놀이터 설비의 열악한 상태에 관심을 기울여 주시기를 바랍니다. 그네가 손상되었고, 페인트가 떨어져 나가고 있고, 미끄럼틀의 볼트 몇 개가 빠져 있습니다. (놀이터) 시설은 우리가 이곳으로 이사 온 이후로 이렇게 형편없는 상태였습니다. 그것은 거기서 노는 아이들에게 위험합니다. 그것을 수리해 주시겠습니까? 이 문제를 해결하기 위해 즉각적인 관심을 두시면 감사하겠습니다. Nina Davis 드림

19

On a two-week trip in the Rocky Mountains, I saw a grizzly bear in its native h_____8) . At first, I felt joy as I watched the bear walk across the land. He stopped every once in a while to turn his head about, s_____9) deeply. He was following the s_____10) of something, and slowly I began to realize that this giant animal was smelling me! I froze. This was no longer a wonderful experience; it was now an i_____11) of survival. The bear's m_____12) was to find meat to eat, and I was clearly on his menu.

로키산맥에서 2주간의 여행 중, 나는 자연 서식지에서 회색곰 한 마리를 보았다. 처음에 나는 그 곰이 땅을 가로질러 걸어가는 모습을 보았을 때 기분이 좋았다. 그것은 이따금 멈춰 서서 고개를 돌려 깊게 코를 킁킁거렸다. 그것은 무언가의 냄새를 따라가고 있었고, 나는 서서히 거대한 이 동물이 내 냄새를 맡고 있다는 것을 깨닫기 시작했다! 나는 얼어붙었다. 이것은 더는 멋진 경험이 아니었고, 이제 생존의 문제였다. 그 곰의 동기는 먹을 고기를 찾는 것이었고, 나는 분명히 그의 메뉴에 올라 있었다.

20

It is **d**_____ **13)** for any of us to **m**_____ **14)** a constant level of attention throughout our working day. We all have body rhythms **c**_____ **15)** by peaks and valleys of energy and **a**_____ **16)** You will achieve more, and feel confident as a benefit, if you schedule your most **d**_____ **17)** tasks at times when you are best able to cope with them. If you haven't thought about energy **p**_____ **18)** before, take a few days to **o**_____ **19)** yourself. Try to note the times when you are at your best. We are all **d**_____ **20)** . For some, the peak will come first thing in the morning, but for others it may take a while to warm up.

우리 중 누구라도 근무일 내내 일정한 수준의 주의집중을 유지하기는 어렵다. 우리 모두 에너지와 기민함의 정점과 저점을 특징으로 하는 신체 리듬을 가지고 있다. 가장 힘든 작업을 그것을 가장 잘 처리할 수 있는 시간에 하도록 계획을 잡으면, 더 많은 것을 이루고 이익으로 자신감을 느낄 것이다. 만약 전에 에너지 정점에 관해 생각해 본 적이 없다면, 며칠 동안 자신을 관찰하라. 자신이 가장 좋은 상태일 때를 알아차리도록 노력하라. 우리는 모두 다르다. 어떤 사람에게는 정점이 아침에 제일 먼저 오지만, 다른 사람에게는 준비되는 데 얼마간의 시간이 걸릴 수도 있다.

21

If we adopt **t**_____ **21)** we need to pay its costs. Thousands of traditional **l**_____ **22)** have been pushed aside by progress, and the lifestyles around those jobs removed. Hundreds of millions of humans today work at jobs they hate, **p**_____ **23)** things they have no love for. Sometimes these jobs cause **p**_____ **24)** pain, disability, or **c**_____ **25)** disease. **T**_____ **26)** creates many new jobs that are certainly dangerous. At the same time, mass **e**_____ **27)** and media train humans to avoid **l**_____ **28)** physical work, to seek jobs working in the digital world. The **d**_____ **29)** of the hands from the head puts a stress on the human mind. Indeed, the **s**_____ **30)** nature of the best-paying jobs is a health risk — for body and mind.

만약 우리가 기술을 받아들이면, 우리는 그것의 비용을 치러야 한다. 수천 개의 전통적인 생계 수단이 발전에 의해 밀려났으며, 그 직업과 관련된 생활 방식이 없어졌다. 오늘날 수억 명의 사람들이 자기가 싫어하는 일자리에서 일하면서, 자신이 아무런 애정을 느끼지 못하는 것들을 생산한다. 때때로 이러한 일자리는 육체적 고통, 장애 또는 만성 질환을 유발한다. 기술은 확실히 위험한 많은 새로운 일자리를 창출한다. 동시에, 대중 교육과 대중 매체는 낮은 기술의 육체노동을 피하고 디지털 세계에서 일하는 직업을 찾도록 인간을 훈련시킨다. 머리로부터 손이 단절되는 것은 인간의 정신에 부담을 준다. 실제로, 가장 보수가 좋은 직업의 주로 앉아서 하는 특성은 신체와 정신에 건강 위험 요소이다.

22

When students are s_____31) their college life, they may a_____32) every course, test, or learning task the same way, using what we like to call "the rubber-stamp approach." Think about it this way: Would you wear a tuxedo to a baseball game? A colorful dress to a f_____33) ? A bathing suit to religious services? Probably not. You know there's a_____34) dress for different o_____35) and settings. S_____36) learners know that "putting on the same clothes" won't work for every class. They are f_____37) learners. They have different s_____38) and know when to use them. They know that you study for m_____39) tests differently than you study for essay tests. And they not only know what to do, but they also know how to do it.

대학 생활을 시작할 때 학생들은 우리가 '고무도장 방식'이라고 부르고 싶은 방법을 이용하여, 모든 과목이나, 시험, 학습 과제를 똑같은 방식으로 접근할지도 모른다. 그것을 이런 식으로 생각해 보라. 여러분은 야구 경기에 턱시도를 입고 가겠는가? 장례식에 화려한 드레스를 입고 가겠는가? 종교적인 예식에 수영복을 입고 가겠는가? 아마 아닐 것이다. 다양한 행사와 상황마다 적합한 옷이 있음을 여러분은 알고 있다. 숙련된 학습자는 '같은 옷을 입는 것'이 모든 수업에 효과가 있지는 않을 것임을 알고 있다. 그들은 유연한 학습자이다. 그들은 다양한 전략을 갖고 있으며 그것을 언제 사용해야 하는지 안다. 그들은 선다형 시험은 논술 시험을 위해 학습하는 것과는 다르게 학습한다는 것을 안다. 그리고 그들은 무엇을 해야 하는지 알고 있을 뿐만 아니라, 그것을 어떻게 해야 하는지도 알고 있다.

23

As the social and e_____40) situation of countries got better, w_____41) levels and working conditions i_____42) . Gradually people were g_____43) more time off. At the same time, forms of t_____44) improved and it became faster and cheaper to get to places. England's industrial r_____45) led to many of these changes. Railways, in the nineteenth century, opened up now famous s_____46) resorts such as Blackpool and Brighton. With the r_____47) came many large hotels. In Canada, for example, the new coast-to-coast railway system made p_____48) the building of such famous hotels as Banff Springs and Chateau Lake Louise in the Rockies. Later, the a_____49) of air t_____50) opened up more of the world and led to t_____51) growth.

국가들의 사회적, 경제적 상황이 더 나아지면서, 임금 수준과 근로 여건이 개선되었다. 점차 사람들은 더 많은 휴가를 받게 되었다. 동시에, 운송 형태가 개선되었고 장소를 이동하는 것이 더 빠르고 더 저렴해졌다. 영국의 산업 혁명이 이러한 변화 중 많은 것을 일으켰다. 19세기에, 철도로 인해 Blackpool과 Brighton 같은 현재 유명한 해안가 리조트가 들어서게 되었다. 철도가 생기면서 많은 대형 호텔이 생겨났다. 예를 들어, 캐나다에서는 새로운 대륙 횡단 철도 시스템이 로키산맥의 Banff Springs와 Chateau Lake Louise 같은 유명한 호텔의 건설을 가능하게 했다. 이후에 항공 운송의 출현은 세계의 더 많은 곳으로 가는 길을 열어 주었고 관광 산업의 성장을 이끌었다.

24

Success can lead you off your i_____52) path and into a c_____53) rut. If you are good at something and are well r_____54) for doing it, you may want to keep doing it even if you stop e_____55) it. The danger is that one day you look around and realize you're so deep in this comfortable rut that you can no longer see the sun or b_____56) fresh air; the sides of the rut have become so slippery that it would take a s_____57) effort to climb out; and, effectively, you're stuck. And it's a situation that many working people worry they're in now. The poor e_____58) market has left them feeling l_____59) in what may be a secure, or even w_____60) — but ultimately unsatisfying — job.

성공은 여러분을 의도한 길에서 벗어나 틀에 박힌 편안한 생활로 이끌 수 있다. 여러분이 어떤 일을 잘하고 그것을 하는 것에 대한 보상을 잘 받는다면, 그것을 즐기지 않게 되더라도 계속 그것을 하고 싶을 수도 있다. 위험한 점은 어느 날 여러분이 주변을 둘러보고, 자신이 틀에 박힌 이 편안한 생활에 너무나 깊이 빠져 있어서 더는 태양을 보거나 신선한 공기를 호흡할 수 없으며, 그 틀에 박힌 생활의 양쪽 면이 너무나 미끄럽게 되어 기어올라 나오려면 초인적인 노력이 필요할 것이고, 사실상 자신이 꼼짝할 수 없다는 것을 깨닫게 된다는 것이다. 그리고 그것은 많은 근로자가 현재 자신이 처해 있다고 걱정하는 상황이다. 열악한 고용 시장이 그들을 안정적이거나 심지어 보수가 좋을 수도 있지만, 궁극적으로는 만족스럽지 못한 일자리에 갇혀 있다고 느끼게 해 놓았다.

25

The above graph s_____61) the number of births and deaths in Korea from 2016 to 2021. The number of births continued to d_____62) throughout the whole period. The gap between the number of births and deaths was the largest in 2016. In 2019, the gap between the number of births and deaths was the smallest, with the number of births s_____63) larger than that of deaths. The number of deaths increased s_____64) during the whole period, e_____65) the period from 2018 to 2019. In 2021, the n_____66) of deaths was larger than that of births.

위 그래프는 2016년부터 2023년까지 한국에서의 출생자 수와 사망자 수를 보여 준다. 출생자 수는 전체 기간 내내 계속 감소했다. 출생자 수와 사망자 수 사이의 차이는 2016년에 가장 컸다. 2019년에는 출생자 수와 사망자 수 사이의 차이가 가장 작았는데, 출생자 수가 사망자 수보다 약간 더 컸다. 사망자 수는 2018년과 2019년까지의 기간을 제외하고 전체 기간 동안 꾸준히 증가했다. 2023년에는 사망자 수가 출생자 수보다 더 컸다.

26

Lilian Bland was born in Kent, England in 1878. Unlike most other girls at the time she wore t_____ 67) and spent her time e_____ 68) adventurous activities like horse riding and hunting. Lilian began her c_____ 69) as a sports and w_____ 70) photographer for British newspapers. In 1910 she became the first woman to design, build, and fly her own airplane. In order to p_____ 71) her to try a slightly safer activity, Lilian's dad bought her a car. Soon Lilian was a master driver and ended up w_____ 72) as a car dealer. She never went back to flying but lived a long and exciting life nonetheless. She married, moved to Canada, and had a kid. E_____ 73) , she moved back to England, and lived there for the rest of her life.

Lilian Bland는 1878년 잉글랜드 Kent에서 태어났다. 그 당시 대부분의 다른 여자아이와 달리 그녀는 바지를 입었고, 승마와 사냥 같은 모험적인 활동을 즐기며 시간을 보냈다. Lilian은 영국 신문사의 스포츠와 야생 동물 사진작가로 자신의 경력을 시작했다. 1910년에 그녀는 자신의 비행기를 설계하고, 제작하고, 비행한 최초의 여성이 되었다. 약간 더 안전한 활동을 하도록 그녀를 설득하기 위해, Lilian의 아버지는 그녀에게 자동차를 사주었다. 곧 Lilian은 뛰어난 운전자가 되었고 결국 자동차 판매원으로 일하게 되었다. 그녀는 결코 비행을 다시 시작하지 않았지만, 그렇더라도 오랫동안 흥미진진한 삶을 살았다. 그녀는 결혼하여 캐나다로 이주했고, 아이를 낳았다. 결국 잉글랜드로 돌아와 거기서 생의 마지막 기간을 보냈다.

29

The most n_____ 74) human characteristic p_____ 75) onto animals is that they can talk in human language. Physically, animal cartoon characters and toys made after animals are also most often d_____ 76) in such a way as to r_____ 77) humans. This is achieved by showing them with h_____ 78) facial features and d_____ 79) front legs to resemble human hands. In more recent a_____ 80) movies the trend has been to show the animals in a more "natural" way. H_____ _81) , they still use their front legs like human hands (for example, lions can pick up and lift small objects with one paw), and they still talk with an a_____ 82) f_____ 83) expression. A general strategy that is used to make the animal characters more emotionally a_____ 84) , both to children and adults, is to give them e_____ 85) and deformed childlike features.

동물에게 투영된 가장 눈에 띄는 인간의 특징은 동물이 인간의 언어로 대화할 수 있다는 점이다. 신체적으로도, 동물 만화 캐릭터와 동물을 본떠 만든 장난감은 또한 인간을 닮게 하는 방식으로 변형되는 경우가 아주 많다. 이것은 인간과 같은 얼굴 특징과 사람의 손을 닮게 변형된 앞다리를 가지고 있는 것으로 그것들을 보여줌으로써 달성된다. 더 최근의 만화 영화에서 추세는 동물을 더 '자연스러운' 방식으로 묘사하는 것이었다. 그러나 그것들은 여전히 사람의 손처럼 앞다리를 사용하고, 여전히 적절한 표정을 지으며 이야기한다. 동물 캐릭터를 아이와 어른 모두에게 더 감정적으로 매력적이게 만들기 위해 이용하는 일반적인 전략은 그것들에 확대되고 변형된 어린이 같은 특징을 부여하는 것이다.

30

The major **p**_____86) shift in the idea of selling came when industrial societies became more **a**_____87) , more **c**_____88) , and more **g**_____89) spread out during the 1940s and 1950s. This forced business to develop closer relations with buyers and **c**_____90) , which in turn made business realize that it was not enough to produce a quality product at a **r**_____91) price. In fact, it was equally **e**_____92) to deliver products that customers actually wanted. Henry Ford produced his best-selling T-model Ford in one color only (black) in 1908, but in modern societies this was no longer possible. The **m**_____93) of society led to a **m**_____94) revolution that destroyed the view that production would create its own demand. Customers, and the **d**_____95) to meet their **d**_____96) and often complex needs, became the focus of business.

산업 사회가 1940년대와 1950년대 동안 더 부유하고, 더 경쟁적이고, 더 지리적으로 퍼져 나가게 되면서 판매 개념에 주요한 철학적 변화가 일어났다. 이로 인해 기업은 구매자 및 고객과 더 긴밀한 관계를 발전시켜야 했고, 이것은 결과적으로 기업이 합리적인 가격에 양질의 제품을 생산하는 것으로는 충분하지 않다는 것을 깨닫게 했다. 사실, 고객이 실제로 원하는 제품을 내놓는 것이 마찬가지로 매우 중요했다. 1908년에 Henry Ford는 자신의 가장 많이 팔렸던 T-모델 Ford를 단 하나의 색상(검은색)으로만 생산했지만, 현대사회에서는 이것이 더 이상 가능하지 않았다. 사회의 현대화는 생산이 그 자체의 수요를 창출할 것이라는 견해를 강화하는 마케팅 혁명으로 이어졌다. 고객과 그들의 다양하고 흔히 복잡한 욕구를 충족하고자 하는 욕망이 기업의 초점이 되었다.

31

People differ in how quickly they can reset their **b**_____97) clocks to **o**_____98) jet lag, and the speed of **r**_____99) depends on the direction of travel. Generally, it's **e**_____100) to fly westward and **l**_____101) your day than it is to fly eastward and shorten it. This east-west difference in jet lag is **s**_____102) enough to have an impact on the **p**_____103) of sports teams. Studies have found that teams flying westward **p**_____104) significantly better than teams flying eastward in professional baseball and college football. A more recent study of more than 46,000 Major League Baseball games **f**_____105) additional evidence that eastward travel is **t**_____106) than westward travel.

시차로 인한 피로감을 극복하기 위해서 자신의 체내 시계를 얼마나 빨리 재설정할 수 있는지는 사람마다 서로 다르며, 그 회복 속도는 이동 방향에 달려 있다. 일반적으로 동쪽으로 비행하여 여러분의 하루를 단축하는 것보다 서쪽으로 비행하여 여러분의 하루를 연장하는 것이 더 쉽다. 시차로 인한 피로감에서 이러한 동서의 차이는 스포츠 팀의 경기력에 영향을 미칠 만큼 충분히 크다. 연구에 따르면 서쪽으로 비행하는 팀이 동쪽으로 비행하는 팀보다 프로 야구와 대학 미식 축구에서 상당히 더 잘한다. 46,000 경기가 넘는 메이저 리그 야구 경기에 대한 더 최근의 연구에 의해 동쪽으로 이동하는 것이 서쪽으로 이동하는 것보다 더 힘들다는 추가적인 증거가 발견되었다.

32

If you want the **c**_____107) that comes from **a**_____108) what you set out to do each day, then it's **i**_____109) to understand how long things are going to take. **O**_____110) about what can be achieved within a certain time frame is a problem. So work on it. Make a practice of **e**_____111) the amount of time needed alongside items on your 'things to do' list, and learn by **e**_____112) when tasks take a greater or lesser time than **e**_____113) .Give attention also to fitting the task to the available time. There are some tasks that you can only set about if you have a **s**_____114) amount of time **a**_____115) . There is no point in trying to **g**_____116) up for such a task when you only have a short period available. So schedule the time you need for the **l**_____117) tasks and put the short tasks into the **s**_____118) moments in between.

만약 매일 하고자 착수하는 일을 성취함으로써 얻게 되는 자신감을 원한다면 일이 얼마나 시간이 걸릴지 아는 것이 중요하다. 어떤 특정 기간 내에 성취될 수 있는 것에 대한 지나친 낙관주의는 문제다. 그러므로 그것을 개선하려고 노력하라. '해야 할 일' 목록에 있는 항목과 함께, 필요한 시간의 양을 추산하는 것을 습관화하고, 과제가 언제 예상보다 더 많은 시간 또는 더 적은 시간이 걸리는지 경험을 통해 배우라. 그 이용 가능한 시간에 과제를 맞추는 것에도 또한 주의를 기울이라. 이용할 수 있는 시간의 양이 상당히 있어야만 시작할 수 있는 몇몇 과제가 있다. 이용할 수 있는 시간이 짧은 시간밖에 없을 때 그런 과제를 위해 준비를 갖추려고 애쓰는 것은 무의미하다. 그러므로 시간이 더 오래 걸리는 과제를 위해 필요한 시간을 계획하고, 그 사이의 남는 시간에 시간이 짧게 걸리는 과제를 배치하라.

33

In Lewis Carroll's *Through the Looking-Glass*, the Red Queen takes Alice on a race through the countryside. They run and they run, but then Alice **d**_____119) that they're still under the same tree that they started **f**_____120) . The Red Queen explains to Alice: "*here*, you see, it takes all the running you can _____121) , to keep in the same place." **B**_____122) sometimes use this Red Queen Effect to explain an **e**_____123) **p**_____124) . If foxes **e**_____125) to run faster so they can catch more rabbits, then only the fastest rabbits will live long enough to make a new generation of bunnies that **r**_____126) even faster — in **w**_____127) case, of course, only the fastest foxes will catch enough rabbits to **t**_____128) and **p**_____129) on their genes. Even though they might run, the two species just stay in place.

Lewis Carroll의 Through the Looking-Glass에서 붉은 여왕은 Alice를 시골을 통과하는 한 경주에 데리고 간다. 그들은 달리고 또 달리지만, 그러다가 Alice는 자신들이 출발했던 나무 아래에 여전히 있음을 발견한다. 붉은 여왕은 Alice에게 "'여기서는' 보다시피 같은 장소에 머물러 있으려면 네가 할 수 있는 모든 뜀박질을 해야 한단다."라고 설명한다. 생물학자들은 때때로 이 '붉은 여왕 효과'를 사용해 진화 원리를 설명한다. 만약 여우가 더 많은 토끼를 잡기 위해 더 빨리 달리도록 진화한다면, 그러면 오직 가장 빠른 토끼만이 충분히 오래 살아 훨씬 더 빨리 달리는 새로운 세대의 토끼를 낳을 텐데, 물론 이 경우 가장 빠른 여우만이 충분한 토끼를 잡아 번성하여 자신들의 유전자를 물려줄 것이다. 그 두 종이 달린다 해도 그것들은 제자리에 머무를 뿐이다.

34

Everything in the world around us was f_____130) in the mind of its creator before it was s_____131) . The houses we live in, the cars we drive, and our clothing — all of these began with an i_____132) . Each idea was then studied, r_____133) and p_____134) before the first nail was driven or the first piece of cloth was cut. Long before the idea was turned into a physical r_____135) , the mind had clearly p_____136) the finished product. The human being d_____137) his or her own future through much the same p_____138) . We begin with an i_____139) about how the f_____140) will be. Over a period of time we r_____141) and p_____142) the v_____143) . Before long, our every thought, decision and activity are all working in harmony to bring into e_____144) what we have mentally c_____145) about the future.

우리 주변 세상의 모든 것은 시작되기 전에 그것을 만들어 낸 사람의 마음속에서 완성되었다. 우리가 사는 집, 우리가 운전하는 자동차, 우리의 옷, 이 모든 것이 아이디어에서 시작했다. 각각의 아이디어는 그런 다음, 첫 번째 못이 박히거나 첫 번째 천 조각이 재단되기 전에, 연구되고, 다듬어지고, 완성되었다. 그 아이디어가 물리적 실체로 바뀌기 훨씬 전에 마음은 완제품을 분명하게 그렸다. 인간은 거의 같은 과정을 통해 자신의 미래를 설계한다. 우리는 미래가 어떨지에 대한 아이디어로 시작한다. 일정 기간에 걸쳐서 우리는 그 비전을 다듬어 완성한다. 머지않아, 우리의 모든 생각, 결정, 활동은 우리가 미래에 대해 머릿속에서 완성한 것을 생겨나게 하려고 모두 조화롭게 작용하게 된다.

35

Whose story it is a_____146) what the story is. Change the main character, and the focus of the story must also c_____147) . If we look at the events through another character's eyes, we will i_____148) them differently. We'll place our s_____149) with someone new. When the c_____150) arises that is the heart of the story, we will be praying for a d_____151) o_____152) . Consider, for example, how the tale of Cinderella would shift if told from the v_____153) of an evil stepsister. *Gone with the Wind* is Scarlett O'Hara's story, but what if we were s_____154) the same events from the v_____155) of Rhett Butler or Melanie Wilkes?

'누구의' 이야기인지가 '무슨' 이야기인지에 영향을 미친다. 주인공을 바꾸면, 이야기의 초점도 틀림없이 바뀐다. 만약 우리가 다른 등장인물의 눈을 통해 사건을 본다면, 우리는 그것을 다르게 해석할 것이다. 우리는 새로운 누군가에게 공감할 것이다. 이야기의 핵심인 갈등이 발생할 때, 우리는 다른 결과를 간절히 바랄 것이다. 예를 들어, 신데렐라 이야기가 사악한 의붓자매의 관점에서 이야기된다면 어떻게 바뀔지 생각해 보라. Gone with the Wind는 Scarlett O'Hara의 이야기이지만, 만약 같은 사건이 Rhett Butler나 Melanie Wilkes의 관점에서 우리에게 제시된다면 어떠할 것인가?

36

In the Old Stone Age, small bands of 20 to 60 people **w**_____156) from place to place in search of food. Once people began **f**_____157) , they could **s**_____158) down near their farms. As a result, towns and villages grew **l**_____159) . Living in **c**_____160) **a**_____161) people to **o**_____162) themselves more **e**_____163) . They could **d**_____164) up the work of producing food and other things they needed. While some workers grew crops, others built new houses and made tools. Village **d**_____165) also learned to work **t**_____166) to do a task **f**_____ _167) . For example, toolmakers could **s**_____168) the work of making stone axes and knives. By working together, they could make **m**_____169) tools in the **s**_____170) amount of time.

구석기 시대에는 20~60명의 작은 무리가 식량을 찾아 이곳저곳을 돌아다녔다. 일단 농사를 짓기 시작하면서, 사람들은 자신들의 농경지 근처에 정착할 수 있었다. 그 결과, 도시와 마을이 더 커졌다. 공동체 생활을 통해 사람들은 자신들을 더 효율적으로 조직할 수 있었다. 그들은 식량과 자신들에게 필요한 다른 것들을 생산하는 일을 나눌 수 있었다. 어떤 노동자들은 농작물을 재배한 반면, 다른 노동자들은 새로운 집을 짓고 도구를 만들었다. 마을 거주자들은 또한 일을 더 빨리 하기 위해 함께 일하는 것도 배웠다. 예를 들어, 도구 제작자들은 돌도끼와 돌칼을 만드는 작업을 함께 할 수 있었다. 함께 일함으로써, 그들은 같은 시간 안에 더 많은 도구를 만들 수 있었다.

37

Natural **p**_____171) **f**_____172) minerals in many ways. For example, hot melted rock material, called magma, **c**_____173) when it **r**_____174) the Earth's surface, or even if it's **t**_____ _175) below the surface. As magma cools, its atoms **l**_____176) heat energy, move **c**_____177) together, and begin to **c**_____178) into **c**_____179) . During this process, **a**_____180) of the different **c**_____181) **a**_____182) themselves into **o**_____183) , **r**_____184) patterns. The type and amount of elements **p**_____185) in a magma partly **d**_____186) which minerals will **f**_____187) . Also, the size of the **c**_____188) that form depends partly on how **r**_____189) the magma **c**_____190) . When magma **c**_____191) slowly, the crystals that form are generally **l**_____192) enough to see with the **u**_____193) eye. This is because the atoms have enough time to move together and form into **l**_____194) crystals. When magma cools **r**_____195) , the crystals that form will be **s**_____196) . In such cases, you can't easily see individual mineral crystals.

자연 과정은 많은 방법으로 광물을 형성한다. 예를 들어, 마그마라고 불리는 뜨거운 용암 물질은 지구의 표면에 도달할 때, 또는 심지어 표면 아래에 갇혔을 때도 식는다. 마그마가 식으면서, 마그마의 원자는 열에너지를 잃고, 서로 더 가까이 이동해, 화합물로 결합하기 시작한다. 이 과정 동안, 서로 다른 화합물의 원자가 질서 있고 반복적인 패턴으로 배열된다. 마그마에 존재하는 원소의 종류와 양이 어떤 광물이 형성될지를 부분적으로 결정한다. 또한, 형성되는 결정의 크기는 부분적으로는 마그마가 얼마나 빨리 식느냐에 달려있다. 마그마가 천천히 식으면, 형성되는 결정은 일반적으로 육안으로 볼 수 있을 만큼 충분히 크다. 이것은 원자가 함께 이동해 더 큰 결정을 형성할 충분한 시간을 가지기 때문이다. 마그마가 빠르게 식으면, 형성되는 결정은 작을 것이다. 그런 경우에는 개별 광물 결정을 쉽게 볼 수 없다.

38

All c_____197) are basically sugars. C_____198) c_____199) are the good carbohydrates for your body. These c_____200) sugar c_____201) are very difficult to b_____202) down and can t_____203) other nutrients like vitamins and minerals in their chains. As they slowly break down, the other nutrients are also r_____204) into your body, and can p_____205) you with fuel for a number of hours. Bad carbohydrates, on the other hand, are s_____206) sugars. Because their structure is not complex, they are easy to break down and h_____207) few nutrients for your body other than the sugars f_____208) which they are made. Your body b_____209) down these carbohydrates rather q_____210) and what it cannot use is c_____211) to fat and s_____212) in the body.

모든 탄수화물은 기본적으로 당이다. 복합 탄수화물은 몸에 좋은 탄수화물이다. 이러한 복당류 화합물은 분해하기 매우 어렵고 비타민과 미네랄 같은 다른 영양소를 그것의 사슬 안에 가두어 둘 수 있다. 그것들이 천천히 분해되면서, 다른 영양소도 여러분의 몸으로 방출되고, 많은 시간 동안 여러분에게 연료를 공급할 수 있다. 반면에 나쁜 탄수화물은 단당류이다. 그것의 구조는 복잡하지 않기 때문에, 그것은 분해되기 쉽고 그것이 만들어지는 당 외에 몸을 위한 영양소를 거의 가지고 있지 않다. 여러분의 몸은 이러한 탄수화물을 상당히 빨리 분해하고 그것(몸)이 사용할 수 없는 것은 지방으로 바뀌어 몸에 저장된다.

39

People commonly make the m_____213) a_____214) that because a person has one type of characteristic, then they a_____215) have other characteristics which go w_____216) it. In one study, university students were given d_____217) of a guest lecturer before he spoke to the group. Half the students r_____218) a description c_____219) the word 'warm', the other half were told the speaker was 'cold'. The guest lecturer then l_____220) a discussion, after w_____221) the students were asked to give their i_____222) of him. As expected, there were large d_____223) between the impressions f_____224) by the students, depending upon their o_____225) information of the lecturer. It was also found that those students who e_____226) the lecturer to be warm tended to i_____227) with him more. This shows that different e_____228) not only a_____229) the i_____230) we form but also our b_____231) and the r_____232) which is formed.

혼히 사람들은 어떤 사람이 한 가지 유형의 특성을 가지고 있기 때문에, 그러면 자동적으로 그것과 어울리는 다른 특성을 가지고 있다는 잘못된 가정을 한다. 한 연구에서, 대학생들은 초청 강사가 그 (대학생) 집단에게 강연을 하기 전에 그 강사에 대한 설명을 들었다. 학생들의 절반은 '따뜻하다'라는 단어가 포함된 설명을 들었고 나머지 절반은 그 강사가 '차갑다'는 말을 들었다. 그러고 나서 그 초청 강사가 토론을 이끌었고, 그 후에 학생들은 그(강사)에 대한 그들의 인상을 말해 달라고 요청받았다. 예상한 대로, 학생들에 의해 형성된 인상 간에는 그 강사에 대한 학생들의 최초 정보에 따라 큰 차이가 있었다. 또한, 그 강사가 따뜻할 것이라 기대한 학생들은 그와 더 많이 소통하는 경향이 있다는 것이 밝혀졌다. 이것은 서로 다른 기대가 우리가 형성하는 인상뿐만 아니라 우리의 행동 및 형성되는 관계에도 영향을 미친다는 것을 보여 준다.

40

To help decide what's r_____233) and what's s_____234) , who's t_____235) and who's not, we look for s_____236) *evidence*. From an e_____237) view, following the group is almost always p_____238) for our p_____239) of s_____240) . "If everyone's doing it, it must be a s_____241) thing to do," explains famous psychologist and best selling writer of *Influence*, Robert Cialdini. While we can frequently see this today in product reviews, even s_____242) c_____243) within the environment can signal t_____244) . Consider this: when you visit a local restaurant, are they busy? Is there a line outside or is it easy to find a seat? It is a h_____245) to wait, but a line can be a p_____246) c_____247) that the food's tasty, and these seats are in d_____248) . More often than not, it's good to a_____249) the p_____250) of those around you.

무엇이 위험하고 무엇이 안전한지, 누구를 신뢰할 수 있고 누구를 신뢰할 수 없는지를 결정하는 것을 돕기 위해, 우리는 '사회적 증거'를 찾는다. 진화의 관점에서 볼 때, 집단을 따르는 것이 거의 항상 우리의 생존 전망에 긍정적이다. "모든 사람이 그것을 하고 있다면, 그것은 해야 할 분별 있는 일인 것이 틀림없다."라고 유명한 심리학자이자 Influence를 쓴 베스트셀러 작가인 Robert Cialdini는 설명한다. 오늘날 상품 평에서 이것을 자주 볼 수 있지만, 환경 내의 훨씬 더 미묘한 신호가 신뢰성을 나타낼 수 있다. 이것을 생각해 보라. 여러분이 어떤 지역의 음식점을 방문할 때, 그들이 바쁜가? 밖에 줄이 있는가, 아니면 자리를 찾기가 쉬운가? 기다리는 것은 성가신 일이지만, 줄은 음식이 맛있고 이곳의 좌석은 수요가 많다는 강력한 신호일 수 있다. 대개는 주변에 있는 사람들의 행동을 따르는 것이 좋다.

41-42

Chess masters s_____251) a chess board in the middle of a game for 5 seconds with 20 to 30 pieces still in play can immediately r_____252) the position of the pieces from m_____253) . Beginners, of course, are able to place only a few. Now take the same pieces and place them on the board r_____254) and the d_____255) is much r_____256) . The expert's a_____257) is only for f_____258) p_____259) — those p_____260) s_____261) in memory. F_____262) with u_____263) patterns, even when it i_____264) the same f_____265) d_____266) , the expert's advantage d_____267) .

체스판을 게임 중간에 20~30개의 말들이 아직 놓여있는 상태로 5초 동안 본 체스의 달인들은 그 말들의 위치를 기억으로부터 즉시 재현할 수 있다. 물론 초보자들은 겨우 몇 개(의 위치)만 기억해 낼 수 있다. 이제 같은 말들을 가져다가 체스판에 무작위로 놓으면 그 차이는 크게 줄어든다. 전문가의 유리함은 익숙한 패턴, 즉 이전에 기억에 저장된 패턴에 대해서만 있다. 익숙하지 않은 패턴에 직면하면, 같은 익숙한 분야와 관련 있는 경우라도 전문가의 유리함은 사라진다.

The **b**_____268) effects of **f**_____269) **s**_____270) on **m**_____271) have been **o**_____272) for many types of **e**_____273) , including music. People with musical training can **r**_____274) short **s**_____275) of musical **n**_____276) more **a**_____277) than those with no musical training when notes follow **u**_____278) **s**_____279) , but the advantage is much reduced when the notes are **o**_____280) **r**_____281) . **E**_____282) also **i**_____ _283) **m**_____284) for sequences of movements. Experienced ballet dancers are able to **r**_____ _285) longer sequences of steps than less experienced dancers, and they can repeat a sequence of steps making up a routine better than steps **o**_____286) **r**_____287) . In each case, memory range is **i**_____288) by the ability to recognize **f**_____289) sequences and patterns.

익숙한 구조가 기억에 미치는 유익한 효과는 음악을 포함하여 많은 유형의 전문 지식에서 관찰되어 왔다. 음표가 전형적인 순서를 따를 때는 음악 훈련을 받은 사람이 음악 훈련을 받지 않은 사람보다 짧은 연속된 악보를 더 정확하게 재현할 수 있지만, 음표가 무작위로 배열되면 그 유리함이 훨씬 줄어든다. 전문 지식은 또한 연속 동작에 대한 기억을 향상시킨다. 숙련된 발레 무용수가 경험이 적은 무용수보다 더 긴 연속 스텝을 반복할 수 있고, 무작위로 배열된 스텝보다 정해진 춤 동작을 이루는 연속 스텝을 더 잘 반복할 수 있다. 각각의 경우, 기억의 범위는 익숙한 순서와 패턴을 인식하는 능력에 의해 늘어난다.

43-45

Once upon a time, there was a king who lived in a beautiful palace. While the king was away, a monster **a**_____290) the gates of the palace. The monster was so ugly and smelly that the guards **f**_____291) in shock. He passed the guards and sat on the king's **t**_____292) . The guards soon came to their senses, went in, and shouted at the monster, **d**_____293) that he get off the throne. With each bad word the guards **u**_____294) , the monster grew more ugly and smelly. The guards got even angrier — they began to **b**_____295) their swords to scare the monster away from the palace. But he just grew bigger and bigger, eventually taking up the whole room. He grew more ugly and smelly than ever. Eventually the king returned. He was wise and kind and saw what was happening. He knew what to do. He smiled and said to the monster, "Welcome to my palace!" He asked the monster **i**_____296) he wanted a cup of coffee. The monster began to grow smaller as he drank the coffee. The king **o**_____297) him some take-out pizza and fries. The guards immediately called for pizza. The monster continued to get smaller with the king's kind gestures. He then **o**_____298) the monster a full body massage. As the guards helped with the **r**_____299) massage, the monster became tiny. With another act of **k**_____300) to the monster, he just disappeared.

옛날 옛적에, 아름다운 궁전에 사는 한 왕이 있었다. 왕이 없는 동안, 한 괴물이 궁전 문으로 접근했다. 그 괴물이 너무 추하고 냄새가 나서 경비병들은 충격으로 얼어붙었다. 그(괴물)는 경비병들을 지나 왕의 왕좌에 앉았다. 경비병들은 곧 정신을 차리고 안으로 들어가 그 괴물을 향해 소리치며 그에게 왕좌에서 내려올 것을 요구했다. 경비병들이 나쁜 말을 사용할 때마다, 그 괴물은 더 추해졌고, 더 냄새가 났다. 경비병들은 한층 더 화가 났다. 그들은 그 괴물을 겁주어 궁전에서 쫓아내려고 칼을 휘두르기 시작했다. 하지만 그는 그저 점점 더 커져서 결국 방 전체를 차지했다. 그는 그 어느 때 보다 더 추해졌고, 더 냄새가 났다. 마침내 왕이 돌아왔다. 그는 현명하고 친절했으며 무슨 일이 일어나고 있는지 알아차렸다. 그는 무엇을 해야 할지 알았다. 그는 미소를 지으며 그 괴물에게 "나의 궁전에 온 것을 환영하오!"라고 말했다. 왕은 그 괴물에게 그가 커피 한 잔을 원하는지 물었다. 괴물은 그 커피를 마시면서 더 작아지기 시작했다. 왕은 그에게 약간의 테이크아웃 피자와 감자튀김을 제안했다. 경비병들은 즉시 피자를 시켰다. 그 괴물은 왕의 친절한 행동에 몸이 계속 더 작아졌다. 그러고 나서 그는 그 괴물에게 전신 마사지를 제안했다. 경비병들이 편안한 마사지를 도와주자 그 괴물은 매우 작아졌다. 그 괴물에게 또 한 번의 친절한 행동을 베풀자, 그는 바로 사라졌다.

18

To whom it may concern,

I am a r_____1) of the Blue Sky Apartment. Recently I observed that the kid zone is in need of repairs. I want you to pay a_____2) to the poor condition of the playground e_____3) in the zone. The swings are damaged, the paint is falling off, and some of the bolts on the slide are missing. The f_____4) have been in this terrible condition s_____5) we moved here. They are dangerous to the children playing there. Would you please have them r_____6) ? I would a_____7) your immediate attention to solve this matter.

Yours sincerely, Nina Davis

19

On a two-week trip in the Rocky Mountains, I saw a grizzly bear in its native h_____8) . At first, I felt joy as I watched the bear walk across the land. He stopped every once in a while to turn his head about, s_____9) deeply. He was following the s_____10) of something, and slowly I began to realize that this giant animal was smelling me! I froze. This was no longer a wonderful experience; it was now an i_____11) of survival. The bear's m_____12) was to find meat to eat, and I was clearly on his menu.

20

It is d_____13) for any of us to m_____14) a constant level of attention throughout our working day. We all have body rhythms c_____15) by peaks and valleys of energy and a_____16) You will achieve more, and feel confident as a benefit, if you schedule your most d_____17) tasks at times when you are best able to cope with them. If you haven't thought about energy p_____18) before, take a few days to o_____19) yourself. Try to note the times when you are at your best. We are all d_____20) . For some, the peak will come first thing in the morning, but for others it may take a while to warm up.

21

If we adopt **t**_____21) we need to pay its costs. Thousands of traditional **l**_____22) have been pushed aside by progress, and the lifestyles around those jobs removed. Hundreds of millions of humans today work at jobs they hate, **p**_____23) things they have no love for. Sometimes these jobs cause **p**_____24) pain, disability, or **c**_____25) disease. **T**_____26) creates many new jobs that are certainly dangerous. At the same time, mass **e**_____27) and media train humans to avoid **l**_____28) physical work, to seek jobs working in the digital world. The **d**_____29) of the hands from the head puts a stress on the human mind. Indeed, the **s**_____30) nature of the best-paying jobs is a health risk — for body and mind.

22

When students are **s**_____31) their college life, they may **a**_____32) every course, test, or learning task the same way, using what we like to call "the rubber-stamp approach." Think about it this way: Would you wear a tuxedo to a baseball game? A colorful dress to a **f**_____33) ? A bathing suit to religious services? Probably not. You know there's **a**_____34) dress for different **o**_____35) and settings. **S**_____36) learners know that "putting on the same clothes" won't work for every class. They are **f**_____37) learners. They have different **s**_____38) and know when to use them. They know that you study for **m**_____39) tests differently than you study for essay tests. And they not only know what to do, but they also know how to do it.

23

As the social and **e**_____40) situation of countries got better, **w**_____41) levels and working conditions **i**_____42) . Gradually people were **g**_____43) more time off. At the same time, forms of **t**_____44) improved and it became faster and cheaper to get to places. England's industrial **r**_____45) led to many of these changes. Railways, in the nineteenth century, opened up now famous **s**_____46) resorts such as Blackpool and Brighton. With the **r**_____47) came many large hotels. In Canada, for example, the new coast-to-coast railway system made **p**_____48) the building of such famous hotels as Banff Springs and Chateau Lake Louise in the Rockies. Later, the **a**_____49) of air **t**_____50) opened up more of the world and led to **t**_____51) growth.

24

Success can lead you off your i_____52) path and into a c_____53) rut. If you are good at something and are well r_____54) for doing it, you may want to keep doing it even if you stop e_____55) it. The danger is that one day you look around and realize you're so deep in this comfortable rut that you can no longer see the sun or b_____56) fresh air; the sides of the rut have become so slippery that it would take a s_____57) effort to climb out; and, effectively, you're stuck. And it's a situation that many working people worry they're in now. The poor e_____58) market has left them feeling l_____59) in what may be a secure, or even w_____60) — but ultimately unsatisfying — job.

25

The above graph s_____61) the number of births and deaths in Korea from 2016 to 2021. The number of births continued to d_____62) throughout the whole period. The gap between the number of births and deaths was the largest in 2016. In 2019, the gap between the number of births and deaths was the smallest, with the number of births s_____63) larger than that of deaths. The number of deaths increased s_____64) during the whole period, e_____65) the period from 2018 to 2019. In 2021, the n_____66) of deaths was larger than that of births.

26

Lilian Bland was born in Kent, England in 1878. Unlike most other girls at the time she wore t_____67) and spent her time e_____68) adventurous activities like horse riding and hunting. Lilian began her c_____69) as a sports and w_____70) photographer for British newspapers. In 1910 she became the first woman to design, build, and fly her own airplane. In order to p_____71) her to try a slightly safer activity, Lilian's dad bought her a car. Soon Lilian was a master driver and ended up w_____72) as a car dealer. She never went back to flying but lived a long and exciting life nonetheless. She married, moved to Canada, and had a kid. E_____73) , she moved back to England, and lived there for the rest of her life.

29

The most **n**_____74) human characteristic **p**_____75) onto animals is that they can talk in human language. Physically, animal cartoon characters and toys made after animals are also most often **d**_____76) in such a way as to **r**_____77) humans. This is achieved by showing them with **h**_____78) facial features and **d**_____79) front legs to resemble human hands. In more recent **a**_____80) movies the trend has been to show the animals in a more "natural" way. **H**_____ _81) , they still use their front legs like human hands (for example, lions can pick up and lift small objects with one paw), and they still talk with an **a**_____82) **f**_____83) expression. A general strategy that is used to make the animal characters more emotionally **a**_____84) , both to children and adults, is to give them **e**_____85) and deformed childlike features.

30

The major **p**_____86) shift in the idea of selling came when industrial societies became more **a**_____87) , more **c**_____88) , and more **g**_____89) spread out during the 1940s and 1950s. This forced business to develop closer relations with buyers and **c**_____90) , which in turn made business realize that it was not enough to produce a quality product at a **r**_____91) price. In fact, it was equally **e**_____92) to deliver products that customers actually wanted. Henry Ford produced his best-selling T-model Ford in one color only (black) in 1908, but in modern societies this was no longer possible. The **m**_____93) of society led to a **m**_____94) revolution that destroyed the view that production would create its own demand. Customers, and the **d**_____95) to meet their **d**_____96) and often complex needs, became the focus of business.

31

People differ in how quickly they can reset their **b**_____97) clocks to **o**_____98) jet lag, and the speed of **r**_____99) depends on the direction of travel. Generally, it's **e**_____100) to fly westward and **l**_____101) your day than it is to fly eastward and shorten it. This east-west difference in jet lag is **s**_____102) enough to have an impact on the **p**_____103) of sports teams. Studies have found that teams flying westward **p**_____104) significantly better than teams flying eastward in professional baseball and college football. A more recent study of more than 46,000 Major League Baseball games **f**_____105) additional evidence that eastward travel is **t**_____ _106) than westward travel.

32

If you want the c_____107) that comes from a_____108) what you set out to do each day, then it's i_____109) to understand how long things are going to take. O_____110) about what can be achieved within a certain time frame is a problem. So work on it. Make a practice of e_____111) the amount of time needed alongside items on your 'things to do' list, and learn by e_____112) when tasks take a greater or lesser time than e_____113) .Give attention also to fitting the task to the available time. There are some tasks that you can only set about if you have a s_____114) amount of time a_____115) . There is no point in trying to g_____116) up for such a task when you only have a short period available. So schedule the time you need for the l_____117) tasks and put the short tasks into the s_____118) moments in between.

33

In Lewis Carroll's *Through the Looking-Glass*, the Red Queen takes Alice on a race through the countryside. They run and they run, but then Alice d_____119) that they're still under the same tree that they started f_____120) . The Red Queen explains to Alice: "*here*, you see, it takes all the running you can _____121) , to keep in the same place." B_____122) sometimes use this Red Queen Effect to explain an e_____123) p_____124) . If foxes e_____125) to run faster so they can catch more rabbits, then only the fastest rabbits will live long enough to make a new generation of bunnies that r_____126) even faster — in w_____127) case, of course, only the fastest foxes will catch enough rabbits to t_____128) and p_____129) on their genes. Even though they might run, the two species just stay in place.

34

Everything in the world around us was f_____130) in the mind of its creator before it was s_____131) . The houses we live in, the cars we drive, and our clothing — all of these began with an i_____132) . Each idea was then studied, r_____133) and p_____134) before the first nail was driven or the first piece of cloth was cut. Long before the idea was turned into a physical r_____135) , the mind had clearly p_____136) the finished product. The human being d_____137) his or her own future through much the same p_____138) . We begin with an i_____139) about how the f_____140) will be. Over a period of time we r_____141) and p_____142) the v_____143) . Before long, our every thought, decision and activity are all working in harmony to bring into e_____144) what we have mentally c_____145) about the future.

35

Whose story it is **a**_____ 146) what the story is. Change the main character, and the focus of the story must also **c**_____ 147) . If we look at the events through another character's eyes, we will **i**_____ 148) them differently. We'll place our **s**_____ 149) with someone new. When the **c**_____ 150) arises that is the heart of the story, we will be praying for a **d**_____ 151) **o**_____ 152) . Consider, for example, how the tale of Cinderella would shift if told from the **v**_____ 153) of an evil stepsister. *Gone with the Wind* is Scarlett O'Hara's story, but what if we were **s**_____ 154) the same events from the **v**_____ 155) of Rhett Butler or Melanie Wilkes?

36

In the Old Stone Age, small bands of 20 to 60 people **w**_____ 156) from place to place in search of food. Once people began **f**_____ 157) , they could **s**_____ 158) down near their farms. As a result, towns and villages grew **l**_____ 159) . Living in **c**_____ 160) **a**_____ 161) people to **o**_____ 162) themselves more **e**_____ 163) . They could **d**_____ 164) up the work of producing food and other things they needed. While some workers grew crops, others built new houses and made tools. Village **d**_____ 165) also learned to work **t**_____ 166) to do a task **f**_____ 167) . For example, toolmakers could **s**_____ 168) the work of making stone axes and knives. By working together, they could make **m**_____ 169) tools in the **s**_____ 170) amount of time.

37

Natural **p**_____ 171) **f**_____ 172) minerals in many ways. For example, hot melted rock material, called magma, **c**_____ 173) when it **r**_____ 174) the Earth's surface, or even if it's **t**_____ 175) below the surface. As magma cools, its atoms **l**_____ 176) heat energy, move **c**_____ 177) together, and begin to **c**_____ 178) into **c**_____ 179) . During this process, **a**_____ 180) of the different **c**_____ 181) **a**_____ 182) themselves into **o**_____ 183) , **r**_____ 184) patterns. The type and amount of elements **p**_____ 185) in a magma partly **d**_____ 186) which minerals will **f**_____ 187) . Also, the size of the **c**_____ 188) that form depends partly on how **r**_____ 189) the magma **c**_____ 190) . When magma **c**_____ 191) slowly, the crystals that form are generally **l**_____ 192) enough to see with the **u**_____ 193) eye. This is because the atoms have enough time to move together and form into **l**_____ 194) crystals. When magma cools **r**_____ 195) , the crystals that form will be **s**_____ 196) . In such cases, you can't easily see individual mineral crystals.

38

All c_____197) are basically sugars. C_____198) c_____199) are the good carbohydrates for your body. These c_____200) sugar c_____201) are very difficult to b_____202) down and can t_____203) other nutrients like vitamins and minerals in their chains. As they slowly break down, the other nutrients are also r_____204) into your body, and can p_____205) you with fuel for a number of hours. Bad carbohydrates, on the other hand, are s_____206) sugars. Because their structure is not complex, they are easy to break down and h_____207) few nutrients for your body other than the sugars f_____208) which they are made. Your body b_____209) down these carbohydrates rather q_____210) and what it cannot use is c_____211) to fat and s_____212) in the body.

39

People commonly make the m_____213) a_____214) that because a person has one type of characteristic, then they a_____215) have other characteristics which go w_____216) it. In one study, university students were given d_____217) of a guest lecturer before he spoke to the group. Half the students r_____218) a description c_____219) the word 'warm', the other half were told the speaker was 'cold'. The guest lecturer then l_____220) a discussion, after w_____221) the students were asked to give their i_____222) of him. As expected, there were large d_____223) between the impressions f_____224) by the students, depending upon their o_____225) information of the lecturer. It was also found that those students who e_____226) the lecturer to be warm tended to i_____227) with him more. This shows that different e_____228) not only a_____229) the i_____230) we form but also our b_____231) and the r_____232) which is formed.

40

To help decide what's **r**_____²³³⁾ and what's **s**_____²³⁴⁾ , who's **t**_____²³⁵⁾ and who's not, we look for **s**_____*²³⁶⁾ evidence.* From an **e**_____²³⁷⁾ view, following the group is almost always **p**_____²³⁸⁾ for our **p**_____²³⁹⁾ of **s**_____²⁴⁰⁾ . "If everyone's doing it, it must be a **s**_____²⁴¹⁾ thing to do," explains famous psychologist and best selling writer of *Influence*, Robert Cialdini. While we can frequently see this today in product reviews, even **s**_____²⁴²⁾ **c**_____²⁴³⁾ within the environment can signal **t**_____²⁴⁴⁾ . Consider this: when you visit a local restaurant, are they busy? Is there a line outside or is it easy to find a seat? It is a **h**_____²⁴⁵⁾ to wait, but a line can be a **p**_____²⁴⁶⁾ **c**_____²⁴⁷⁾ that the food's tasty, and these seats are in **d**_____²⁴⁸⁾ . More often than not, it's good to **a**_____²⁴⁹⁾ the **p**_____²⁵⁰⁾ of those around you.

41-42

Chess masters **s**_____²⁵¹⁾ a chess board in the middle of a game for 5 seconds with 20 to 30 pieces still in play can immediately **r**_____²⁵²⁾ the position of the pieces from **m**_____²⁵³⁾ . Beginners, of course, are able to place only a few. Now take the same pieces and place them on the board **r**_____²⁵⁴⁾ and the **d**_____²⁵⁵⁾ is much **r**_____²⁵⁶⁾ . The expert's **a**_____²⁵⁷⁾ is only for **f**_____²⁵⁸⁾ **p**_____²⁵⁹⁾ — those **p**_____²⁶⁰⁾ **s**_____²⁶¹⁾ in memory. **F**_____²⁶²⁾ with **u**_____²⁶³⁾ patterns, even when it **i**_____²⁶⁴⁾ the same **f**_____²⁶⁵⁾ **d**_____²⁶⁶⁾ , the expert's advantage **d**_____²⁶⁷⁾ .

The **b**_____²⁶⁸⁾ effects of **f**_____²⁶⁹⁾ **s**_____²⁷⁰⁾ on **m**_____²⁷¹⁾ have been **o**_____²⁷²⁾ for many types of **e**_____²⁷³⁾ , including music. People with musical training can **r**_____²⁷⁴⁾ short **s**_____²⁷⁵⁾ of musical **n**_____²⁷⁶⁾ more **a**_____²⁷⁷⁾ than those with no musical training when notes follow **u**_____²⁷⁸⁾ **s**_____²⁷⁹⁾ , but the advantage is much reduced when the notes are **o**_____²⁸⁰⁾ **r**_____²⁸¹⁾ . **E**_____²⁸²⁾ also **i**_____²⁸³⁾ **m**_____²⁸⁴⁾ for sequences of movements. Experienced ballet dancers are able to **r**_____²⁸⁵⁾ longer sequences of steps than less experienced dancers, and they can repeat a sequence of steps making up a routine better than steps **o**_____²⁸⁶⁾ **r**_____²⁸⁷⁾ . In each case, memory range is **i**_____²⁸⁸⁾ by the ability to recognize **f**_____²⁸⁹⁾ sequences and patterns.

43-45

Once upon a time, there was a king who lived in a beautiful palace. While the king was away, a monster a_____290) the gates of the palace. The monster was so ugly and smelly that the guards f_____291) in shock. He passed the guards and sat on the king's t_____292) . The guards soon came to their senses, went in, and shouted at the monster, d_____293) that he get off the throne. With each bad word the guards u_____294) , the monster grew more ugly and smelly. The guards got even angrier — they began to b_____295) their swords to scare the monster away from the palace. But he just grew bigger and bigger, eventually taking up the whole room. He grew more ugly and smelly than ever. Eventually the king returned. He was wise and kind and saw what was happening. He knew what to do. He smiled and said to the monster, "Welcome to my palace!" He asked the monster i_____296) he wanted a cup of coffee. The monster began to grow smaller as he drank the coffee. The king o_____297) him some take-out pizza and fries. The guards immediately called for pizza. The monster continued to get smaller with the king's kind gestures. He then o_____298) the monster a full body massage. As the guards helped with the r_____299) massage, the monster became tiny. With another act of k_____300) to the monster, he just disappeared.

2021 고1 3월 모의고사

❶ voca ❷ text ❸ [/] ❹ ____ ❺ quiz 1 ❻ quiz 2 ❼ quiz 3 ❽ quiz 4 ❾ quiz 5

☑ **다음 글을 읽고 물음에 답하시오.** (18)

They are dangerous to the children playing there. Would you please have them repaired?

To whom it may concern, I am a resident of the Blue Sky Apartment. (①) Recently I observed that the kid zone is in need of repairs. (②) I want you to pay attention to the poor condition of the playground equipment in the zone. (③) The swings are damaged, the paint is falling off, and some of the bolts on the slide are missing. (④) The facilities have been in this terrible condition since we moved here. (⑤) I would appreciate your immediate attention to solve this matter. Yours sincerely, Nina Davis

1. ¹⁾글의 흐름으로 보아, 주어진 문장이 들어가기에 가장 적절한 곳은?

☑ **다음 글을 읽고 물음에 답하시오.** (19)

He was following the scent of something, and slowly I began to realize that this giant animal was smelling me!

On a two-week trip in the Rocky Mountains, I saw a grizzly bear in its native habitat. (①) At first, I felt joy as I watched the bear walk across the land. He stopped every once in a while to turn his head about, sniffing deeply. (②) I froze. (③) This was no longer a wonderful experience; (④) it was now an issue of survival. (⑤) The bear's motivation was to find meat to eat, and I was clearly on his menu.

2. ²⁾글의 흐름으로 보아, 주어진 문장이 들어가기에 가장 적절한 곳은?

☑ **다음 글을 읽고 물음에 답하시오.** (20)

Try to note the times when you are at your best.

It is difficult for any of us to maintain a constant level of attention throughout our working day. (①) We all have body rhythms characterised by peaks and valleys of energy and alertness. (②) You will achieve more, and feel confident as a benefit, if you schedule your most demanding tasks at times when you are best able to cope with them. (③) If you haven't thought about energy peaks before, take a few days to observe yourself. (④) We are all different. (⑤) For some, the peak will come first thing in the morning, but for others it may take a while to warm up.

3. ³⁾글의 흐름으로 보아, 주어진 문장이 들어가기에 가장 적절한 곳은?

☑ **다음 글을 읽고 물음에 답하시오.** (21)

At the same time, mass education and media train humans to avoid low-tech physical work, to seek jobs working in the digital world.

If we adopt technology, we need to pay its costs. (①) Thousands of traditional livelihoods have been pushed aside by progress, and the lifestyles around those jobs removed. (②) Hundreds of millions of humans today work at jobs they hate, producing things they have no love for. (③) Sometimes these jobs cause physical pain, disability, or chronic disease. (④) Technology creates many new jobs that are certainly dangerous. (⑤) The divorce of the hands from the head puts a stress on the human mind. Indeed, the sedentary nature of the best-paying jobs is a health risk — for body and mind.

4. ⁴⁾글의 흐름으로 보아, 주어진 문장이 들어가기에 가장 적절한 곳은?

☑ **다음 글을 읽고 물음에 답하시오.** (22)

Skillful learners know that "putting on the same clothes" won't work for every class.

When students are starting their college life, they may approach every course, test, or learning task the same way, using what we like to call "the rubber-stamp approach". (①) Think about it this way: Would you wear a tuxedo to a baseball game? A colorful dress to a funeral? A bathing suit to religious services? (②) Probably not. You know there's appropriate dress for different occasions and settings. (③) They are flexible learners. They have different strategies and know when to use them. (④) They know that you study for multiple-choice tests differently than you study for essay tests. (⑤) And they not only know what to do, but they also know how to do it.

5. 5)글의 흐름으로 보아, 주어진 문장이 들어가기에 가장 적절한 곳은?

☑ **다음 글을 읽고 물음에 답하시오.** (22)

They are flexible learners. They have different strategies and know when to use them.

When students are starting their college life, they may approach every course, test, or learning task the same way, using what we like to call "the rubber-stamp approach". (①) Think about it this way: Would you wear a tuxedo to a baseball game? A colorful dress to a funeral? A bathing suit to religious services? (②) Probably not. You know there's appropriate dress for different occasions and settings. (③) Skillful learners know that "putting on the same clothes" won't work for every class. (④) They know that you study for multiple-choice tests differently than you study for essay tests. (⑤) And they not only know what to do, but they also know how to do it.

6. 6)글의 흐름으로 보아, 주어진 문장이 들어가기에 가장 적절한 곳은?

☑ **다음 글을 읽고 물음에 답하시오.** (23)

With the railways came many large hotels.

As the social and economic situation of countries got better, wage levels and working conditions improved. (①) Gradually people were given more time off. At the same time, forms of transport improved and it became faster and cheaper to get to places. (②) England's industrial revolution led to many of these changes. (③) Railways, in the nineteenth century, opened up now famous seaside resorts such as Blackpool and Brighton. (④) In Canada, for example, the new coast-to-coast railway system made possible the building of such famous hotels as Banff Springs and Chateau Lake Louise in the Rockies. (⑤) Later, the arrival of air transport opened up more of the world and led to tourism growth.

7. 7)글의 흐름으로 보아, 주어진 문장이 들어가기에 가장 적절한 곳은?

☑ **다음 글을 읽고 물음에 답하시오.** (24)

The danger is that one day you look around and realize you're so deep in this comfortable rut that you can no longer see the sun or breathe fresh air;

Success can lead you off your intended path and into a comfortable rut. (①) If you are good at something and are well rewarded for doing it, you may want to keep doing it even if you stop enjoying it. (②) the sides of the rut have become so slippery that it would take a superhuman effort to climb out; and, effectively, you're stuck. (③) And it's a situation that many working people worry they're in now. (④) The poor employment market has left them feeling locked in what may be a secure, or even well-paying — but ultimately unsatisfying — job.(⑤)

8. 8)글의 흐름으로 보아, 주어진 문장이 들어가기에 가장 적절한 곳은?

☑ **다음 글을 읽고 물음에 답하시오.** (26)

> In order to persuade her to try a slightly safer activity, Lilian's dad bought her a car.

Lilian Bland was born in Kent, England in 1878. Unlike most other girls at the time she wore trousers and spent her time enjoying adventurous activities like horse riding and hunting. (①) Lilian began her career as a sports and wildlife photographer for British newspapers. (②) In 1910 she became the first woman to design, build, and fly her own airplane. (③) Soon Lilian was a master driver and ended up working as a car dealer. (④) She never went back to flying but lived a long and exciting life nonetheless. (⑤) She married, moved to Canada, and had a kid. Eventually, she moved back to England, and lived there for the rest of her life.

9. 9)글의 흐름으로 보아, 주어진 문장이 들어가기에 가장 적절한 곳은?

☑ **다음 글을 읽고 물음에 답하시오.** (29)

> However, they still use their front legs like human hands.

The most noticeable human characteristic projected onto animals is that they can talk in human language. (①) Physically, animal cartoon characters and toys made after animals are also most often deformed in such a way as to resemble humans. (②) This is achieved by showing them with humanlike facial features and deformed front legs to resemble human hands. (③) In more recent animated movies the trend has been to show the animals in a more "natural" way. (④) For example, lions can pick up and lift small objects with one paw. And they still talk with an appropriate facial expression. (⑤) A general strategy that is used to make the animal characters more emotionally appealing, both to children and adults, is to give them enlarged and deformed childlike features.

10. 10)글의 흐름으로 보아, 주어진 문장이 들어가기에 가장 적절한 곳은?

☑ **다음 글을 읽고 물음에 답하시오.** (30)

> In fact, it was equally essential to deliver products that customers actually wanted.

The major philosophical shift in the idea of selling came when industrial societies became more affluent, more competitive, and more geographically spread out during the 1940s and 1950s. (①) This forced business to develop closer relations with buyers and clients, which in turn made business realize that it was not enough to produce a quality product at a reasonable price. (②) Henry Ford produced his best-selling T-model Ford in one color only (black) in 1908, but in modern societies this was no longer possible. (③) The modernization of society led to a marketing revolution that destroyed the view that production would create its own demand. (④) Customers, and the desire to meet their diverse and often complex needs, became the focus of business.(⑤)

11. 11)글의 흐름으로 보아, 주어진 문장이 들어가기에 가장 적절한 곳은?

☑ **다음 글을 읽고 물음에 답하시오.** (31)

> This east-west difference in jet lag is sizable enough to have an impact on the performance of sports teams.

Jet leg is the feeling of tiredness and confusion that people experience after making a long journey by plane to a place where the time is different from the place they left. (①) People differ in how quickly they can reset their biological clocks to overcome jet lag. (②) Alao, the speed of recovery depends on the direction of travel. (③) Generally, it's easier to fly westward and lengthen your day than it is to fly eastward and shorten it. (④) Studies have found that teams flying westward perform significantly better than teams flying eastward in professional baseball and college football. (⑤) A more recent study of more than 46,000 Major League Baseball games found additional evidence that eastward travel is tougher than westward travel.

12. 12)글의 흐름으로 보아, 주어진 문장이 들어가기에 가장 적절한 곳은?

☑ **다음 글을 읽고 물음에 답하시오.** (32)

> There are some tasks that you can only set about if you have a significant amount of time available.

If you want the confidence that comes from achieving what you set out to do each day, then it's important to understand how long things are going to take. (①) Over-optimism about what can be achieved within a certain time frame is a problem. (②) So work on it. Make a practice of estimating the amount of time needed alongside items on your 'things to do' list, and learn by experience when tasks take a greater or lesser time than expected. (③) Give attention also to fitting the task to the available time. (④) There is

no point in trying to gear up for such a task when you only have a short period available. (⑤) So schedule the time you need for the longer tasks and put the short tasks into the spare moments in between.

13. 13)글의 흐름으로 보아, 주어진 문장이 들어가기에 가장 적절한 곳은?

☑ **다음 글을 읽고 물음에 답하시오.** (32)

> There is no point in trying to gear up for such a task when you only have a short period available.

If you want the confidence that comes from achieving what you set out to do each day, then it's important to understand how long things are going to take. (①) Over-optimism about what can be achieved within a certain time frame is a problem. (②) So work on it. Make a practice of estimating the amount of time needed alongside items on your 'things to do' list, and learn by experience when tasks take a greater or lesser time than expected. (③) Give attention also to fitting the task to the available time. (④) There are some tasks that you can only set about if you have a significant amount of time available. (⑤) So schedule the time you need for the longer tasks and put the short tasks into the spare moments in between.

14. 14)글의 흐름으로 보아, 주어진 문장이 들어가기에 가장 적절한 곳은?

☑ **다음 글을 읽고 물음에 답하시오.** (33)

> If foxes evolve to run faster so they can catch more rabbits, then only the fastest rabbits will live long enough to make a new generation of bunnies that run even faster.

In Lewis Carroll's Through the Looking-Glass, the Red Queen takes Alice on a race through the countryside. (①) They run and they run, but then Alice discovers that they're still under the same tree that they started from. (②) The Red Queen explains to Alice: "here, you see, it takes all the running you can do, to keep in the same place". (③) Biologists sometimes use this Red Queen Effect to explain an evolutionary principle. (④) In which case, of course, only the fastest foxes will catch enough rabbits to thrive and pass on their genes. (⑤) Even though they might run, the two species just stay in place.

15. 15)글의 흐름으로 보아, 주어진 문장이 들어가기에 가장 적절한 곳은?

☑ **다음 글을 읽고 물음에 답하시오.** (34)

> The human being designs his or her own future through much the same process.

Everything in the world around us was finished in the mind of its creator before it was started. (①) The houses we live in, the cars we drive, and our clothing — all of these began with an idea. (②) Each idea was then studied, refined and perfected before the first nail was driven or the first piece of cloth was cut. (③) Long before the idea was turned into a physical reality, the mind had clearly pictured the finished product. (④) We begin with an idea about how the future will be. Over a period of time we refine and perfect the vision. (⑤) Before long, our every thought, decision and activity are all working in harmony to bring into existence what we have mentally concluded about the future.

16. 16)글의 흐름으로 보아, 주어진 문장이 들어가기에 가장 적절한 곳은?

☑ **다음 글을 읽고 물음에 답하시오.** (35)

> When the conflict arises that is the heart of the story, we will be praying for a different outcome.

Whose story it is affects what the story is. (①) Change the main character, and the focus of the story must also change. (②) If we look at the events through another character's eyes, we will interpret them differently. (③) We'll place our sympathies with someone new. (④) Consider, for example, how the tale of Cinderella would shift if told from the viewpoint of an evil stepsister. (⑤) Gone with the Wind is Scarlett O'Hara's story, but what if we were shown the same events from the viewpoint of Rhett Butler or Melanie Wilkes?

17. 17)글의 흐름으로 보아, 주어진 문장이 들어가기에 가장 적절한 곳은?

☑ **다음 글을 읽고 물음에 답하시오.** (35)

> Consider, for example, how the tale of Cinderella would shift if told from the viewpoint of an evil stepsister.

Whose story it is affects what the story is. (①) Change the main character, and the focus of the story must also change. (②) If we look at the events through another character's eyes, we will interpret them differently. (③) We'll place our sympathies with someone new. (④) When the conflict arises that is the heart of the story, we will be praying for a different outcome. (⑤) Gone with the Wind is Scarlett O'Hara's story, but what if we were shown the same events from the viewpoint of Rhett Butler or Melanie Wilkes?

18. 18)글의 흐름으로 보아, 주어진 문장이 들어가기에 가장 적절한 곳은?

☑ **다음 글을 읽고 물음에 답하시오.** (36)

As a result, towns and villages grew larger.

In the Old Stone Age, small bands of 20 to 60 people wandered from place to place in search of food. (①) Once people began farming, they could settle down near their farms. (②) Living in communities allowed people to organize themselves more efficiently. They could divide up the work of producing food and other things they needed. (③) While some workers grew crops, others built new houses and made tools. (④) Village dwellers also learned to work together to do a task faster. (⑤) For example, toolmakers could share the work of making stone axes and knives. By working together, they could make more tools in the same amount of time.

19. 19)글의 흐름으로 보아, 주어진 문장이 들어가기 에 가장 적절한 곳은?

☑ **다음 글을 읽고 물음에 답하시오.** (37)

Also, the size of the crystals that form depends partly on how rapidly the magma cools.

Natural processes form minerals in many ways. For example, hot melted rock material, called magma, cools when it reaches the Earth's surface, or even if it's trapped below the surface. (①) As magma cools, its atoms lose heat energy, move closer together, and begin to combine into compounds. (②) During this process, atoms of the different compounds arrange themselves into orderly, repeating patterns. (③) The type and amount of elements present in a magma partly determine which minerals will form. (④) When magma cools slowly, the crystals that form are generally large enough to see with the unaided eye. (⑤) This is because the atoms have enough time to move together and form into larger crystals. When magma cools rapidly, the crystals that form will be small. In such cases, you can't easily see individual mineral crystals.

20. 20)글의 흐름으로 보아, 주어진 문장이 들어가기 에 가장 적절한 곳은?

☑ **다음 글을 읽고 물음에 답하시오.** (38)

Bad carbohydrates, on the other hand, are simple sugars.

All carbohydrates are basically sugars. (①) Complex carbohydrates are the good carbohydrates for your body. (②) These complex sugar compounds are very difficult to break down and can trap other nutrients like vitamins and minerals in their chains. (③) As they slowly break down, the other nutrients are also released into your body, and can provide you with fuel for a number of hours. (④) Because their structure is not complex, they are easy to break down and hold few nutrients for your body other than the sugars from which they are made. (⑤) Your body breaks down these carbohydrates rather quickly and what it cannot use is converted to fat and stored in the body.

21. 21)글의 흐름으로 보아, 주어진 문장이 들어가기 에 가장 적절한 곳은?

☑ **다음 글을 읽고 물음에 답하시오.** (38)

Because their structure is not complex, they are easy to break down and hold few nutrients for your body other than the sugars from which they are made.

All carbohydrates are basically sugars. (①) Complex carbohydrates are the good carbohydrates for your body. (②) These complex sugar compounds are very difficult to break down and can trap other nutrients like vitamins and minerals in their chains. (③) As they slowly break down, the other nutrients are also released into your body, and can provide you with fuel for a number of hours. (④) Bad carbohydrates, on the other hand, are simple sugars. (⑤) Your body breaks down these carbohydrates rather quickly and what it cannot use is converted to fat and stored in the body.

22. 22)글의 흐름으로 보아, 주어진 문장이 들어가기 에 가장 적절한 곳은?

☑ **다음 글을 읽고 물음에 답하시오.** (39)

> As expected, there were large differences between the impressions formed by the students, depending upon their original information of the lecturer.

People commonly make the mistaken assumption that because a person has one type of characteristic, then they automatically have other characteristics which go with it. (①) In one study, university students were given descriptions of a guest lecturer before he spoke to the group. (②) Half the students received a description containing the word 'warm', the other half were told the speaker was 'cold'. (③) The guest lecturer then led a discussion, after which the students were asked to give their impressions of him. (④) It was also found that those students who expected the lecturer to be warm tended to interact with him more. (⑤) This shows that different expectations not only affect the impressions we form but also our behaviour and the relationship which is formed.

23. 23)글의 흐름으로 보아, 주어진 문장이 들어가기에 가장 적절한 곳은?

☑ **다음 글을 읽고 물음에 답하시오.** (40)

> While we can frequently see this today in product reviews, even subtler cues within the environment can signal trustworthiness. Consider this: when you visit a local restaurant, are they busy?

To help decide what's risky and what's safe, who's trustworthy and who's not, we look for social evidence. (①) From an evolutionary view, following the group is almost always positive for our prospects of survival. (②) "If everyone's doing it, it must be a sensible thing to do", explains famous psychologist and best selling writer of Influence, Robert Cialdini. (③) Is there a line outside or is it easy to find a seat? (④) It is a hassle to wait, but a line can be a powerful cue that the food's tasty, and these seats are in demand. (⑤) More often than not, it's good to adopt the practices of those around you.

24. 24)글의 흐름으로 보아, 주어진 문장이 들어가기에 가장 적절한 곳은?

☑ **다음 글을 읽고 물음에 답하시오.** (41, 42)

> People with musical training can reproduce short sequences of musical notation more accurately than those with no musical training when notes follow conventional sequences, but the advantage is much reduced when the notes are ordered randomly.

Chess masters shown a chess board in the middle of a game for 5 seconds with 20 to 30 pieces still in play can immediately reproduce the position of the pieces from memory. (①) Beginners, of course, are able to place only a few. Now take the same pieces and place them on the board randomly and the difference is much reduced. (②) The expert's advantage is only for familiar patterns — those previously stored in memory. (③) Faced with unfamiliar patterns, even when it involves the same familiar domain, the expert's advantage disappears. (④) The beneficial effects of familiar structure on memory have been observed for many types of expertise, including music. (⑤) Expertise also improves memory for sequences of movements. Experienced ballet dancers are able to repeat longer sequences of steps than less experienced dancers, and they can repeat a sequence of steps making up a routine better than steps ordered randomly. In each case, memory range is increased by the ability to recognize familiar sequences and patterns.

25. 25)글의 흐름으로 보아, 주어진 문장이 들어가기에 가장 적절한 곳은?

☑ 다음 글을 읽고 물음에 답하시오. (41, 42)

> The beneficial effects of familiar structure on memory have been observed for many types of expertise, including music.

Chess masters shown a chess board in the middle of a game for 5 seconds with 20 to 30 pieces still in play can immediately reproduce the position of the pieces from memory. (①) Beginners, of course, are able to place only a few. Now take the same pieces and place them on the board randomly and the difference is much reduced. (②) The expert's advantage is only for familiar patterns — those previously stored in memory. (③) Faced with unfamiliar patterns, even when it involves the same familiar domain, the expert's advantage disappears. (④) People with musical training can reproduce short sequences of musical notation more accurately than those with no musical training when notes follow conventional sequences, but the advantage is much reduced when the notes are ordered randomly. (⑤) Expertise also improves memory for sequences of movements. Experienced ballet dancers are able to repeat longer sequences of steps than less experienced dancers, and they can repeat a sequence of steps making up a routine better than steps ordered randomly. In each case, memory range is increased by the ability to recognize familiar sequences and patterns.

26. 26)글의 흐름으로 보아, 주어진 문장이 들어가기에 가장 적절한 곳은?

☑ 다음 글을 읽고 물음에 답하시오. (43, 44, 45)

> Eventually the king returned. He was wise and kind and saw what was happening. He knew what to do. He smiled and said to the monster, "Welcome to my palace"!

Once upon a time, there was a king who lived in a beautiful palace. While the king was away, a monster approached the gates of the palace. (①) The monster was so ugly and smelly that the guards froze in shock. He passed the guards and sat on the king's throne. (②) The guards soon came to their senses, went in, and shouted at the monster, demanding that he get off the throne. With each bad word the guards used, the monster grew more ugly and smelly. (③) The guards got even angrier — they began to brandish their swords to scare the monster away from the palace. But he just grew bigger and bigger, eventually taking up the whole room. He grew more ugly and smelly than ever. (④) He asked the monster if he wanted a cup of coffee. The monster began to grow smaller as he drank the coffee. The king offered him some take-out pizza and fries. (⑤) The guards immediately called for pizza. The monster continued to get smaller with the king's kind gestures. He then offered the monster a full body massage. As the guards helped with the relaxing massage, the monster became tiny. With another act of kindness to the monster, he just disappeared.

27. 27)글의 흐름으로 보아, 주어진 문장이 들어가기에 가장 적절한 곳은?

1. 28) 18

To whom it may concern, I am a resident of the Blue Sky Apartment.

(A) They are dangerous to the children playing there. Would you please have them repaired?

(B) The swings are damaged, the paint is falling off, and some of the bolts on the slide are missing. The facilities have been in this terrible condition since we moved here.

(C) Recently I observed that the kid zone is in need of repairs. I want you to pay attention to the poor condition of the playground equipment in the zone.

(D) I would appreciate your immediate attention to solve this matter. Yours sincerely, Nina Davis

2. 29) 19

On a two-week trip in the Rocky Mountains, I saw a grizzly bear in its native habitat.

(A) At first, I felt joy as I watched the bear walk across the land. He stopped every once in a while to turn his head about, sniffing deeply.

(B) The bear's motivation was to find meat to eat, and I was clearly on his menu.

(C) He was following the scent of something, and slowly I began to realize that this giant animal was smelling me! I froze.

(D) This was no longer a wonderful experience; it was now an issue of survival.

3. 30) 20

It is difficult for any of us to maintain a constant level of attention throughout our working day.

(A) If you haven't thought about energy peaks before, take a few days to observe yourself.

(B) We all have body rhythms characterised by peaks and valleys of energy and alertness. You will achieve more, and feel confident as a benefit, if you schedule your most demanding tasks at times when you are best able to cope with them.

(C) We are all different.

(D) Try to note the times when you are at your best.

(E) For some, the peak will come first thing in the morning, but for others it may take a while to warm up.

4. 31) 21

If we adopt technology, we need to pay its costs.

(A) The divorce of the hands from the head puts a stress on the human mind.

(B) At the same time, mass education and media train humans to avoid low-tech physical work, to seek jobs working in the digital world.

(C) Thousands of traditional livelihoods have been pushed aside by progress, and the lifestyles around those jobs removed. Hundreds of millions of humans today work at jobs they hate, producing things they have no love for.

(D) Indeed, the sedentary nature of the best-paying jobs is a health risk — for body and mind.

(E) Sometimes these jobs cause physical pain, disability, or chronic disease. Technology creates many new jobs that are certainly dangerous.

5. 32) ²²

When students are starting their college life, they may approach every course, test, or learning task the same way, using what we like to call "the rubber-stamp approach."

(A) Probably not. You know there's appropriate dress for different occasions and settings. Skillful learners know that "putting on the same clothes" won't work for every class.

(B) They know that you study for multiple-choice tests differently than you study for essay tests. And they not only know what to do, but they also know how to do it.

(C) Think about it this way: Would you wear a tuxedo to a baseball game? A colorful dress to a funeral? A bathing suit to religious services?

(D) They are flexible learners. They have different strategies and know when to use them.

6. 33) ²³

As the social and economic situation of countries got better, wage levels and working conditions improved.

(A) Gradually people were given more time off. At the same time, forms of transport improved and it became faster and cheaper to get to places.

(B) England's industrial revolution led to many of these changes. Railways, in the nineteenth century, opened up now famous seaside resorts such as Blackpool and Brighton.

(C) Later, the arrival of air transport opened up more of the world and led to tourism growth.

(D) With the railways came many large hotels. In Canada, for example, the new coast-to-coast railway system made possible the building of such famous hotels as Banff Springs and Chateau Lake Louise in the Rockies.

7. 34) ²⁴

Success can lead you off your intended path and into a comfortable rut.

(A) And it's a situation that many working people worry they're in now.

(B) The danger is that one day you look around and realize you're so deep in this comfortable rut that you can no longer see the sun or breathe fresh air; the sides of the rut have become so slippery that it would take a superhuman effort to climb out; and, effectively, you're stuck.

(C) The poor employment market has left them feeling locked in what may be a secure, or even well-paying — but ultimately unsatisfying — job.

(D) If you are good at something and are well rewarded for doing it, you may want to keep doing it even if you stop enjoying it.

8. 35) ²⁶

Lilian Bland was born in Kent, England in 1878.

(A) She married, moved to Canada, and had a kid. Eventually, she moved back to England, and lived there for the rest of her life.

(B) In order to persuade her to try a slightly safer activity, Lilian's dad bought her a car. Soon Lilian was a master driver and ended up working as a car dealer. She never went back to flying but lived a long and exciting life nonetheless.

(C) Unlike most other girls at the time she wore trousers and spent her time enjoying adventurous activities like horse riding and hunting. Lilian began her career as a sports and wildlife photographer for British newspapers. In 1910 she became the first woman to design, build, and fly her own airplane.

9. 36) 29

The most noticeable human characteristic projected onto animals is that they can talk in human language.

(A) In more recent animated movies the trend has been to show the animals in a more "natural" way.

(B) A general strategy that is used to make the animal characters more emotionally appealing, both to children and adults, is to give them enlarged and deformed childlike features.

(C) However, they still use their front legs like human hands (for example, lions can pick up and lift small objects with one paw), and they still talk with an appropriate facial expression.

(D) Physically, animal cartoon characters and toys made after animals are also most often deformed in such a way as to resemble humans. This is achieved by showing them with humanlike facial features and deformed front legs to resemble human hands.

10. 37) 30

The major philosophical shift in the idea of selling came when industrial societies became more affluent, more competitive, and more geographically spread out during the 1940s and 1950s.

(A) This forced business to develop closer relations with buyers and clients, which in turn made business realize that it was not enough to produce a quality product at a reasonable price. In fact, it was equally essential to deliver products that customers actually wanted.

(B) Customers, and the desire to meet their diverse and often complex needs, became the focus of business.

(C) Henry Ford produced his best-selling T-model Ford in one color only (black) in 1908, but in modern societies this was no longer possible. The modernization of society led to a marketing revolution that destroyed the view that production would create its own demand.

11. 38) 31

People differ in how quickly they can reset their biological clocks to overcome jet lag, and the speed of recovery depends on the direction of travel.

(A) Studies have found that teams flying westward perform significantly better than teams flying eastward in professional baseball and college football.

(B) A more recent study of more than 46,000 Major League Baseball games found additional evidence that eastward travel is tougher than westward travel.

(C) Generally, it's easier to fly westward and lengthen your day than it is to fly eastward and shorten it. This east-west difference in jet lag is sizable enough to have an impact on the performance of sports teams.

12. 39) [32]

If you want the confidence that comes from achieving what you set out to do each day, then it's important to understand how long things are going to take.

(A) Make a practice of estimating the amount of time needed alongside items on your 'things to do' list, and learn by experience when tasks take a greater or lesser time than expected. Give attention also to fitting the task to the available time.

(B) There are some tasks that you can only set about if you have a significant amount of time available. There is no point in trying to gear up for such a task when you only have a short period available.

(C) So schedule the time you need for the longer tasks and put the short tasks into the spare moments in between.

(D) Over-optimism about what can be achieved within a certain time frame is a problem. So work on it.

13. 40) [33]

In Lewis Carroll's Through the Looking-Glass, the Red Queen takes Alice on a race through the countryside.

(A) Biologists sometimes use this Red Queen Effect to explain an evolutionary principle. If foxes evolve to run faster so they can catch more rabbits, then only the fastest rabbits will live long enough to make a new generation of bunnies that run even faster — in which case, of course, only the fastest foxes will catch enough rabbits to thrive and pass on their genes.

(B) They run and they run, but then Alice discovers that they're still under the same tree that they started from. The Red Queen explains to Alice: "here, you see, it takes all the running you can do, to keep in the same place."

(C) Even though they might run, the two species just stay in place.

14. 41) [34]

Everything in the world around us was finished in the mind of its creator before it was started.

(A) The houses we live in, the cars we drive, and our clothing — all of these began with an idea. Each idea was then studied, refined and perfected before the first nail was driven or the first piece of cloth was cut. Long before the idea was turned into a physical reality, the mind had clearly pictured the finished product.

(B) Over a period of time we refine and perfect the vision. Before long, our every thought, decision and activity are all working in harmony to bring into existence what we have mentally concluded about the future.

(C) The human being designs his or her own future through much the same process. We begin with an idea about how the future will be.

15. 42) 35

> Whose story it is affects what the story is.

(A) Consider, for example, how the tale of Cinderella would shift if told from the viewpoint of an evil stepsister.

(B) Gone with the Wind is Scarlett O'Hara's story, but what if we were shown the same events from the viewpoint of Rhett Butler or Melanie Wilkes?

(C) We'll place our sympathies with someone new. When the conflict arises that is the heart of the story, we will be praying for a different outcome.

(D) Change the main character, and the focus of the story must also change. If we look at the events through another character's eyes, we will interpret them differently.

16. 43) 36

> In the Old Stone Age, small bands of 20 to 60 people wandered from place to place in search of food.

(A) For example, toolmakers could share the work of making stone axes and knives. By working together, they could make more tools in the same amount of time.

(B) Living in communities allowed people to organize themselves more efficiently. They could divide up the work of producing food and other things they needed.

(C) Once people began farming, they could settle down near their farms. As a result, towns and villages grew larger.

(D) While some workers grew crops, others built new houses and made tools. Village dwellers also learned to work together to do a task faster.

17. 44) 37

> Natural processes form minerals in many ways.

(A) The type and amount of elements present in a magma partly determine which minerals will form. Also, the size of the crystals that form depends partly on how rapidly the magma cools. When magma cools slowly, the crystals that form are generally large enough to see with the unaided eye.

(B) This is because the atoms have enough time to move together and form into larger crystals. When magma cools rapidly, the crystals that form will be small. In such cases, you can't easily see individual mineral crystals.

(C) For example, hot melted rock material, called magma, cools when it reaches the Earth's surface, or even if it's trapped below the surface. As magma cools, its atoms lose heat energy, move closer together, and begin to combine into compounds. During this process, atoms of the different compounds arrange themselves into orderly, repeating patterns.

18. 45) 38

> All carbohydrates are basically sugars.

(A) As they slowly break down, the other nutrients are also released into your body, and can provide you with fuel for a number of hours. Bad carbohydrates, on the other hand, are simple sugars.

(B) Because their structure is not complex, they are easy to break down and hold few nutrients for your body other than the sugars from which they are made. Your body breaks down these carbohydrates rather quickly and what it cannot use is converted to fat and stored in the body.

(C) Complex carbohydrates are the good carbohydrates for your body. These complex sugar compounds are very difficult to break down and can trap other nutrients like vitamins and minerals in their chains.

19. 46) ³⁹

People commonly make the mistaken assumption that because a person has one type of characteristic, then they automatically have other characteristics which go with it.

(A) It was also found that those students who expected the lecturer to be warm tended to interact with him more.

(B) In one study, university students were given descriptions of a guest lecturer before he spoke to the group. Half the students received a description containing the word 'warm', the other half were told the speaker was 'cold'.

(C) This shows that different expectations not only affect the impressions we form but also our behaviour and the relationship which is formed.

(D) As expected, there were large differences between the impressions formed by the students, depending upon their original information of the lecturer.

(E) The guest lecturer then led a discussion, after which the students were asked to give their impressions of him.

20. 47) ⁴⁰

To help decide what's risky and what's safe, who's trustworthy and who's not, we look for social evidence.

(A) Is there a line outside or is it easy to find a seat? It is a hassle to wait, but a line can be a powerful cue that the food's tasty, and these seats are in demand.

(B) While we can frequently see this today in product reviews, even subtler cues within the environment can signal trustworthiness. Consider this: when you visit a local restaurant, are they busy?

(C) From an evolutionary view, following the group is almost always positive for our prospects of survival. "If everyone's doing it, it must be a sensible thing to do," explains famous psychologist and best selling writer of Influence, Robert Cialdini.

(D) More often than not, it's good to adopt the practices of those around you.

21. 48) 41, 42

Chess masters shown a chess board in the middle of a game for 5 seconds with 20 to 30 pieces still in play can immediately reproduce the position of the pieces from memory.

(A) Faced with unfamiliar patterns, even when it involves the same familiar domain, the expert's advantage disappears. The beneficial effects of familiar structure on memory have been observed for many types of expertise, including music.

(B) Experienced ballet dancers are able to repeat longer sequences of steps than less experienced dancers, and they can repeat a sequence of steps making up a routine better than steps ordered randomly. In each case, memory range is increased by the ability to recognize familiar sequences and patterns.

(C) Beginners, of course, are able to place only a few. Now take the same pieces and place them on the board randomly and the difference is much reduced. The expert's advantage is only for familiar patterns — those previously stored in memory.

(D) People with musical training can reproduce short sequences of musical notation more accurately than those with no musical training when notes follow conventional sequences, but the advantage is much reduced when the notes are ordered randomly. Expertise also improves memory for sequences of movements.

22. 49) 43, 44, 45

Once upon a time, there was a king who lived in a beautiful palace.

(A) With each bad word the guards used, the monster grew more ugly and smelly. The guards got even angrier — they began to brandish their swords to scare the monster away from the palace. But he just grew bigger and bigger, eventually taking up the whole room. He grew more ugly and smelly than ever.

(B) Eventually the king returned. He was wise and kind and saw what was happening. He knew what to do. He smiled and said to the monster, "Welcome to my palace!"

(C) While the king was away, a monster approached the gates of the palace. The monster was so ugly and smelly that the guards froze in shock. He passed the guards and sat on the king's throne. The guards soon came to their senses, went in, and shouted at the monster, demanding that he get off the throne.

(D) The monster continued to get smaller with the king's kind gestures. He then offered the monster a full body massage. As the guards helped with the relaxing massage, the monster became tiny. With another act of kindness to the monster, he just disappeared.

(E) He asked the monster if he wanted a cup of coffee. The monster began to grow smaller as he drank the coffee. The king offered him some take-out pizza and fries. The guards immediately called for pizza.

2021 고1 3월 모의고사

❶ voca ❷ text ❸ [/] ❹ ____ ❺ quiz 1 ❻ quiz 2 ❼ quiz 3 ❽ quiz 4 ❾ quiz 5

1. 1)**밑줄 친 부분 중, 어법, 혹은 문맥상 어색한 곳을 고르시오.** 2023_고1_3_18번

To whom it may concern,
I am a resident of the Blue Sky Apartment. Recently I ① **observed** that the kid zone is in ② **need** of repairs. I want you to pay attention to the poor condition of the playground equipment in the zone. The swings are ③ **damaged** , the paint is falling off, and some of the bolts on the slide are missing. The facilities have been in this terrible condition since we moved here. They are dangerous to the children ④ **playing** there. Would you please have them ⑤ **repairing** ? I would appreciate your immediate attention to solve this matter.
Yours sincerely,
Nina Davis

2. 2)**밑줄 친 부분 중, 어법, 혹은 문맥상 어색한 곳을 고르시오.** 2023_고1_3_19번

On a two-week trip in the Rocky Mountains, I saw a grizzly bear in its native habitat . At first, I felt joy as I watched the bear ① **walk** across the land. He stopped every once in a while to turn his head about, sniffing deeply. He was following the scent of something, and slowly I began to realize ② **what** this giant animal was smelling ③ **me** ! I froze. This was no longer a wonderful experience; it was now an issue of ④ **survival** . The bear's ⑤ **motivation** was to find meat to eat, and I was clearly on his menu.

3. 3)**밑줄 친 부분 중, 어법, 혹은 문맥상 어색한 곳을 고르시오.** 2023_고1_3_20번

It is difficult ① **for** any of us to maintain a constant level of attention throughout our working day. We all have body rhythms characterised by peaks and valleys of energy and alertness. You will achieve more, and feel confident as a benefit, if you schedule your most demanding tasks at times when you are best able to cope ② **with**. If you haven't thought about energy peaks before, take a few days to observe ③ **yourself** . Try to note the times ④ **when** you are at your best. We are all ⑤ **different** . For some, the peak will come first thing in the morning, but for others it may take a while to warm up.

4. 4)**밑줄 친 부분 중, 어법, 혹은 문맥상 어색한 곳을 고르시오.** 2023_고1_3_21번

If we adopt technology, we need to pay its costs. Thousands of traditional livelihoods have been pushed aside by ① **progress** , and the lifestyles around those jobs removed. Hundreds of millions of humans today work at jobs they hate, producing things they have no ② **love for**. Sometimes these jobs cause physical pain, disability, or chronic disease. Technology creates many new jobs that are certainly dangerous . At the same time, mass education and media train humans to avoid low-tech physical work, to ③ **seek** jobs working in the digital world. The ④ **integration** of the hands from the head puts a stress on the human mind. Indeed, the ⑤ **sedentary** nature of the best-paying jobs is a health risk — for body and mind.

5. ⁵⁾밑줄 친 부분 중, 어법, 혹은 문맥상 어색한 곳을 고르시오. 2023_고1_3_22번

When students are starting their college life, they may approach every course, test, or learning task the same way, using ① **what** we like to call "the rubber-stamp approach". Think about it this way: Would you wear a tuxedo to a baseball game? A colorful dress to a funeral? A bathing suit to religious services? Probably not. You know there's appropriate dress for different occasions and settings. Skillful learners know ② **what** "putting on the same clothes" won't work for every ③ **class**. They are flexible learners. They have different strategies and know when to use them. They know ④ **that** you study for multiple-choice tests ⑤ **differently** than you study for essay tests. And they not only know what to do, but they also know how to do it.

6. ⁶⁾밑줄 친 부분 중, 어법, 혹은 문맥상 어색한 곳을 고르시오. 2023_고1_3_23번

As the social and economic situation of countries got better, wage levels and working conditions ① **improved** . Gradually people were given more time off . At the same time, forms of transport improved and it became faster and cheaper to get to places. England's ② **industrious** revolution led to many of these changes. Railways, in the nineteenth century, opened up now famous seaside resorts such as Blackpool and Brighton. With the railways ③ **came** many large hotels. In Canada, for example, the new coast-to-coast railway system made ④ **possible** the building of such famous hotels as Banff Springs and Chateau Lake Louise in the Rockies. Later, the arrival of air transport opened up more of the world and led to tourism ⑤ **growth** .

7. ⁷⁾밑줄 친 부분 중, 어법, 혹은 문맥상 어색한 곳을 고르시오. 2023_고1_3_24번

Success can lead you off your ① **intended** path and into a comfortable rut. If you are good at something and are well ② **awarded** for doing it, you may want to keep doing it even if you stop enjoying it. The danger is that one day you look around and realize you're so deep in this ③ **comfortable** rut that you can no longer see the sun or breathe fresh air; the sides of the rut have become so slippery that it would take a superhuman effort to climb out; and, effectively, you're ④ **stuck** . And it's a situation ⑤ **that** many working people worry they're in now. The poor employment market has left them feeling locked in what may be a secure, or even well-paying — but ultimately unsatisfying — job.

8. ⁸⁾밑줄 친 부분 중, 어법, 혹은 문맥상 어색한 곳을 고르시오. 2023_고1_3_25번

The above graph shows the number of births and deaths in Korea from 2016 to 2021. The number of ① **births** continued to decrease throughout the whole period. The gap between the number of births and deaths was the largest in 2016. In 2019, the gap between the number of births and ② **deaths** was the smallest, with the number of births slightly larger than that of deaths. The number of deaths increased steadily ③ **during** the whole period, except the period from 2018 to 2019. In 2021, the number of deaths ④ **were** larger than ⑤ **that** of births.

9. 9)밑줄 친 부분 중, 어법, 혹은 문맥상 어색한 곳을 고르시오. 2023_고1_3_26번

Lilian Bland was born in Kent, England in 1878. Unlike most other girls at the time she wore trousers and spent her time ① **enjoying** adventurous activities like horse riding and hunting. Lilian began her career as a sports and wildlife photographer for British newspapers. In 1910 she became the first woman to design, build, and fly her own airplane. In order to persuade her to ② **trying** a slightly safer activity, Lilian's dad bought her a car. Soon Lilian was a master driver and ended up ③ **working** as a car dealer. She never went back to flying but lived a long and ④ **exciting** life nonetheless. She married, moved to Canada, and had a kid. Eventually, she moved back to England, and lived there for the rest of her life.

10. 10)밑줄 친 부분 중, 어법, 혹은 문맥상 어색한 곳을 고르시오. 2023_고1_3_29번

The most noticeable human characteristic projected onto animals is that they can talk in human language. ① **Physically** , animal cartoon characters and toys made after animals are also most often ② **deformed** in such a way as to resemble humans. This is achieved by showing them with humanlike facial features and deformed front legs to resemble human hands. In more recent animated movies the trend has been to show the animals in a more "natural" way. However , they still use their front legs like human hands (for example, lions can pick up and lift small objects with one paw), and they still talk with an appropriate facial expression. A general strategy that ③ **is used to** ④ **making** the animal characters more emotionally ⑤ **appealing** , both to children and adults, is to give them enlarged and deformed childlike features.

11. 11)밑줄 친 부분 중, 어법, 혹은 문맥상 어색한 곳을 고르시오. 2023_고1_3_30번

The major philosophical shift in the idea of selling came when industrial societies became more affluent , more competitive, and more geographically spread out during the 1940s and 1950s. This forced business ① **develop** closer relations with buyers and clients, which in turn made business ② **realize** that it was not enough to produce a ③ **quality** product at a reasonable price. In fact, it was equally essential to deliver products that customers actually wanted . Henry Ford produced his best-selling T-model Ford in one color only (black) in 1908, but in modern societies this was no longer possible. The modernization of society led to a marketing revolution that destroyed the view that production would create its own ④ **demand** . Customers, and the desire to meet their diverse and often complex ⑤ **needs** , became the focus of business.

12. 12)밑줄 친 부분 중, 어법, 혹은 문맥상 어색한 곳을 고르시오. 2023_고1_3_31번

People differ in how quickly they can reset their biological clocks to ① **overcome** jet lag, and the speed of ② **recovery** depends on the direction of travel. Generally, it's easier to fly westward and lengthen your day than it is to fly eastward and ③ **shorten** it. This east-west difference in jet lag is sizable enough to have an impact on the performance of sports teams. Studies have found that teams flying westward perform significantly ④ **better** than teams flying eastward in professional baseball and college football. A more recent study of more than 46,000 Major League Baseball games found additional evidence that eastward travel is ⑤ **easier** than westward travel.

13. 13)밑줄 친 부분 중, 어법, 혹은 문맥상 어색한 곳을 고르시오. 2023_고1_3_32번

If you want the confidence that comes from achieving ① **what** you set out to do each day, then it's important to understand how long things are going to take. Over-optimism about what can be achieved within a certain time frame is a problem. So work on it. Make a practice of estimating the amount of time needed alongside items on your 'things to do' list, and learn by experience ② **when** tasks take a greater or lesser time than expected. Give attention also to fitting the task to the available time. There are some tasks ③ **when** you can only set about if you have a ④ **significant** amount of time available. There is no point in trying to gear up for such a task when you only have a short period available. So schedule the time you need for the longer tasks and put the ⑤ **short** tasks into the spare moments in between.

14. 14)밑줄 친 부분 중, 어법, 혹은 문맥상 어색한 곳을 고르시오. 2023_고1_3_33번

In Lewis Carroll's Through the Looking-Glass, the Red Queen takes Alice on a race through the countryside. They run and they run, but then Alice ① **discovers** that they're still under the same tree that they started from. The Red Queen explains to Alice: "here, you see, it takes all the running you can do, to keep in the same place". Biologists sometimes use this Red Queen Effect to explain an ② **evolutionary** principle . If foxes ③ **evolve** to run faster so they can catch more rabbits, then only the fastest rabbits will live long enough to make a new generation of bunnies that run even faster — in which case, of course, only the fastest foxes will catch enough rabbits to ④ **collapse** and ⑤ **pass on** their genes. Even though they might run, the two species just stay in place.

15. 15)밑줄 친 부분 중, 어법, 혹은 문맥상 어색한 곳을 고르시오. 2023_고1_3_34번

Everything in the world around us was ① **finished** in the mind of its creator before it was ② **started** . The houses we live in, the cars we drive, and our clothing — all of these began with an ③ **object** . Each idea was then studied, refined and perfected before the first nail was driven or the first piece of cloth was cut. Long before the idea was turned into a physical reality, the mind had clearly pictured the finished product. The human being designs his or her own future through much the same ④ **process** . We begin with an idea about how the future will be. Over a period of time we refine and perfect the ⑤ **vision** . Before long, our every thought, decision and activity are all working in harmony to bring into existence what we have mentally concluded about the future.

16. 16)밑줄 친 부분 중, 어법, 혹은 문맥상 어색한 곳을 고르시오. 2023_고1_3_35번

Whose story it is ① **affects** what the story is. Change the main character, and the focus of the story must also change. ② **If we look** at the events through another character's eyes, we will interpret them differently. We'll place our sympathies with ③ **someone new** . When the conflict ④ **arises** that is the heart of the story, we will be praying for a different outcome . Consider, for example, how the tale of Cinderella would shift if told from the viewpoint of an evil stepsister. Gone with the Wind is Scarlett O'Hara's story, but what if we were ⑤ **showing** the same events from the viewpoint of Rhett Butler or Melanie Wilkes?

17. 17)**밑줄 친 부분 중, 어법, 혹은 문맥상 어색한 곳을 고르시오.** 2023_고1_3_36번

In the Old Stone Age, small bands of 20 to 60 people wandered from place to place in search of food. Once people began farming, they could settle down near their farms. As a result , towns and villages grew ① **larger** . Living in communities allowed people ② **organize** themselves more efficiently. They could divide up the work of producing food and other things they needed. ③ **While** some workers grew crops, others built new houses and made tools. Village dwellers also learned to work together to ④ **do** a task faster. ⑤ **For example**, toolmakers could share the work of making stone axes and knives. By working together, they could make more tools in the same amount of time.

18. 18)**밑줄 친 부분 중, 어법, 혹은 문맥상 어색한 곳을 고르시오.** 2023_고1_3_37번

Natural processes form minerals in many ways. For example, hot melted rock material, ① **called** magma, cools when it reaches the Earth's surface, or even if it's trapped below the surface. As magma cools, its atoms ② **gain** heat energy, move ③ **closer** together, and begin to combine into compounds . During this process, atoms of the different compounds arrange themselves into orderly , repeating patterns. The type and amount of elements present in a magma partly determine ④ **which** minerals will form. Also, the size of the crystals that form depends partly on how ⑤ **rapidly** the magma cools. When magma cools slowly, the crystals that form are generally large enough to see with the unaided eye. This is because the atoms have enough time to move together and form into larger crystals. When magma cools rapidly, the crystals that form will be small . In such cases, you can't easily see individual mineral crystals.

19. 19)**밑줄 친 부분 중, 어법, 혹은 문맥상 어색한 곳을 고르시오.** 2023_고1_3_38번

All carbohydrates are basically sugars. Complex carbohydrates are the good carbohydrates for your body. These complex sugar compounds are very ① **easy** to break down and can ② **trap** other nutrients like vitamins and minerals in their chains. As they slowly break down, the other nutrients are also ③ **released** into your body, and can provide you with fuel for a number of hours. Bad carbohydrates, on the other hand, are simple sugars. ④ **Because** their structure is not complex, they are easy to break down and hold ⑤ **few** nutrients for your body other than the sugars from which they are made. Your body breaks down these carbohydrates rather quickly and what it cannot use is converted to fat and stored in the body.

20. 20)**밑줄 친 부분 중, 어법, 혹은 문맥상 어색한 곳을 고르시오.** 2023_고1_3_39번

People commonly make the mistaken assumption that because a person has one type of characteristic, then they automatically have other characteristics which go with it. In one study, university students were given descriptions of a guest lecturer before he spoke to the group. Half the students received a ① **description** ② **containing** the word 'warm', the other half were told the speaker was 'cold'. The guest lecturer then led a discussion, ③ **which** the students were asked to give their impressions of him. As expected, there were large ④ **differences** between the impressions formed by the students, depending upon their original information of the lecturer. It was also found that those students who expected the lecturer to be warm tended to interact with him more. This shows that different ⑤ **expectations** not only affect the impressions we form but also our behaviour and the relationship which is formed.

21. 21)**밑줄 친 부분 중, 어법, 혹은 문맥상 어색한 곳을 고르시오.** 2023_고1_3_40번

To help decide what's risky and what's safe, who's trustworthy and who's not, we look for social evidence. From an ① **evolutionary** view, following the group is almost always ② **negative** for our prospects of survival. "If everyone's doing it, it must be a ③ **sensible** thing to do", explains famous psychologist and best selling writer of Influence, Robert Cialdini. While we can frequently see this today in product reviews, even subtler cues within the environment can signal trustworthiness. Consider this: when you visit a local restaurant, are they busy? Is there a line outside or is it easy to find a seat? It is a hassle to wait, but a line can be a ④ **powerful** cue that the food's tasty, and these seats are in demand. More often than not, it's good to ⑤ **adopt** the practices of those around you.

22. 22)**밑줄 친 부분 중, 어법, 혹은 문맥상 어색한 곳을 고르시오.** 2023_고1_3_41, 42번

Chess masters shown a chess board in the middle of a game for 5 seconds with 20 to 30 pieces still in play can immediately ① **replenish** the position of the pieces from memory. Beginners, of course, are able to place only a few . Now take the same pieces and place them on the board randomly and the difference is much ② **reduced** . The expert's advantage is only for ③ **familiar** patterns — those previously stored in memory. Faced with unfamiliar patterns, even when it involves the same familiar domain , the expert's advantage disappears . The beneficial effects of familiar structure on memory have been observed for many types of expertise, including music. People with musical training can reproduce short sequences of musical notation more accurately than those with no musical training when notes follow usual sequences, but the advantage is much reduced when the notes are ordered randomly. Expertise also improves memory for sequences of movements. Experienced ballet dancers are able to repeat longer sequences of steps than ④ **less** experienced dancers, and they can repeat a sequence of steps making up a routine better than steps ordered randomly. In each case, memory range is ⑤ **increased** by the ability to recognize familiar sequences and patterns.

23. 23)**밑줄 친 부분 중, 어법, 혹은 문맥상 어색한 곳을 고르시오.** 2023_고1_3_43, 44. 45번

Once upon a time, there was a king who lived in a beautiful palace. ① **While** the king was away, a monster ② **approached** the gates of the palace. The monster was so ugly and smelly that the guards froze in shock. He passed the guards and sat on the king's throne. The guards soon came to their senses, went in, and shouted at the monster, demanding ③ **that** he get off the throne. With each bad ④ **word** the guards used, the monster grew more ugly and smelly. The guards got even angrier — they began to brandish their swords to scare the monster away from the palace. But he just grew bigger and bigger, eventually ⑤ **took** up the whole room. He grew more ugly and smelly than ever. Eventually the king returned. He was wise and kind and saw what was happening. He knew what to do. He smiled and said to the monster, "Welcome to my palace"! He asked the monster if he wanted a cup of coffee. The monster began to grow smaller as he drank the coffee. The king offered him some take-out pizza and fries. The guards immediately called for pizza. The monster continued to get smaller with the king's kind gestures. He then offered the monster a full body massage. As the guards helped with the relaxing massage, the monster became tiny. With another act of kindness to the monster, he just disappeared.

2021 고1 3월 모의고사

❶ voca   ❷ text   ❸ [/]   ❹ _____   ❺ quiz 1   ❻ quiz 2   ❼ quiz 3   ❽ quiz 4   ❾ quiz 5

1. 1)**밑줄 친 ⓐ~ⓖ 중 어법, 혹은 문맥상 어휘의 사용이 어색한 것끼리 짝지어진 것을 고르시오.** 2023_고1_3_18번

To whom it may concern,
I am a resident of the Blue Sky Apartment. Recently I ⓐ **observed** that the kid zone is in ⓑ **need** of repairs. I want you to pay attention to the poor condition of the playground equipment in the zone. The swings are ⓒ **damaging** , the paint is falling off, and some of the bolts on the slide ⓓ **is** missing. The facilities ⓔ **were** in this terrible condition since we moved here. They are dangerous to the children ⓕ **playing** there. Would you please have them ⓖ **repairing** ? I would appreciate your immediate attention to solve this matter.
Yours sincerely, Nina Davis

① ⓐ, ⓓ, ⓔ   ② ⓐ, ⓑ, ⓒ, ⓕ   ③ ⓑ, ⓒ, ⓓ, ⓖ
④ ⓑ, ⓓ, ⓔ, ⓕ   ⑤ ⓒ, ⓓ, ⓔ, ⓖ

2. 2)**밑줄 친 ⓐ~ⓕ 중 어법, 혹은 문맥상 어휘의 사용이 어색한 것끼리 짝지어진 것을 고르시오.** 2023_고1_3_19번

On a two-week trip in the Rocky Mountains, I saw a grizzly bear in its native ⓐ **habitat** . At first, I felt joy as I watched the bear ⓑ **walk** across the land. He stopped every once in a while to turn his head about, sniffing deeply. He was following the scent of something, and slowly I began to realize ⓒ **that** this giant animal was smelling ⓓ **me** ! I froze. This was no longer a wonderful experience; it was now an issue of ⓔ **pleasure** . The bear's ⓕ **simulation** was to find meat to eat, and I was clearly on his menu.

① ⓐ, ⓕ   ② ⓑ, ⓕ   ③ ⓔ, ⓕ
④ ⓐ, ⓓ, ⓔ   ⑤ ⓑ, ⓒ, ⓔ

3. 3)**밑줄 친 ⓐ~ⓖ 중 어법, 혹은 문맥상 어휘의 사용이 어색한 것끼리 짝지어진 것을 고르시오.** 2023_고1_3_20번

It is difficult ⓐ **for** any of us to maintain a ⓑ **flexible** level of attention throughout our working day. We all have body rhythms characterised by peaks and valleys of energy and alertness. You will achieve more, and feel confident as a benefit, if you schedule your most ⓒ **demanded** tasks at times when you are best able to cope ⓓ **with**. If you haven't thought about energy peaks before, take a few days to observe ⓔ **you** . Try to note the times ⓕ **when** you are at your best. We are all ⓖ **different** . For some, the peak will come first thing in the morning, but for others it may take a while to warm up.

① ⓐ, ⓕ, ⓖ   ② ⓑ, ⓓ, ⓖ   ③ ⓒ, ⓓ, ⓕ
④ ⓐ, ⓑ, ⓓ, ⓔ   ⑤ ⓑ, ⓒ, ⓓ, ⓔ

4. 4)**밑줄 친 ⓐ~ⓚ 중 어법, 혹은 문맥상 어휘의 사용이 어색한 것끼리 짝지어진 것을 고르시오.** 2023_고1_3_21번

If we ⓐ **adopt** technology, we need to pay its costs. Thousands of traditional livelihoods have been ⓑ **pushed** aside by ⓒ **progress** , and the lifestyles around those jobs removed. Hundreds of millions of humans today work at jobs they hate, producing things they have no ⓓ **love for** . Sometimes these jobs cause physical pain, disability, or chronic disease. Technology creates many new jobs that are certainly ⓔ **dangerous** . At the same time, ⓕ **mess** education and media train humans to ⓖ **avoid** low-tech physical work, to ⓗ **sick** jobs ⓘ **working** in the digital world. The ⓙ **integration** of the hands from the head puts a stress on the human mind. Indeed, the ⓚ **rudimentary** nature of the best-paying jobs is a health risk — for body and mind.

① ⓓ, ⓚ   ② ⓐ, ⓓ, ⓕ   ③ ⓑ, ⓔ, ⓘ
④ ⓓ, ⓗ, ⓚ   ⑤ ⓕ, ⓗ, ⓙ, ⓚ

5. 5)**밑줄 친 ⓐ~ⓘ 중 어법, 혹은 문맥상 어휘의 사용이 어색한 것끼리 짝지어진 것을 고르시오.** 2023_고1_3_22번

When students are starting their college life, they may ⓐ **approach** every course, test, or learning task the same way, using ⓑ **that** we like to call "the rubber-stamp approach". Think about it this way: Would you wear a tuxedo to a baseball game? A colorful dress to a funeral? A bathing suit to religious services? Probably not. You know there's appropriate dress for different occasions and settings. Skillful learners know ⓒ **what** "putting on the same clothes" won't work for

every ⓓ **classes** . They are ⓔ **flexible** learners. They have different strategies and know when to use them. They know ⓕ **that** you study for multiple-choice tests ⓖ **differently** than you study for essay tests. And they not only know ⓗ **how** to do, but they also know ⓘ **how** to do it.

① ⓐ, ⓑ, ⓓ   ② ⓐ, ⓕ, ⓘ   ③ ⓒ, ⓓ, ⓔ
④ ⓑ, ⓒ, ⓓ, ⓗ   ⑤ ⓒ, ⓓ, ⓖ, ⓗ

6. 6)**밑줄 친 ⓐ~ⓖ 중 어법, 혹은 문맥상 어휘의 사용이 어색한 것끼리 짝지어진 것을 고르시오.** 2023_고1_3_23번

As the social and economic situation of countries got better, wage levels and working conditions ⓐ **retreated** . Gradually people were given more time ⓑ **off** . At the same time, forms of transport improved and it became faster and cheaper to get to places. England's ⓒ **industrial** ⓓ **revolution** led to many of these changes. Railways, in the nineteenth century, opened up now famous seaside resorts such as Blackpool and Brighton. With the railways ⓔ **coming** many large hotels. In Canada, for example, the new coast-to-coast railway system made ⓕ **possible** the building of such famous hotels as Banff Springs and Chateau Lake Louise in the Rockies. Later, the arrival of air transport opened up more of the world and led to tourism ⓖ **growth** .

① ⓐ, ⓓ   ② ⓐ, ⓔ   ③ ⓐ, ⓕ   ④ ⓔ, ⓖ
⑤ ⓑ, ⓓ, ⓖ

7. ⁷⁾**밑줄 친 ⓐ~ⓛ 중 어법, 혹은 문맥상 어휘의 사용이 어색한 것끼리 짝지어진 것을 고르시오.** ^{2023_}
고1_3_24번

Success can lead you off your ⓐ **pretended** path and into a ⓑ **revolutionary** rut. If you are good at something and are well ⓒ **rewarded** for doing it, you may want to keep ⓓ **to do** it even if you stop enjoying it. The danger is that one day you look around and realize you're so deep in this ⓔ **comfortable** rut ⓕ **that** you can no longer see the sun or breathe fresh air; the sides of the rut have become so slippery ⓖ **which** it would take a superhuman effort to climb out; and, effectively, you're ⓗ **stuck** . And it's a situation ⓘ **that** many working people worry they're in now. The poor employment market has left them feeling ⓙ **locked** in ⓚ **what** may be a secure, or even well-paying — but ultimately ⓛ **unsatisfying** — job.

① ⓐ, ⓑ, ⓔ   ② ⓐ, ⓑ, ⓙ   ③ ⓐ, ⓑ, ⓓ, ⓖ
④ ⓐ, ⓔ, ⓖ, ⓚ   ⑤ ⓒ, ⓖ, ⓘ, ⓙ

8. ⁸⁾**밑줄 친 ⓐ~ⓗ 중 어법, 혹은 문맥상 어휘의 사용이 어색한 것끼리 짝지어진 것을 고르시오.** ^{2023_}
고1_3_25번

The above graph shows ⓐ **the** number of births and deaths in Korea from 2016 to 2021. The number of ⓑ **birth** continued to decrease throughout the whole period. The gap between the number of births and deaths ⓒ **were** the largest in 2016. In 2019, the gap between the number of births and ⓓ **deaths** was the smallest, with the number of births slightly larger than ⓔ **that** of deaths. The number of deaths increased steadily ⓕ **while** the whole period, except the period from 2018 to 2019. In 2021, the number of deaths ⓖ **was** larger than ⓗ **those** of births.

① ⓒ, ⓖ   ② ⓐ, ⓒ, ⓓ   ③ ⓑ, ⓓ, ⓔ
④ ⓑ, ⓓ, ⓖ   ⑤ ⓑ, ⓒ, ⓕ, ⓗ

9. ⁹⁾**밑줄 친 ⓐ~ⓓ 중 어법, 혹은 문맥상 어휘의 사용이 어색한 것끼리 짝지어진 것을 고르시오.** ^{2023_}
고1_3_26번

Lilian Bland was born in Kent, England in 1878. Unlike most other girls at the time she wore trousers and spent her time ⓐ **to enjoy** adventurous activities like horse riding and hunting. Lilian began her career as a sports and wildlife photographer for British newspapers. In 1910 she became the first woman to design, build, and fly her own airplane. In order to persuade her to ⓑ **trying** a slightly safer activity, Lilian's dad bought her a car. Soon Lilian was a master driver and ended up ⓒ **working** as a car dealer. She never went back to flying but lived a long and ⓓ **excited** life nonetheless. She married, moved to Canada, and had a kid. Eventually, she moved back to England, and lived there for the rest of her life.

① ⓐ, ⓒ   ② ⓑ, ⓒ   ③ ⓐ, ⓑ, ⓓ
④ ⓐ, ⓒ, ⓓ   ⑤ ⓑ, ⓒ, ⓓ

10. 10)밑줄 친 ⓐ~ⓜ 중 어법, 혹은 문맥상 어휘의 사용이 어색한 것끼리 짝지어진 것을 고르시오.
2023_고1_3_29번

The most noticeable human characteristic ⓐ **projected** onto animals ⓑ **are** that they can talk in human language. ⓒ **Verbally** , animal cartoon characters and toys ⓓ **made** after animals are also most often ⓔ **deformed** in such a way as to ⓕ **resemble** humans. This is achieved by showing them with humanlike facial features and deformed front legs to ⓖ **resemble with** human hands. In more recent animated movies the trend ⓗ **has** been to show the animals in a more "natural" way. ⓘ **However** , they still use their front legs like human hands (for example, lions can pick up and lift small objects with one paw), and they still talk with an appropriate facial expression. A general strategy that ⓙ **is used to** ⓚ **make** the animal characters more emotionally ⓛ **appealing** , both to children and adults, is to give them enlarged and deformed ⓜ **childlike** features.

① ⓕ, ⓖ   ② ⓑ, ⓒ, ⓓ   ③ ⓑ, ⓒ, ⓖ
④ ⓓ, ⓕ, ⓛ   ⑤ ⓑ, ⓘ, ⓙ, ⓜ

11. 11)밑줄 친 ⓐ~ⓞ 중 어법, 혹은 문맥상 어휘의 사용이 어색한 것끼리 짝지어진 것을 고르시오.
2023_고1_3_30번

The major ⓐ **philosophical** shift in the idea of selling came when ⓑ **industrial** societies became more ⓒ **affluent** , more competitive, and more ⓓ **geographically** spread out ⓔ **during** the 1940s and 1950s. This forced business ⓕ **to develop** ⓖ **closer** relations with buyers and clients, which in turn made business ⓗ **realize** that it was not enough to produce a ⓘ **quality** product at a reasonable price. In fact, it was equally essential to deliver products that customers actually ⓙ **bought** . Henry

Ford produced his best-selling T-model Ford in one color only (black) in 1908, but in modern societies this was no longer possible. The modernization of society led to a marketing ⓚ **revolution** that destroyed the view ⓛ **that** ⓜ **demand** would create its own ⓝ **demand** . Customers, and the desire to meet their diverse and often complex ⓞ **productions** , became the focus of business.

① ⓐ, ⓞ   ② ⓖ, ⓛ, ⓞ   ③ ⓖ, ⓜ, ⓞ   ④ ⓙ, ⓜ, ⓞ   ⑤ ⓑ, ⓓ, ⓗ, ⓙ

12. 12)밑줄 친 ⓐ~ⓙ 중 어법, 혹은 문맥상 어휘의 사용이 어색한 것끼리 짝지어진 것을 고르시오.
2023_고1_3_31번

People differ in how ⓐ **quickly** they can reset their biological clocks to ⓑ **overwhelm** jet lag, and the speed of ⓒ **recovery** depends on the direction of travel. Generally, it's easier to fly westward and ⓓ **lengthen** your day than it is to fly eastward and ⓔ **shorten** it. This east-west difference in jet lag is sizable enough to have an impact on the performance of sports teams. Studies have found that teams ⓕ **flied** westward perform significantly ⓖ **better** than teams ⓗ **flying** eastward in professional baseball and college football. A more recent study of more than 46,000 Major League Baseball games found additional evidence ⓘ **that** eastward travel is ⓙ **easier** than westward travel.

① ⓑ, ⓓ   ② ⓐ, ⓔ, ⓕ   ③ ⓑ, ⓕ, ⓙ   ④ ⓒ, ⓓ, ⓕ, ⓗ   ⑤ ⓓ, ⓖ, ⓘ, ⓙ

13. 13)밑줄 친 ⓐ~ⓘ 중 어법, 혹은 문맥상 어휘의 사용이 어색한 것끼리 짝지어진 것을 고르시오.

2023_고1_3_32번

If you want the confidence that comes from achieving ⓐ **what** you set out to do each day, then it's important to understand how long things are going to take. ⓑ **Over-pessimism** about ⓒ **what** can be achieved within a certain time frame is a problem. So work on it. Make a practice of ⓓ **estimating** the amount of time needed alongside items on your 'things to do' list, and learn by experience ⓔ **when** tasks take a greater or lesser time than expected. Give attention also to fitting the task to the available time. There are some tasks ⓕ **when** you can only set about if you have a ⓖ **minimum** amount of time available. There is no point in trying to ⓗ **gear** up for such a task when you only have a short period available. So schedule the time you need for the longer tasks and put the ⓘ **long** tasks into the spare moments in between.

① ⓔ, ⓗ, ⓘ ② ⓐ, ⓒ, ⓓ, ⓕ ③ ⓑ, ⓔ, ⓕ, ⓖ
④ ⓑ, ⓕ, ⓖ, ⓗ ⑤ ⓑ, ⓕ, ⓖ, ⓘ

14. 14)밑줄 친 ⓐ~ⓘ 중 어법, 혹은 문맥상 어휘의 사용이 어색한 것끼리 짝지어진 것을 고르시오.

2023_고1_3_33번

In Lewis Carroll's Through the Looking-Glass, the Red Queen takes Alice on a race through the countryside. They run and they run, but then Alice ⓐ **discovers** ⓑ **that** they're still under the same tree ⓒ **that** they started from. The Red Queen explains to Alice: "here, you see, it takes all the running you can do, to keep in the same place". Biologists sometimes use this Red Queen Effect to

explain an ⓓ **revolutionary** ⓔ **principle**. If foxes ⓕ **evolve** to run faster so they can catch more rabbits, then only the ⓖ **fastest** rabbits will live long enough to make a new generation of bunnies that run even faster — in which case, of course, only the fastest foxes will catch enough rabbits to ⓗ **collapse** and ⓘ **pass on** their genes. Even though they might run, the two species just stay in place.

① ⓐ, ⓗ ② ⓑ, ⓓ ③ ⓒ, ⓓ ④ ⓓ, ⓗ
⑤ ⓔ, ⓖ

15. 15)밑줄 친 ⓐ~ⓚ 중 어법, 혹은 문맥상 어휘의 사용이 어색한 것끼리 짝지어진 것을 고르시오.

2023_고1_3_34번

Everything in the world around us was ⓐ **finished** in the mind of its creator before it was ⓑ **finished**. The houses we live in, the cars we drive, and our clothing — all of these began with an ⓒ **idea**. Each idea was then studied, refined and perfected before the first nail was driven or the first piece of cloth was cut. Long ⓓ **before** the idea was turned into a ⓔ **physical** reality, the mind had clearly pictured the finished product. The human being designs his or her own ⓕ **future** through much the same ⓖ **process**. We begin with ⓗ **an idea** about how the future will be. Over a period of time we refine and perfect the ⓘ **vision**. Before long, our every thought, decision and activity are all working in harmony to bring into ⓙ **existence** what we have mentally ⓚ **excluded** about the future.

① ⓐ, ⓔ ② ⓐ, ⓚ ③ ⓑ, ⓗ
④ ⓑ, ⓚ ⑤ ⓔ, ⓘ

16. ¹⁶⁾밑줄 친 ⓐ~ⓗ 중 어법, 혹은 문맥상 어휘의 사용이 어색한 것끼리 짝지어진 것을 고르시오.
2023_고1_3_35번

Whose story it is ⓐ **affect** what the story is. ⓑ **If you change** the main character, and the focus of the story must also change. ⓒ **If we look** at the events through another character's eyes, we will interpret them differently. We'll place our sympathies with ⓓ **someone new**. When the conflict ⓔ **raises** that is the heart of the story, we will be praying for a different ⓕ **outcome** . Consider, for example, how the tale of Cinderella would shift if ⓖ **told** from the viewpoint of an evil stepsister. Gone with the Wind is Scarlett O'Hara's story, but what if we were ⓗ **shown** the same events from the viewpoint of Rhett Butler or Melanie Wilkes?

① ⓐ, ⓒ   ② ⓐ, ⓑ, ⓓ   ③ ⓐ, ⓑ, ⓔ
④ ⓐ, ⓒ, ⓓ   ⑤ ⓐ, ⓔ, ⓖ

17. ¹⁷⁾밑줄 친 ⓐ~ⓗ 중 어법, 혹은 문맥상 어휘의 사용이 어색한 것끼리 짝지어진 것을 고르시오.
2023_고1_3_36번

In the Old Stone Age, small bands of 20 to 60 people ⓐ **wondered** from place to place in search of food. Once people began farming, they could settle down near their farms. ⓑ **As a result** , towns and villages grew ⓒ **smaller** . Living in ⓓ **communities** allowed people ⓔ **to organize** themselves more efficiently. They could divide up the work of producing food and other things they needed. ⓕ **During** some workers grew crops, others built new houses and made tools. Village dwellers also learned to work together to ⓖ **do** a task faster. ⓗ **On the other hand**, toolmakers

could share the work of making stone axes and knives. By working together, they could make more tools in the same amount of time.

① ⓐ, ⓑ   ② ⓑ, ⓔ, ⓖ   ③ ⓓ, ⓖ, ⓗ   ④ ⓐ, ⓒ, ⓓ, ⓗ   ⑤ ⓐ, ⓒ, ⓕ, ⓗ

18. ¹⁸⁾밑줄 친 ⓐ~ⓟ 중 어법, 혹은 문맥상 어휘의 사용이 어색한 것끼리 짝지어진 것을 고르시오.
2023_고1_3_37번

Natural ⓐ **progresses** form minerals in many ways. For example, hot melted rock material, ⓑ **called** magma, cools when it ⓒ **reaches** the Earth's surface, or even if it's trapped below the surface. As magma cools, its atoms ⓓ **lose** heat energy, move ⓔ **closer** together, and begin to combine into ⓕ **compounds** . ⓖ **During** this process, atoms of the different compounds ⓗ **arrange** themselves into ⓘ **order** , repeating patterns. The type and amount of elements ⓙ **present** in a magma partly determine ⓚ **which** minerals will form. Also, the size of the crystals that ⓛ **form** depends partly on how ⓜ **rapid** the magma cools. When magma cools slowly, the crystals that form are generally large enough to see with the unaided eye. This is ⓝ **because** the atoms have enough time to move together and form into larger crystals. When magma cools rapidly, the crystals that form will be ⓞ **small** . In such cases, you ⓟ **can** easily see individual mineral crystals.

① ⓐ, ⓑ, ⓟ   ② ⓒ, ⓖ, ⓘ   ③ ⓕ, ⓘ, ⓟ
④ ⓐ, ⓘ, ⓜ, ⓟ   ⑤ ⓓ, ⓖ, ⓙ, ⓚ

19. 19)밑줄 친 ⓐ~ⓘ 중 어법, 혹은 문맥상 어휘의 사용이 어색한 것끼리 짝지어진 것을 고르시오.

2023_고1_3_38번

All carbohydrates are basically sugars. Complex carbohydrates are the good carbohydrates for your body. These complex sugar compounds are very ⓐ **difficult** to break down and can ⓑ **release** other nutrients like vitamins and minerals in their chains. As they slowly break down, the other nutrients are also ⓒ **relieved** into your body, and can provide you ⓓ **for** fuel for ⓔ **a** number of hours. Bad carbohydrates, on the other hand, are simple sugars. ⓕ **Because** their structure is not complex, they are easy to break down and hold ⓖ **few** nutrients for your body other than the sugars ⓗ **from which** they are made. Your body breaks down these carbohydrates rather quickly and ⓘ **what** it cannot use is converted to fat and stored in the body.

① ⓐ, ⓕ, ⓖ   ② ⓐ, ⓖ, ⓗ   ③ ⓑ, ⓒ, ⓓ
④ ⓓ, ⓔ, ⓕ   ⑤ ⓐ, ⓔ, ⓖ, ⓘ

20. 20)밑줄 친 ⓐ~ⓝ 중 어법, 혹은 문맥상 어휘의 사용이 어색한 것끼리 짝지어진 것을 고르시오.

2023_고1_3_39번

People commonly make the ⓐ **organized** ⓑ **assumption** ⓒ **that** because a person has one type of characteristic, then they automatically have other characteristics which ⓓ **go** with it. In one study, university students were given ⓔ **prescription** of a guest lecturer before he spoke to the group. Half the students received a ⓕ **description** ⓖ **containing** the word 'warm', the other half were told the speaker was 'cold'. The guest lecturer then led a discussion, ⓗ **after which** the students ⓘ **were asked** to give their impressions of him. As expected, there were large ⓙ **differences** between the impressions ⓚ **formed** by the students, depending upon their original information of the lecturer. It was also found that those students who expected the lecturer to be warm tended to ⓛ **interact** with him more. This shows that different ⓜ **expectations** not only ⓝ **affect** the impressions we form but also our behaviour and the relationship which is formed.

① ⓐ, ⓔ   ② ⓐ, ⓙ   ③ ⓔ, ⓙ
④ ⓖ, ⓙ   ⑤ ⓖ, ⓝ

21. 21)밑줄 친 ⓐ~ⓖ 중 어법, 혹은 문맥상 어휘의 사용이 어색한 것끼리 짝지어진 것을 고르시오.

2023_고1_3_40번

To help decide what's risky and what's safe, who's trustworthy and who's not, we look for ⓐ **physical** evidence. From an ⓑ **evolutionary** view, following the group is almost always ⓒ **positive** for our prospects of survival. "If everyone's doing it, it must be a ⓓ **sensible** thing to do", explains famous psychologist and best selling writer of Influence, Robert Cialdini. While we can frequently see this today in product reviews, even ⓔ **subtler** cues within the environment can signal trustworthiness. Consider this: when you visit a local restaurant, are they busy? Is there a line outside or is it easy to find a seat? It is a hassle to wait, but a line can be a ⓕ **meaningless** cue that the food's tasty, and these seats are in demand. More often than not, it's good to ⓖ **adapt to** the practices of those around you.

① ⓐ, ⓒ   ② ⓐ, ⓔ, ⓖ   ③ ⓐ, ⓕ, ⓖ
④ ⓒ, ⓔ, ⓖ   ⑤ ⓔ, ⓕ, ⓖ

22. 22)밑줄 친 ⓐ~ⓟ 중 어법, 혹은 문맥상 어휘의 사용이 어색한 것끼리 짝지어진 것을 고르시오.
2023_고1_3_41, 42번

Chess masters ⓐ **shown** a chess board in the middle of a game for 5 seconds with 20 to 30 pieces still in play can immediately ⓑ **replenish** the position of the pieces from memory. Beginners, of course, are able to place only a ⓒ **few** . Now take the same pieces and place them on the board randomly and the difference is much ⓓ **reduced** . The expert's advantage is only for ⓔ **familiar** patterns — those previously stored in memory. Faced with ⓕ **unfamiliar** patterns, even when it involves the same familiar ⓖ **domain** , the expert's advantage ⓗ **is disappeared** . The beneficial effects of familiar structure on memory have been ⓘ **observed** for many types of expertise, including music. People with musical training can ⓙ **reproduce** short sequences of musical ⓚ **notation** more accurately than those with no musical training when notes follow ⓛ **usual** sequences, but the advantage is ⓜ **less** reduced when the notes are ordered randomly. Expertise also improves memory for sequences of movements. Experienced ballet dancers are able to repeat ⓝ **shorter** sequences of steps than ⓞ **less** experienced dancers, and they can repeat a sequence of steps making up a routine better than steps ordered randomly. In each case, memory range is ⓟ **increased** by the ability to recognize familiar sequences and patterns.

① ⓔ, ⓜ   ② ⓑ, ⓙ, ⓜ   ③ ⓖ, ⓛ, ⓝ
④ ⓑ, ⓗ, ⓜ, ⓝ   ⑤ ⓕ, ⓖ, ⓗ, ⓘ

23. 23)밑줄 친 ⓐ~ⓘ 중 어법, 혹은 문맥상 어휘의 사용이 어색한 것끼리 짝지어진 것을 고르시오.
2023_고1_3_43, 44. 45번

Once upon a time, there was a king who lived in a beautiful palace. ⓐ **While** the king was away, a monster ⓑ **approached** the gates of the palace. The monster was so ugly and smelly ⓒ **which** the guards froze in shock. He passed the guards and sat on the king's throne. The guards soon came to their senses, went in, and shouted at the monster, demanding ⓓ **what** he get off the throne. With each bad ⓔ **words** the guards used, the monster grew more ugly and smelly. The guards got even angrier — they began to brandish their swords to scare the monster away from the palace. But he just grew bigger and bigger, eventually ⓕ **took** up the whole room. He grew more ugly and smelly than ever. Eventually the king returned. He was wise and kind and saw ⓖ **what** was happening. He knew what to do. He smiled and said to the monster, "Welcome to my palace"! He asked the monster if he wanted a cup of coffee. The monster began to grow smaller as he drank the coffee. The king offered him some take-out pizza and fries. The guards immediately called for pizza. The monster continued to get smaller with the king's kind gestures. He then offered the monster a full body massage. ⓗ **As** the guards helped with the relaxing massage, the monster became tiny. ⓘ **With** another act of kindness to the monster, he just disappeared.

① ⓒ, ⓗ   ② ⓑ, ⓒ, ⓔ   ③ ⓑ, ⓓ, ⓘ   ④ ⓐ, ⓒ, ⓕ, ⓘ   ⑤ ⓒ, ⓓ, ⓔ, ⓕ

2021 고1 3월 모의고사

❶ voca   ❷ text   ❸ [/]   ❹ ____   ❺ quiz 1   ❻ quiz 2   ❼ quiz 3   ❽ quiz 4   ❾ quiz 5

1. 1)밑줄 부분 중 어법, 혹은 문맥상 어휘의 쓰임이 어색한 것을 올바르게 고쳐 쓰시오. (3개) 2023_고1_3_18번

To whom it may concern,

I am a resident of the Blue Sky Apartment. Recently I ① **observed** that the kid zone is in ② **favor** of repairs. I want you to pay attention to the poor condition of the playground equipment in the zone. The swings are ③ **damaged** , the paint is falling off, and some of the bolts on the slide ④ **are** missing. The facilities ⑤ **were** in this terrible condition since we moved here. They are dangerous to the children ⑥ **are playing** there. Would you please have them ⑦ **repaired** ? I would appreciate your immediate attention to solve this matter.

Yours sincerely,

Nina Davis

기호	어색한 표현		올바른 표현
( )	_____	⇨	_____
( )	_____	⇨	_____
( )	_____	⇨	_____

2. 2)밑줄 부분 중 어법, 혹은 문맥상 어휘의 쓰임이 어색한 것을 올바르게 고쳐 쓰시오. (3개) 2023_고1_3_19번

On a two-week trip in the Rocky Mountains, I saw a grizzly bear in its native ① **inhabitant** . At first, I felt joy as I watched the bear ② **walk** across the land. He stopped every once in a while to turn his head about, sniffing deeply. He was following the scent of something, and slowly I began to realize ③ **what** this giant animal was smelling ④ **me** ! I froze. This was no longer a wonderful experience; it was now an issue of ⑤ **survival** . The bear's ⑥ **simulation** was to find meat to eat, and I was clearly on his menu.

기호	어색한 표현		올바른 표현
( )	_____	⇨	_____
( )	_____	⇨	_____
( )	_____	⇨	_____

3. 3)밑줄 부분 중 어법, 혹은 문맥상 어휘의 쓰임이 어색한 것을 올바르게 고쳐 쓰시오. (5개) ^{2023_고1_3_20번}

It is difficult ① **for** any of us to maintain a ② **flexible** level of attention throughout our working day. We all have body rhythms characterised by peaks and valleys of energy and alertness. You will achieve more, and feel confident as a benefit, if you schedule your most ③ **demanded** tasks at times when you are best able to cope ④ **with**. If you haven't thought about energy peaks before, take a few days to observe ⑤ **yourself** . Try to note the times ⑥ **which** you are at your best. We are all ⑦ **similar** . For some, the peak will come first thing in the morning, but for others it may take a while to warm up.

기호	어색한 표현		올바른 표현
( )	_____	⇨	_____
( )	_____	⇨	_____
( )	_____	⇨	_____
( )	_____	⇨	_____
( )	_____	⇨	_____

4. 4)밑줄 부분 중 어법, 혹은 문맥상 어휘의 쓰임이 어색한 것을 올바르게 고쳐 쓰시오. (9개) ^{2023_고1_3_21번}

If we ① **adopt** technology, we need to pay its costs. Thousands of traditional livelihoods have been ② **pushing** aside by ③ **process** , and the lifestyles around those jobs removed. Hundreds of millions of humans today work at jobs they hate, producing things they have no ④ **love**. Sometimes these jobs cause physical pain, disability, or chronic disease. Technology creates many new jobs that are certainly ⑤ **safe** . At the same time, ⑥ **mass** education and media train humans to ⑦ **accept** low-tech physical work, to ⑧ **sick** jobs ⑨ **worked** in the digital world. The ⑩ **integration** of the hands from the head puts a stress on the human mind. Indeed, the ⑪ **rudimentary** nature of the best-paying jobs is a health risk — for body and mind.

기호	어색한 표현		올바른 표현
( )	_____	⇨	_____
( )	_____	⇨	_____
( )	_____	⇨	_____
( )	_____	⇨	_____
( )	_____	⇨	_____
( )	_____	⇨	_____
( )	_____	⇨	_____
( )	_____	⇨	_____
( )	_____	⇨	_____

5. 5)밑줄 부분 중 어법, 혹은 문맥상 어휘의 쓰임이 어색한 것을 올바르게 고쳐 쓰시오. (3개) 2023_고1_3_22번

When students are starting their college life, they may ① **approach** every course, test, or learning task the same way, using ② **that** we like to call "the rubber-stamp approach". Think about it this way: Would you wear a tuxedo to a baseball game? A colorful dress to a funeral? A bathing suit to religious services? Probably not. You know there's appropriate dress for different occasions and settings. Skillful learners know ③ **that** "putting on the same clothes" won't work for every ④ **class** . They are ⑤ **inflexible** learners. They have different strategies and know when to use them. They know ⑥ **that** you study for multiple-choice tests ⑦ **different** than you study for essay tests. And they not only know ⑧ **what** to do, but they also know ⑨ **how** to do it.

기호	어색한 표현		올바른 표현
( )	_____	⇨	_____
( )	_____	⇨	_____
( )	_____	⇨	_____

6. 6)밑줄 부분 중 어법, 혹은 문맥상 어휘의 쓰임이 어색한 것을 올바르게 고쳐 쓰시오. (1개) 2023_고1_3_23번

As the social and economic situation of countries got better, wage levels and working conditions ① **improved** . Gradually people were given more time ② **off** . At the same time, forms of transport improved and it became faster and cheaper to get to places. England's ③ **industrious** ④ **revolution** led to many of these changes. Railways, in the nineteenth century, opened up now famous seaside resorts such as Blackpool and Brighton. With the railways ⑤ **came** many large hotels. In Canada, for example, the new coast-to-coast railway system made ⑥ **possible** the building of such famous hotels as Banff Springs and Chateau Lake Louise in the Rockies. Later, the arrival of air transport opened up more of the world and led to tourism ⑦ **growth** .

기호	어색한 표현		올바른 표현
( )	_____	⇨	_____

7. 7)밑줄 부분 중 어법, 혹은 문맥상 어휘의 쓰임이 어색한 것을 올바르게 고쳐 쓰시오. (2개) 2023_고1_3_24번

Success can lead you off your ① **intended** path and into a ② **comfortable** rut. If you are good at something and are well ③ **rewarded** for doing it, you may want to keep ④ **doing** it even if you stop enjoying it. The danger is that one day you look around and realize you're so deep in this ⑤ **comfortable** rut ⑥ **that** you can no longer see the sun or breathe fresh air; the sides of the rut have become so slippery ⑦ **which** it would take a superhuman effort to climb out; and, effectively, you're ⑧ **stuck** . And it's a situation ⑨ **that** many working people worry they're in now. The poor employment market has left them feeling ⑩ **locked** in ⑪ **that** may be a secure, or even well-paying — but ultimately ⑫ **unsatisfying** — job.

기호	어색한 표현		올바른 표현
( )	_____	⇨	_____
( )	_____	⇨	_____

8. 8)밑줄 부분 중 <u>어법, 혹은 문맥상 어휘</u>의 쓰임이 어색한 것을 올바르게 고쳐 쓰시오. (8개) ^{2023_고1_3_25번}

The above graph shows ① <u>a</u> number of births and deaths in Korea from 2016 to 2021. The number of ② <u>birth</u> continued to decrease throughout the whole period. The gap between the number of births and deaths ③ <u>were</u> the largest in 2016. In 2019, the gap between the number of births and ④ <u>death</u> was the smallest, with the number of births slightly larger than ⑤ <u>those</u> of deaths. The number of deaths increased steadily ⑥ <u>while</u> the whole period, except the period from 2018 to 2019. In 2021, the number of deaths ⑦ <u>were</u> larger than ⑧ <u>those</u> of births.

기호	어색한 표현		올바른 표현
( )	_____	⇨	_____
( )	_____	⇨	_____
( )	_____	⇨	_____
( )	_____	⇨	_____
( )	_____	⇨	_____
( )	_____	⇨	_____
( )	_____	⇨	_____
( )	_____	⇨	_____

9. 9)밑줄 부분 중 <u>어법, 혹은 문맥상 어휘</u>의 쓰임이 어색한 것을 올바르게 고쳐 쓰시오. (2개) ^{2023_고1_3_26번}

Lilian Bland was born in Kent, England in 1878. Unlike most other girls at the time she wore trousers and spent her time ① <u>enjoying</u> adventurous activities like horse riding and hunting. Lilian began her career as a sports and wildlife photographer for British newspapers. In 1910 she became the first woman to design, build, and fly her own airplane. In order to persuade her to ② <u>try</u> a slightly safer activity, Lilian's dad bought her a car. Soon Lilian was a master driver and ended up ③ <u>work</u> as a car dealer. She never went back to flying but lived a long and ④ <u>excited</u> life nonetheless. She married, moved to Canada, and had a kid. Eventually, she moved back to England, and lived there for the rest of her life.

기호	어색한 표현		올바른 표현
( )	_____	⇨	_____
( )	_____	⇨	_____

10. 10)밑줄 부분 중 어법, 혹은 문맥상 어휘의 쓰임이 어색한 것을 올바르게 고쳐 쓰시오. (5개) 2023_고1_3_29번

The most noticeable human characteristic ① **projected** onto animals ② **is** that they can talk in human language. ③ **Verbally** , animal cartoon characters and toys ④ **made** after animals are also most often ⑤ **deformed** in such a way as to ⑥ **resemble** humans. This is achieved by showing them with humanlike facial features and deformed front legs to ⑦ **resemble with** human hands. In more recent animated movies the trend ⑧ **has** been to show the animals in a more "natural" way. ⑨ **However** , they still use their front legs like human hands (for example, lions can pick up and lift small objects with one paw), and they still talk with an appropriate facial expression. A general strategy that ⑩ **used to** ⑪ **making** the animal characters more emotionally ⑫ **appealed** , both to children and adults, is to give them enlarged and deformed ⑬ **childlike** features.

기호	어색한 표현		올바른 표현
( )	_____	⇨	_____
( )	_____	⇨	_____
( )	_____	⇨	_____
( )	_____	⇨	_____
( )	_____	⇨	_____

11. 11)밑줄 부분 중 어법, 혹은 문맥상 어휘의 쓰임이 어색한 것을 올바르게 고쳐 쓰시오. (3개) 2023_고1_3_30번

The major ① **philosophical** shift in the idea of selling came when ② **industrial** societies became more ③ **fluent** , more competitive, and more ④ **geographically** spread out ⑤ **while** the 1940s and 1950s. This forced business ⑥ **to develop** ⑦ **closer** relations with buyers and clients, which in turn made business ⑧ **realize** that it was not enough to produce a ⑨ **quality** product at a reasonable price. In fact, it was equally essential to deliver products that customers actually ⑩ **wanted** . Henry Ford produced his best-selling T-model Ford in one color only (black) in 1908, but in modern societies this was no longer possible. The modernization of society led to a marketing ⑪ **revolution** that destroyed the view ⑫ **which** ⑬ **production** would create its own ⑭ **demand** . Customers, and the desire to meet their diverse and often complex ⑮ **needs** , became the focus of business.

기호	어색한 표현		올바른 표현
( )	_____	⇨	_____
( )	_____	⇨	_____
( )	_____	⇨	_____

12. 12)밑줄 부분 중 어법, 혹은 문맥상 어휘의 쓰임이 어색한 것을 올바르게 고쳐 쓰시오. (9개) 2023_고1_3_31번

People differ in how ① **quickly** they can reset their biological clocks to ② **overwhelm** jet lag, and the speed of ③ **discovery** depends on the direction of travel. Generally, it's easier to fly westward and ④ **shorten** your day than it is to fly eastward and ⑤ **lengthen** it. This east-west difference in jet lag is sizable enough to have an impact on the performance of sports teams. Studies have found that teams ⑥ **flied** westward perform significantly ⑦ **worse** than teams ⑧ **flied** eastward in professional baseball and college football. A more recent study of more than 46,000 Major League Baseball games found additional evidence ⑨ **which** eastward travel is ⑩ **easier** than westward travel.

기호	어색한 표현		올바른 표현
( )	_____	⇨	_____
( )	_____	⇨	_____
( )	_____	⇨	_____
( )	_____	⇨	_____
( )	_____	⇨	_____
( )	_____	⇨	_____
( )	_____	⇨	_____
( )	_____	⇨	_____
( )	_____	⇨	_____

13. 13)밑줄 부분 중 어법, 혹은 문맥상 어휘의 쓰임이 어색한 것을 올바르게 고쳐 쓰시오. (4개) 2023_고1_3_32번

If you want the confidence that comes from achieving ① **what** you set out to do each day, then it's important to understand how long things are going to take. ② **Over-optimism** about ③ **that** can be achieved within a certain time frame is a problem. So work on it. Make a practice of ④ **estimating** the amount of time needed alongside items on your 'things to do' list, and learn by experience ⑤ **when** tasks take a greater or lesser time than expected. Give attention also to fitting the task to the available time. There are some tasks ⑥ **that** you can only set about if you have a ⑦ **minimum** amount of time available. There is no point in trying to ⑧ **give** up for such a task when you only have a short period available. So schedule the time you need for the longer tasks and put the ⑨ **long** tasks into the spare moments in between.

기호	어색한 표현		올바른 표현
( )	_____	⇨	_____
( )	_____	⇨	_____
( )	_____	⇨	_____
( )	_____	⇨	_____

14. 14)밑줄 부분 중 어법, 혹은 문맥상 어휘의 쓰임이 어색한 것을 올바르게 고쳐 쓰시오. (8개) ^{2023_고1_3_33번}

In Lewis Carroll's Through the Looking-Glass, the Red Queen takes Alice on a race through the countryside. They run and they run, but then Alice ① **recovers** ② **what** they're still under the same tree ③ **from which** they started from. The Red Queen explains to Alice: "here, you see, it takes all the running you can do, to keep in the same place". Biologists sometimes use this Red Queen Effect to explain an ④ **evolutionary** ⑤ **principal** . If foxes ⑥ **revolve** to run faster so they can catch more rabbits, then only the ⑦ **slowest** rabbits will live long enough to make a new generation of bunnies that run even faster — in which case, of course, only the fastest foxes will catch enough rabbits to ⑧ **collapse** and ⑨ **stop** their genes. Even though they might run, the two species just stay in place.

기호	어색한 표현		올바른 표현
( )	_____	⇨	_____
( )	_____	⇨	_____
( )	_____	⇨	_____
( )	_____	⇨	_____
( )	_____	⇨	_____
( )	_____	⇨	_____
( )	_____	⇨	_____
( )	_____	⇨	_____

15. 15)밑줄 부분 중 어법, 혹은 문맥상 어휘의 쓰임이 어색한 것을 올바르게 고쳐 쓰시오. (6개) ^{2023_고1_3_34번}

Everything in the world around us was ① **started** in the mind of its creator before it was ② **finished** . The houses we live in, the cars we drive, and our clothing — all of these began with an ③ **idea** . Each idea was then studied, refined and perfected before the first nail was driven or the first piece of cloth was cut. Long ④ **after** the idea was turned into a ⑤ **philosophical** reality, the mind had clearly pictured the finished product. The human being designs his or her own ⑥ **future** through much the same ⑦ **progress** . We begin with ⑧ **an idea** about how the future will be. Over a period of time we refine and perfect the ⑨ **vision** . Before long, our every thought, decision and activity are all working in harmony to bring into ⑩ **existence** what we have mentally ⑪ **excluded** about the future.

기호	어색한 표현		올바른 표현
( )	_____	⇨	_____
( )	_____	⇨	_____
( )	_____	⇨	_____
( )	_____	⇨	_____
( )	_____	⇨	_____
( )	_____	⇨	_____

16. 16)밑줄 부분 중 **어법, 혹은 문맥상 어휘의 쓰임이** 어색한 것을 올바르게 고쳐 쓰시오. **(1개)** 2023_고1_3_35번

Whose story it is ① **affects** what the story is. ② **Change** the main character, and the focus of the story must also change. ③ **If we look** at the events through another character's eyes, we will interpret them differently. We'll place our sympathies with ④ **someone new**. When the conflict ⑤ **raises** that is the heart of the story, we will be praying for a different ⑥ **outcome** . Consider, for example, how the tale of Cinderella would shift if ⑦ **told** from the viewpoint of an evil stepsister. Gone with the Wind is Scarlett O'Hara's story, but what if we were ⑧ **shown** the same events from the viewpoint of Rhett Butler or Melanie Wilkes?

기호   어색한 표현   올바른 표현

(   ) _____ ⇨ _____

17. 17)밑줄 부분 중 **어법, 혹은 문맥상 어휘의 쓰임이** 어색한 것을 올바르게 고쳐 쓰시오. **(3개)** 2023_고1_3_36번

In the Old Stone Age, small bands of 20 to 60 people ① **wandered** from place to place in search of food. Once people began farming, they could settle down near their farms. ② **As a result** , towns and villages grew ③ **larger** . Living in ④ **communities** allowed people ⑤ **organize** themselves more efficiently. They could divide up the work of producing food and other things they needed. ⑥ **While** some workers grew crops, others built new houses and made tools. Village dwellers also learned to work together to ⑦ **doing** a task faster. ⑧ **On the other hand**, toolmakers could share the work of making stone axes and knives. By working together, they could make more tools in the same amount of time.

기호   어색한 표현   올바른 표현

(   ) _____ ⇨ _____

(   ) _____ ⇨ _____

(   ) _____ ⇨ _____

18. 18)**밑줄 부분 중 어법, 혹은 문맥상 어휘의 쓰임이 어색한 것을 올바르게 고쳐 쓰시오. (15개)** 2023_고1_3_37번

Natural ① **progresses** form minerals in many ways. For example, hot melted rock material, ② **which called** magma, cools when it ③ **arrives** the Earth's surface, or even if it's trapped below the surface. As magma cools, its atoms ④ **gain** heat energy, move ⑤ **farther** together, and begin to combine into ⑥ **entities** . ⑦ **While** this process, atoms of the different compounds ⑧ **arrange** themselves into ⑨ **order** , repeating patterns. The type and amount of elements ⑩ **absent** in a magma partly determine ⑪ **that** minerals will form. Also, the size of the crystals that ⑫ **deform** depends partly on how ⑬ **rapid** the magma cools. When magma cools slowly, the crystals that form are generally large enough to see with the unaided eye. This is ⑭ **why** the atoms have enough time to move together and form into larger crystals. When magma cools rapidly, the crystals that form will be ⑮ **large** . In such cases, you ⑯ **can** easily see individual mineral crystals.

기호	어색한 표현		올바른 표현
( )	_____	⇨	_____
( )	_____	⇨	_____
( )	_____	⇨	_____
( )	_____	⇨	_____
( )	_____	⇨	_____
( )	_____	⇨	_____
( )	_____	⇨	_____
( )	_____	⇨	_____
( )	_____	⇨	_____
( )	_____	⇨	_____
( )	_____	⇨	_____
( )	_____	⇨	_____
( )	_____	⇨	_____
( )	_____	⇨	_____
( )	_____	⇨	_____

19. 19)**밑줄 부분 중 어법, 혹은 문맥상 어휘의 쓰임이 어색한 것을 올바르게 고쳐 쓰시오. (2개)** 2023_고1_3_38번

All carbohydrates are basically sugars. Complex carbohydrates are the good carbohydrates for your body. These complex sugar compounds are very ① **difficult** to break down and can ② **trap** other nutrients like vitamins and minerals in their chains. As they slowly break down, the other nutrients are also ③ **released** into your body, and can provide you ④ **for** fuel for ⑤ **a** number of hours. Bad carbohydrates, on the other hand, are simple sugars. ⑥ **Because** their structure is not complex, they are easy to break down and hold ⑦ **little** nutrients for your body other than the sugars ⑧ **from which** they are made. Your body breaks down these carbohydrates rather quickly and ⑨ **what** it cannot use is converted to fat and stored in the body.

기호	어색한 표현		올바른 표현
( )	_____	⇨	_____
( )	_____	⇨	_____

20. **20)밑줄 부분 중 어법, 혹은 문맥상 어휘의 쓰임이 어색한 것을 올바르게 고쳐 쓰시오. (8개)** 2023_고1_3_39번

People commonly make the ① **organized** ② **consumption** ③ **which** because a person has one type of characteristic, then they automatically have other characteristics which ④ **goes** with it. In one study, university students were given ⑤ **prescription** of a guest lecturer before he spoke to the group. Half the students received a ⑥ **inscription** ⑦ **containing** the word 'warm', the other half were told the speaker was 'cold'. The guest lecturer then led a discussion, ⑧ **after which** the students ⑨ **asked** to give their impressions of him. As expected, there were large ⑩ **differences** between the impressions ⑪ **formed** by the students, depending upon their original information of the lecturer. It was also found that those students who expected the lecturer to be warm tended to ⑫ **transact** with him more. This shows that different ⑬ **expectations** not only ⑭ **affect** the impressions we form but also our behaviour and the relationship which is formed.

기호	어색한 표현		올바른 표현
( )	_____	⇨	_____
( )	_____	⇨	_____
( )	_____	⇨	_____
( )	_____	⇨	_____
( )	_____	⇨	_____
( )	_____	⇨	_____
( )	_____	⇨	_____
( )	_____	⇨	_____

21. **21)밑줄 부분 중 어법, 혹은 문맥상 어휘의 쓰임이 어색한 것을 올바르게 고쳐 쓰시오. (4개)** 2023_고1_3_40번

To help decide what's risky and what's safe, who's trustworthy and who's not, we look for ① **social** evidence. From an ② **evolutionary** view, following the group is almost always ③ **negative** for our prospects of survival. "If everyone's doing it, it must be a ④ **sensitive** thing to do", explains famous psychologist and best selling writer of Influence, Robert Cialdini. While we can frequently see this today in product reviews, even ⑤ **bolder** cues within the environment can signal trustworthiness. Consider this: when you visit a local restaurant, are they busy? Is there a line outside or is it easy to find a seat? It is a hassle to wait, but a line can be a ⑥ **meaningless** cue that the food's tasty, and these seats are in demand. More often than not, it's good to ⑦ **adopt** the practices of those around you.

기호	어색한 표현		올바른 표현
( )	_____	⇨	_____
( )	_____	⇨	_____
( )	_____	⇨	_____
( )	_____	⇨	_____

22. 22)밑줄 부분 중 어법, 혹은 문맥상 어휘의 쓰임이 어색한 것을 올바르게 고쳐 쓰시오. (14개) 2023_고1_3_41, 42번

Chess masters ① **was shown** a chess board in the middle of a game for 5 seconds with 20 to 30 pieces still in play can immediately ② **replenish** the position of the pieces from memory. Beginners, of course, are able to place only a ③ **little** . Now take the same pieces and place them on the board randomly and the difference is much ④ **increased** . The expert's advantage is only for ⑤ **novel** patterns — those previously stored in memory. Faced with ⑥ **familiar** patterns, even when it involves the same familiar ⑦ **pattern** , the expert's advantage ⑧ **is disappeared** . The beneficial effects of familiar structure on memory have been ⑨ **observing** for many types of expertise, including music. People with musical training can ⑩ **produce** short sequences of musical ⑪ **rotation** more accurately than those with no musical training when notes follow ⑫ **usual** sequences, but the advantage is ⑬ **much** reduced when the notes are ordered randomly. Expertise also improves memory for sequences of movements. Experienced ballet dancers are able to repeat ⑭ **shorter** sequences of steps than ⑮ **more** experienced dancers, and they can repeat a sequence of steps making up a routine better than steps ordered randomly. In each case, memory range is ⑯ **reduced** by the ability to recognize familiar sequences and patterns.

기호	어색한 표현		올바른 표현
( )	_____	⇨	_____
( )	_____	⇨	_____
( )	_____	⇨	_____
( )	_____	⇨	_____
( )	_____	⇨	_____
( )	_____	⇨	_____
( )	_____	⇨	_____
( )	_____	⇨	_____
( )	_____	⇨	_____
( )	_____	⇨	_____
( )	_____	⇨	_____
( )	_____	⇨	_____
( )	_____	⇨	_____
( )	_____	⇨	_____

23. ²³⁾밑줄 부분 중 <u>어법, 혹은 문맥상 어휘의 쓰임이 어색한 것을 올바르게 고쳐 쓰시오. (7개)</u> ^{2023_고1_3_43, 44.}
^{45번}

Once upon a time, there was a king who lived in a beautiful palace. ① **While** the king was away, a monster ② **approached to** the gates of the palace. The monster was so ugly and smelly ③ **which** the guards froze in shock. He passed the guards and sat on the king's throne. The guards soon came to their senses, went in, and shouted at the monster, demanding ④ **what** he get off the throne. With each bad ⑤ **words** the guards used, the monster grew more ugly and smelly. The guards got even angrier — they began to brandish their swords to scare the monster away from the palace. But he just grew bigger and bigger, eventually ⑥ **took** up the whole room. He grew more ugly and smelly than ever. Eventually the king returned. He was wise and kind and saw ⑦ **that** was happening. He knew what to do. He smiled and said to the monster, "Welcome to my palace"! He asked the monster if he wanted a cup of coffee. The monster began to grow smaller as he drank the coffee. The king offered him some take-out pizza and fries. The guards immediately called for pizza. The monster continued to get smaller with the king's kind gestures. He then offered the monster a full body massage. ⑧ **With** the guards helped with the relaxing massage, the monster became tiny. ⑨ **With** another act of kindness to the monster, he just disappeared.

기호	어색한 표현		올바른 표현
( )	_____	⇨	_____
( )	_____	⇨	_____
( )	_____	⇨	_____
( )	_____	⇨	_____
( )	_____	⇨	_____
( )	_____	⇨	_____
( )	_____	⇨	_____

2021 고1 3월 모의고사

❶ voca   ❷ text   ❸ [/]   ❹ ____   ❺ quiz 1   ❻ quiz 2   ❼ quiz 3   ❽ quiz 4   ❾ quiz 5

☑ **다음 글을 읽고 물음에 답하시오.** (2023_고1_3_18번)

To whom it may concern, I am a resident of the Blue Sky Apartment. Recently I observed that the kid zone is ^{필요로 하는} _____ repairs. I want you to pay attention to the poor condition of the playground ^{장비,설비} _____ in the zone. The swings are damaged, the paint is falling off, and some of the bolts on the slide are missing. The ^{시설} _____ have been in this terrible condition since we moved here. They are dangerous to the children playing there. Would you please have them repaired? I would appreciate your ^{즉각적인} _____ attention to solve this matter. Yours sincerely, Nina Davis

1. ¹⁾힌트를 참고하여 각 빈칸에 알맞은 단어를 쓰시오.

☑ **다음 글을 읽고 물음에 답하시오.** (2023_고1_3_19번)

On a two-week trip in the Rocky Mountains, I saw a grizzly bear in its ^{천연의} _____ ^{서식지} _____. At first, I felt joy as I watched the bear walk across the land. (가) <u>그는 깊은 숨을 들이마시며 시선을 돌리려 때때로 멈추었다.</u> He was following the ^{향기} _____ of something, and slowly I began to realize that this giant animal was smelling me! I froze. This was no longer a wonderful ^{경험} _____; it was now an issue of ^{생존} _____. The bear's ^{동기} _____ was to find meat to eat, and I was clearly on his menu.

2. ²⁾힌트를 참고하여 각 빈칸에 알맞은 단어를 쓰시오.

3. ³⁾위 글에 주어진 (가)의 한글과 같은 의미를 가지도록, 각각의 주어진 단어들을 알맞게 배열하시오.

(가) turn / while / head / a / his / stopped / deeply / every / sniffing / He / in / to / about, / once

☑ **다음 글을 읽고 물음에 답하시오.** (2023_고1_3_20번)

It is difficult for any of us to maintain a constant level of attention throughout our working day. We all have body rhythms ^{특성화하다} _____ by ^{정점} _____ and valleys of energy and ^{기민함} _____. You will ^{성취하다} _____ more, and feel ^{자신감 넘치는} _____ as a benefit, (가) <u>몸의 컨디션이 가장 좋을 때 가장 까다로운 일을 하기로 한다면</u>. ⓐ <u>If you haven't think about energy peaks before, take a few days observing yourself.</u> Try to note the times when you are at your best. We are all different. For some, the peak will come first thing in the morning, but for others it may take a while to warm up.

4. 4)힌트를 참고하여 각 <u>빈칸에 알맞은</u> 단어를 쓰시오.

5. 5)밑줄 친 ⓐ에서, 어법 혹은 문맥상 어색한 부분을 찾아 올바르게 고쳐 쓰시오.

   ⓐ   잘못된 표현   바른 표현

   (   ) ⇨ (   )

   (   ) ⇨ (   )

6. 6)위 글에 주어진 (가)의 한글과 같은 의미를 가지도록, 각각의 주어진 단어들을 알맞게 배열하시오.

(가) with / you / your / cope / tasks / best / you / most / at / able / demanding / schedule / times / when / are / to / if / them

☑ 다음 글을 읽고 물음에 답하시오. (2023_고1_3_21번)

If we ^{받아들이다} _____ technology, we need to pay its costs. Thousands of traditional ^{생계수단} _____ ⓐ have pushed aside by progress, and the lifestyles around those jobs been removed. ⓑ Hundreds of millions of humans today work at jobs they hate, produce things they have no love. Sometimes these jobs cause physical pain, ^{장애} _____, or ^{만성의} _____ ^{질환} _____. Technology creates many new jobs that are certainly dangerous. (가) 동시에 대중 교육과 미디어는 인간으로 하여금 육체 노동 대신 디지털 세상에서 일하게끔 만들고 있다. The ^{이혼} _____ of the hands from the head puts a stress on the human mind. ^{물론} _____, the ^{앉아있는 경향의} _____ nature of the best-paying jobs is a health ^{위험요소} _____ - for body and mind.

7. 7)힌트를 참고하여 각 빈칸에 알맞은 단어를 쓰시오.

8. 8)밑줄 친 ⓐ~ⓑ에서, 어법 혹은 문맥상 어색한 부분을 찾아 올바르게 고쳐 쓰시오.

   ⓐ   잘못된 표현   바른 표현

   (   ) ⇨ (   )

   (   ) ⇨ (   )

   ⓑ   잘못된 표현   바른 표현

   (   ) ⇨ (   )

   (   ) ⇨ (   )

9. 9)위 글에 주어진 (가)의 한글과 같은 의미를 가지도록, 각각의 주어진 단어들을 알맞게 배열하시오.

(가) jobs / mass / train / the / time, / low-tech / avoid / digital / to / working / world / to / work, / physical / the / seek / media / in / humans / At / and / education / same

☑ 다음 글을 읽고 물음에 답하시오. (2023_고1_3_22번)

When students are starting their college life, they may ^{접근하다} _____ every course, test, or learning task the same way, using what we like to call the rubber-stamp approach. Think about it this way: Would you wear a ^{연미복} _____ to a baseball game? A colorful dress to a ^{장례식} _____? A ^{수영복} _____ to ^{종교의식, 예배} _____? Probably not. You know there's appropriate dress for different occasions and settings. ^{숙련된} _____ learners know that putting on the same clothes won't work for every class. They are ^{유연한} _____ learners. They have different ^{전략} _____ and know when to use them. They know that you study for ^{다지선다 시험} _____ differently than you study for ^{논술형시험} _____. (가) 그리고 그들은 무엇을 해야 할 지 알고 있을 뿐만 아니라 어떻게 해야 하는지도 알고 있다.

10. ¹⁰⁾힌트를 참고하여 각 빈칸에 알맞은 단어를 쓰시오.

11. ¹¹⁾위 글에 주어진 (가)의 한글과 같은 의미를 가지도록, 각각의 주어진 단어들을 알맞게 배열하시오.

(가) to / only / to / what / they / know / not / how / they / but / do / know / do, / also / And / it

☑ **다음 글을 읽고 물음에 답하시오.** (2023_고1_3_23번)

(가) 국가의 사회적, 경제적 상황이 좋아짐에 따라 임금 수준과 근로 조건도 개선되었다. ^{서서히} _____ people were given more ^{휴식 시간} _____. At the same time, forms of transport improved and it became faster and cheaper to get to places. England's ^{산업혁명} _____ led to many of these changes. ^{철도} _____, in the nineteenth ^{세기} _____, opened up now famous seaside resorts such as Blackpool and Brighton. With the railways came many large hotels. In Canada, for example, the new coast-to-coast ^{철도} _____ system made possible the building of such famous hotels as Banff Springs and Chateau Lake Louise in the Rockies. (나) 이후 항공 교통 시대의 도래는 더 많은 세계를 열었고 관광을 성장하게 하였다.

12. ¹²⁾힌트를 참고하여 각 <u>빈칸에 알맞은</u> 단어를 쓰시오.

13. ¹³⁾위 글에 주어진 (가) ~ (나)의 한글과 같은 의미를 가지도록, 각각의 주어진 단어들을 알맞게 배열하시오.

(가) and / improved / levels / conditions / wage / got / the / social / As / of / countries / situation / better, / working / and / economic

(나) arrival / of / up / more / tourism / led / transport / of / growth / world / to / opened / air / the / and / the / Later,

☑ **다음 글을 읽고 물음에 답하시오.** (2023_고1_3_24번)

Success can lead you off your ^{의도된} _____ ^{경로} _____ and into a comfortable ^{틀에 박힌 생활} _____. ⓐ If you are good at something and be well rewarded to be done it, you may want to keep doing it even if you stop enjoying it. The danger is that one day you look around and realize you're so deep in this comfortable ^{틀에 박힌 생활} _____ that you can no longer see the sun or breathe fresh air; the sides of the ^{틀에} ^{박힌 생활} _____ have become so ^{미끄러운} _____ that it would take a ^{초인적인} _____ ^{노력,수고} _____ to ^{빠져나} ^{오다} _____; and, ^{효과적으로} _____, you're ^{갇힌,끼인} _____. (가) 그리고 많은 노동자들이 현재 처한 상황이다. ⓑ The poor employment market has left them felt locked in what may be a secure, or even well-paying but ultimate unsatisfying job.

14. ¹⁴⁾힌트를 참고하여 각 <u>빈칸에 알맞은</u> 단어를 쓰시오.

15. ¹⁵⁾밑줄 친 ⓐ~ⓑ에서, 어법 혹은 문맥상 어색한 부분을 찾아 올바르게 고쳐 쓰시오.

   ⓐ   잘못된 표현   바른 표현

   (   ) ⇨ (   )

   (   ) ⇨ (   )

   ⓑ   잘못된 표현   바른 표현

   (   ) ⇨ (   )

   (   ) ⇨ (   )

16. ¹⁶⁾위 글에 주어진 (가)의 한글과 같은 의미를 가지도록, 각각의 주어진 단어들을 알맞게 배열하시오.

(가) situation / And / now / many / that / they're / it's / working / worry / a / in / people

☑ **다음 글을 읽고 물음에 답하시오.** (2023_고1_3_25번)

The above graph shows the number of births and deaths in Korea from 2016 to 2021. The number of births continued to ^{감소하다} _____ ^{~동안} _____ the whole period. The gap between the number of births and deaths was the largest in 2016. In 2019, the gap between the number of births and deaths was the smallest, with the number of births ^{근소하게} _____ larger than that of deaths. The number of deaths ^{증가하다} _____ ^{지속적으로} _____ during the whole period, ^{~를 제외하고} _____ the period from 2018 to 2019. In 2021, the number of deaths was larger than that of births for the first time.

17. ¹⁷⁾힌트를 참고하여 각 <u>빈칸에 알맞은</u> 단어를 쓰시오.

☑ **다음 글을 읽고 물음에 답하시오.** (2023_고1_3_26번)

Lilian Bland was born in Kent, England in 1878. ^{~와 달리} _____ most other girls at the time she wore ^{바지} _____ and spent her time enjoying ^{모험적인} _____ ^{활동} _____ like horse riding and hunting. Lilian began her ^{직업, 경력} _____ as a sports and ^{야생} _____ photographer for British newspapers. In 1910 she became the first woman to design, build, and fly her own airplane. (가) <u>조금이라도 안전한 활동을 하도록 설득하기 위해 Lilian의 아버지는 그녀에게 차를 사 주었다.</u> Soon Lilian was a master driver and ended up working as a ^{자동차 판매원} _____. She never went back to flying but lived a long and exciting life ^{그럼에도 불구하고} _____. She married, moved to Canada, and had a kid. ^{마침내} _____, she moved back to England, and lived there for the rest of her life.

18. ¹⁸⁾힌트를 참고하여 각 <u>빈칸에 알맞은</u> 단어를 쓰시오.

19. ¹⁹⁾위 글에 주어진 (가)의 한글과 같은 의미를 가지도록, 각각의 주어진 단어들을 알맞게 배열하시오.

(가) try / her / persuade / Lilian's / to / In / bought / activity, / a / her / order / car / to / slightly / a / dad / safer

☑ **다음 글을 읽고 물음에 답하시오.** (2023_고1_3_29번)

The most ^{주목할 만한} _____ human characteristic projected onto animals is that they can talk in human language. ⓐ Physically, animal cartoon characters and toys made after animals are also most often to deform in such a way as resembled humans. This is achieved by showing them with humanlike facial features and deformed front legs to resemble human hands. In more recent animated movies the trend has been to show the animals in a more natural way. However, they still use their front legs like human hands (for example, lions can pick up and lift small objects with one paw), and they still talk with an ^{적합한} _____ facial ^{표현} _____. (가) 동물 캐릭터를 어른과 아이 모두에게 정서적으로 통하도록 만드는 일반적인 전략은 과장하고 어린 아이처럼 변형하는 것이다.

20. ²⁰⁾힌트를 참고하여 각 빈칸에 알맞은 단어를 쓰시오.

21. ²¹⁾밑줄 친 ⓐ에서, 어법 혹은 문맥상 어색한 부분을 찾아 올바르게 고쳐 쓰시오.

ⓐ　　　잘못된 표현　　　　　　바른 표현

(　　　　　) ⇨ (　　　　　　)

(　　　　　) ⇨ (　　　　　　)

22. ²²⁾위 글에 주어진 (가)의 한글과 같은 의미를 가지도록, 각각의 주어진 단어들을 알맞게 배열하시오.

(가) to / adults, / to / animal / more / give / deformed / and / emotionally / both / enlarged / used / that / characters / the / is / childlike / and / A / features / strategy / to / them / is / appealing, / make / general / children

☑ **다음 글을 읽고 물음에 답하시오.** (2023_고1_3_30번)

The major ^{철학적} _____ ^{변화} _____ in the idea of selling came when industrial societies became more ^{풍부한} _____, more ^{경쟁적인} _____, and more ^{지리적으로} _____ ^{확산하다} _____ during the 1940s and 1950s. (가) <u>이것은 기업으로 하여금 구매자 및 고객과 긴밀한 관계를 발전시키도록 했고, 이는 기업이 합리적인 가격에 양질의 제품을 생산하는 것만으로는 충분하지 않다는 것을 깨닫게 했다.</u> In fact, it was ^{마찬가지로} _____ ^{필수적인, 중요한} _____ to deliver products that customers actually wanted. Henry Ford produced his best-selling T-model Ford in one color only (black) in 1908, but in modern societies this was no longer possible. (나) <u>사회의 현대화는 생산이 수요를 만든다는 관점을 파괴하는 마케팅 혁명으로 이어졌다</u>. Customers, and the desire to meet their ^{다양한} _____ and often ^{복잡한} _____ needs, became the focus of business.

23. 23)힌트를 참고하여 각 빈칸에 알맞은 단어를 쓰시오.

24. 24)위 글에 주어진 (가) ~ (나)의 한글과 같은 의미를 가지도록, 각각의 주어진 단어들을 알맞게 배열하시오.

(가) not / buyers / in / made / a / to / which / with / a / turn / relations / it / develop / closer / product / business / This / price / clients, / forced / to / at / was / quality / enough / produce / that / business / reasonable / and / realize

(나) the / demand / marketing / would / to / view / revolution / its / led / a / The / modernization / own / that / of / create / destroyed / society / production / that

☑ **다음 글을 읽고 물음에 답하시오.** (2023_고1_3_31번)

ⓐ <u>People differ from how quick they can reset their biological clocks to overcoming jet lag, and the</u> <u>speed of recovery depends of the direction of travel.</u> ^{일반적으로} _____, it's easier to fly westward and ^늘 ^{이다} _____ your day than it is to fly eastward and ^{줄이다} _____ it. (가) <u>동서간 시차의 차이는 스포츠 팀</u> <u>의 경기력에 영향을 주기에 충분히 큰 것이다.</u> ^{연구} _____ have found that teams flying westward perform ^{상당히} _____ better than teams flying eastward in professional baseball and college football. (나) <u>46,000개가 넘는 메이저 리그 야구 경기에 대한 최근의 연구에서 동쪽으로의 여행이 서쪽으로의 여행보다 더</u> <u>힘들다는 추가적인 단서를 발견했다.</u>

25. ²⁵⁾힌트를 참고하여 각 <u>빈칸에 알맞은</u> 단어를 쓰시오.

26. ²⁶⁾밑줄 친 ⓐ에서, 어법 혹은 문맥상 어색한 부분을 찾아 올바르게 고쳐 쓰시오.

ⓐ	잘못된 표현		바른 표현
(	)	⇨ (	)
(	)	⇨ (	)
(	)	⇨ (	)
(	)	⇨ (	)

27. ²⁷⁾위 글에 주어진 (가) ~ (나)의 한글과 같은 의미를 가지도록, 각각의 주어진 단어들을 알맞게 배열하시오.

(가) sports / of / difference / an / teams / impact / on / east-west / in / jet / sizable / lag / to / the / is / performance / enough / This / have

(나) of / westward / games / Major / found / recent / study / 46,000 / travel / League / is / tougher / Baseball / more / evidence / travel / than / that / more / additional / A / than / eastward

☑ 다음 글을 읽고 물음에 답하시오. (2023_고1_3_32번)

(가) 매일 계획한 일을 완수하는 자신감을 얻고 싶다면, 일이 얼마나 소요되는지 이해하는 것이 중요하다. 과도한

낙관주의 _____ about what can be achieved within a certain 기간 _____ is a problem. So work on it. Make a practice of estimating the amount of time needed alongside items on your 'things to do' list, and learn by experience when tasks take a greater or lesser time than expected. ⓐ Give attention also to be fit the task to the available time. There are some tasks that you can only set about if you have a 중요한 _____ amount of time available. ⓑ There is no point in trial to gear up for a such task when you only have a short period available. So schedule the time you need for the longer tasks and put the short tasks into the spare moments between.

28. 28)힌트를 참고하여 각 빈칸에 알맞은 단어를 쓰시오.

29. 29)밑줄 친 ⓐ~ⓑ에서, 어법 혹은 문맥상 어색한 부분을 찾아 올바르게 고쳐 쓰시오.

ⓐ   잘못된 표현   바른 표현

(   ) ⇨ (   )

ⓑ   잘못된 표현   바른 표현

(   ) ⇨ (   )

(   ) ⇨ (   )

(   ) ⇨ (   )

30. 30)위 글에 주어진 (가)의 한글과 같은 의미를 가지도록, 각각의 주어진 단어들을 알맞게 배열하시오.

(가) take / to / long / want / what / achieving / confidence / day, / going / it's / you / you / are / important / the / to / do / If / out / then / each / how / that / set / to / understand / from / comes / things

☑ **다음 글을 읽고 물음에 답하시오.** (2023_고1_3_33번)

In Lewis Carroll's Through the Looking-Glass, the Red Queen takes Alice on a race through the countryside. They run and they run, but then Alice ^{발견하다, 깨닫다} _____ that they're still under the same tree that they started from. The Red Queen explains to Alice: here, you see, it takes all the running you can do, to keep in the same place. ^{생물학자} _____ sometimes use this Red Queen Effect to explain an ^{진화} _____ ^{원칙} _____. If foxes ^{진화하다} _____ to run faster so they can catch more rabbits, then only the fastest rabbits will live long enough to make a new generation of bunnies that run even faster in which case, of course, only the fastest foxes will catch enough rabbits to ^{번성하다, 번창하다} _____ and pass on their ^{유전자} _____. Even though they might run, the two species just stay in place.

31. 31)힌트를 참고하여 각 빈칸에 알맞은 단어를 쓰시오.

32. 32)힌트를 참고하여 각 빈칸에 알맞은 단어를 쓰시오.

33. 33)위 글에 주어진 (가)의 한글과 같은 의미를 가지도록, 각각의 주어진 단어들을 알맞게 배열하시오.

(가) pictured / a / finished / the / physical / the / before / was / idea / reality, / turned / product / into / clearly / the / mind / had / Long

☑ **다음 글을 읽고 물음에 답하시오.** (2023_고1_3_34번)

Everything in the world around us was finished in the mind of its creator before it was started. The houses we live in, the cars we drive, and our clothing? all of these began with an idea. Each idea was then studied, refined and perfected before the first nail was driven or the first piece of cloth was cut. (가) 그 아이디어가 물리적 형태를 띠기 이미 오래 전, 완성된 형태가 마음 속에 선명하게 그려졌다. The human being designs his or her own future through much the same ^{과정} _____. We begin with an idea about how the future will be. Over a period of time we refine and perfect the vision. ⓐ <u>Before long, our every thought, decision and activity are all working on harmony to bring existence what we have mentally conclude about the future.</u>

1. ³⁴⁾힌트를 참고하여 각 빈칸에 알맞은 단어를 쓰시오.

2. ³⁵⁾밑줄 친 ⓐ에서, 어법 혹은 문맥상 어색한 부분을 찾아 올바르게 고쳐 쓰시오.

ⓐ 잘못된 표현	바른 표현
( ) ⇨ (	)
( ) ⇨ (	)
( ) ⇨ (	)

3. ³⁶⁾위 글에 주어진 (가)의 한글과 같은 의미를 가지도록, 각각의 주어진 단어들을 알맞게 배열하시오.

(가) the / a / Long / turned / into / pictured / physical / product / mind / the / finished / before / the / idea / reality, / had / was / clearly

☑ **다음 글을 읽고 물음에 답하시오.** (2023_고1_3_35번)

Whose story it is ^{영향을 주다} _____ what the story is. Change the main character, and the focus of the story must also change. (가) <u>만일 우리가 사건을 다른 인물의 시각으로 바라보면, 그들을 달리 해석할 것이다</u>. We'll place our ^{공감} _____ with someone new. When the ^{갈등} _____ ^{일어나다} _____ that is the heart of the story, we will be praying for a different ^{결과} _____. Consider, for example, how the tale of Cinderella would shift if told from the ^{시각} _____ of an evil stepsister. Gone with the Wind is Scarlett O'Hara's story, but what if we were shown the same events from the viewpoint of Rhett Butler or Melanie Wilkes?

34. ³⁷⁾힌트를 참고하여 각 <u>빈칸에 알맞은</u> 단어를 쓰시오.

35. ³⁸⁾위 글에 주어진 (가)의 한글과 같은 의미를 가지도록, 각각의 주어진 단어들을 알맞게 배열하시오.

(가) will / interpret / them / through / the / we / If / character's / another / events / look / we / eyes, / differently / at

☑ **다음 글을 읽고 물음에 답하시오.** (2023_고1_3_36번)

In the Old Stone Age, small bands of 20 to 60 people ^{헤매다} _____ from place to place ^{~를 찾아서} _____ food. Once people began farming, they could ^{정착하다} _____ near their farms. ^{그 결과} _____, towns and villages grew larger. ⓐ <u>Living in communities allowed people organizing themselves more efficient.</u> They could divide up the work of producing food and other things they needed. While some workers grew ^{작물} _____, others built new houses and made tools. Village ^{거주인} _____ also learned to work together to do a task faster. For example, toolmakers could share the work of making stone axes and knives. By working together, they could make more tools in the same amount of time.

36. ³⁹⁾힌트를 참고하여 각 <u>빈칸에 알맞은</u> 단어를 쓰시오.

37. ⁴⁰⁾밑줄 친 ⓐ에서, 어법 혹은 문맥상 어색한 부분을 찾아 올바르게 고쳐 쓰시오.

    ⓐ   잘못된 표현   바른 표현

    (   ) ⇨ (   )

    (   ) ⇨ (   )

38. ⁴¹⁾힌트를 참고하여 각 <u>빈칸에 알맞은</u> 단어를 쓰시오.

☑ 다음 글을 읽고 물음에 답하시오. (2023_고1_3_37번)

Natural processes ^{형성하다, 만들다} _____ ^{광물} _____ in many ways. For example, hot melted rock material, called magma, cools when it reaches the Earth's surface, or even if it's ^{갇힌} _____ below the surface. As magma cools, its ^{원자} _____ lose heat energy, move closer together, and begin to ^{결합하다} _____ into ^{화합물} _____. (가) 이 과정 동안 서로 다른 화합물의 원자들은 규칙적이고 반복적인 패턴으로 배열됩니다. The type and amount of ^{성분} _____ present in a magma partly ^{정의하다, 결정하다} _____ which minerals will form. Also, the size of the ^{결정} _____ that form depends partly on how ^{빠르게} _____ the magma cools. (나) 마그마가 천천히 냉각되면 결정은 일반적으로 육안으로 관찰할 수 있을 만큼 크게 형성된다. This is because the atoms have enough time to move together and form into larger crystals. When magma cools rapidly, the crystals that form will be small. In such cases, you can't easily see ^{개별적인} _____ mineral crystals.

1. 42)힌트를 참고하여 각 빈칸에 알맞은 단어를 쓰시오.

2. 43)위 글에 주어진 (가) ~ (나)의 한글과 같은 의미를 가지도록, 각각의 주어진 단어들을 알맞게 배열하시오.

(가) the / orderly, / patterns / atoms / compounds / different / of / this / arrange / repeating / themselves / During / process, / into

(나) see / crystals / magma / enough / cools / the / that / generally / with / unaided / eye. / slowly, / are / form / When / to / the / large

☑ **다음 글을 읽고 물음에 답하시오.** (2023_고1_3_38번)

All 탄수화물 _____ are basically sugars. 복합 탄수화물 _____ are the good carbohydrates for your body. These complex sugar compounds are very difficult to 쪼개지다, 분해되다 _____ and can trap other 영양소 _____ like vitamins and minerals in their chains. As they slowly break down, the other nutrients are also 방출하다 _____ into your body, and can provide you with 연료 ____ for a number of hours. Bad carbohydrates, on the other hand, are simple sugars. (가) 구조가 복잡하기 않은 까닭에 그것들은 분해되기 쉽고 구성된 당류 외에 당신의 몸을 위한 영양소는 적게 가지고 있다. Your body breaks down these carbohydrates rather quickly and what it cannot use is converted to fat and 저장된 _____ in the body.

39. 44)힌트를 참고하여 각 빈칸에 알맞은 단어를 쓰시오.

40. 45)위 글에 주어진 (가)의 한글과 같은 의미를 가지도록, 각각의 주어진 단어들을 알맞게 배열하시오.

(가) are / to / which / break / and / the / nutrients / from / body / easy / down / they / hold / is / complex, / their / than / other / sugars / are / for / Because / structure / they / made. / not / few / your

☑ 다음 글을 읽고 물음에 답하시오. (2023_고1_3_39번)

People commonly make the ^{잘못된} _____ ^{추정} _____ that because a person has one type of characteristic, then they ^{자동적으로} _____ have other characteristics which go with it. (가) <u>한 연구에서, 대학생들은 강의 전 초청된 강의자에 대한 정보를 주었다.</u> Half the students received a description ^{포함하는} _____ the word 'warm', the other half were told the speaker was 'cold'. The guest lecturer then led a ^{토론} _____, after which the students were asked to give their ^{인상} _____ of him. As expected, there were large differences between the impressions formed by the students, depending upon their original information of the lecturer.] It was also found that those students who expected the lecturer to be warm tended to ^{소통하다, 상호작용하다} _____ with him more. (나) <u>이는 다른 기대감은 우리가 형성하는 인상 뿐 아니라 우리의 행동과 관계 형성에까지 영향을 준다는 것을 보여준다.</u>

41. 46)힌트를 참고하여 각 빈칸에 알맞은 단어를 쓰시오.

42. 47)위 글에 주어진 (가) ~ (나)의 한글과 같은 의미를 가지도록, 각각의 주어진 단어들을 알맞게 배열하시오.

(가) one / descriptions / were / group. / guest / before / the / he / students / to / a / spoke / university / of / lecturer / In / study, / given

(나) also / impressions / shows / but / we / form / is / only / not / affect / and / the / relationship / different / which / that / This / formed. / the / behaviour / our / expectations

☑ **다음 글을 읽고 물음에 답하시오.** (2023_고1_3_40번)

To help decide what's ^(위험한, 실패할 수 있는) _____ and what's safe, who's ^(신뢰할 만한, 믿음직한) _____ and who's not, we look for social evidence. (가) 진화론적 관점으로는 무리를 따르는 것은 생존을 전망하는 데 있어 거의 언제나 긍정적이다. If everyone's doing it, it must be a ^(합리적인) _____ thing to do, ^(설명하다) _____ famous psychologist and bestselling writer of ^(영향, 영향력) _____, Robert Cialdini. While we can ^(자주) _____ see this today in product reviews, even ^(미묘한) _____ ^(단서) _____ within the environment can ^(신호를 주다) _____ trustworthiness. Consider this: when you visit a local restaurant, are they busy? Is there a line outside or is it easy to find a seat? ⓐ It is a hassle to wait, but a line can be a powerful cue which the food's tasty, and these seats are in demanding. More often than not, it's good to adopt the practices of those around you.

43. ^(48)힌트를 참고하여 각 빈칸에 알맞은 단어를 쓰시오.

44. ^(49)밑줄 친 ⓐ에서, 어법 혹은 문맥상 어색한 부분을 찾아 올바르게 고쳐 쓰시오.

ⓐ	잘못된 표현		바른 표현
(	) ⇨ (	)
(	) ⇨ (	)

45. ^(50)위 글에 주어진 (가)의 한글과 같은 의미를 가지도록, 각각의 주어진 단어들을 알맞게 배열하시오.

(가) survival. / evolutionary / positive / our / / always / is / following / the / prospects / almost / view, / From / group / an / for / of

☑ **다음 글을 읽고 물음에 답하시오.** (2023_고1_3_41, 42번)

Chess masters shown a chess board in the middle of a game for 5 seconds with 20 to 30 pieces still in play can ^{즉시} _____ ^{재현하다} _____ the position of the pieces from memory. ⓐ <u>Beginners, of course, able to place an only few.</u> Now take the same pieces and place them on the board random and the difference is much reduced. The expert's ^{유리한 점, 이} _____ is only for ^{익숙한} _____ stored in memory. Faced with unfamiliar patterns, even when it ^{포함하다} _____ the same familiar ^{범위, 영토, 영역} _____, the expert's advantage ^{사라지다} _____. (가) 기억에 대한 친숙한 구조에서 오는 유익한 효과는 음악을 포함해 많은 분야에서 관찰되어져 왔다. People with musical training can reproduce short ^{진행, 배열, 순서} _____ of ^{악보} _____ more ^{정확하게} _____ than those with no musical training when notes follow conventional sequences, but the advantage is much ^{감소된} _____ when the notes are ordered randomly. ^{전문지식} _____ also improves memory for sequences of movements. Experienced ballet dancers are able to repeat longer sequences of steps than less experienced dancers, and they can ^{되풀이하다} _____ a sequence of steps making up a routine better than steps ordered randomly. In each case, memory ^{범위, 범주} _____ is increased by the ability to ^{인지하다} _____ familiar sequences and patterns.

46. 51)힌트를 참고하여 각 빈칸에 알맞은 단어를 쓰시오.

47. 52)밑줄 친 ⓐ에서, 어법 혹은 문맥상 어색한 부분을 찾아 올바르게 고쳐 쓰시오.

    ⓐ   잘못된 표현   바른 표현

    (   ) ⇨ (   )

    (   ) ⇨ (   )

    (   ) ⇨ (   )

48. 53)위 글에 주어진 (가)의 한글과 같은 의미를 가지도록, 각각의 주어진 단어들을 알맞게 배열하시오.

(가) familiar / beneficial / been / many / observed / music. / memory / have / of / The / structure / on / effects / types / of / for / expertise, / including

☑ **다음 글을 읽고 물음에 답하시오.** (2023_고1_3_43, 44. 45번)

Once upon a time, there was a king who lived in a beautiful palace. While the king was away, a monster approached the gates of the palace. The monster was so ugly and smelly that the ^{경비병}_____ froze in shock. He passed the guards and sat on the king's ^{왕좌}_____. The guards soon came to their senses, went in, and shouted at the monster, demanding that he ^{내리다}_____ the throne. With each bad word the guards used, the monster grew more ugly and smelly. The guards got even angrier they began to ^{휘두르다}_____ their swords to scare the monster away from the palace. (가) <u>그러나 그는 그냥 계속 커지고 또 커져서, 결국은 온 방을 차지하며 되었다.</u> He grew more ugly and smelly than ever. Eventually the king returned. He was wise and kind and saw what was happening. He knew what to do. He smiled and said to the monster, Welcome to my palace! He asked the monster if he wanted a cup of coffee. The monster began to grow smaller as he drank the coffee. The king offered him some take-out pizza and fries. The guards ^{즉시}_____ called for pizza. The monster continued to get smaller with the king's kind gestures. He then offered the monster a full body massage. As the guards helped with the relaxing massage, the monster became tiny. With another act of kindness to the monster, he just disappeared.

49. ⁵⁴⁾힌트를 참고하여 각 빈칸에 알맞은 단어를 쓰시오.

50. ⁵⁵⁾위 글에 주어진 (가)의 한글과 같은 의미를 가지도록, 각각의 주어진 단어들을 알맞게 배열하시오.

(가) bigger, / grew / up / taking / and / eventually / he / whole / the / room. / bigger / But / just

보듬영어

정답

WORK BOOK

———

2023년 고1 3월 모의고사 내신대비용 WorkBook & 변형문제

Answers

1) whom
2) that
3) to
4) equipment
5) falling
6) playing
7) repaired
8) native
9) watched
10) walk
11) to turn
12) sniffing
13) following
14) that
15) a grizzly bear
16) motivation
17) any
18) maintain
19) characterised
20) confident
21) demanding
22) cope
23) the most demanding task
24) thought
25) take
26) adopt
27) its
28) pushed
29) removed
30) work
31) producing
32) 목적격 관계대명사 that/which
33) physical
34) avoid
35) working
36) puts
37) sedentary
38) approach
39) same
40) the rubber-stamp approach; approaching every course, test, or learning task the same way
41) that
42) flexible
43) different
44) them
45) that
46) differently
47) what
48) how
49) improved
50) given
51) transport
52) it
53) opened
54) came
55) possible
56) Success
57) intended
58) rewarded
59) 당신이 잘하는 무언가
60) doing
61) enjoying
62) that
63) that
64) breathe
65) that
66) left
67) what
68) the
69) continued
70) was
71) was
72) that
73) Unlike
74) enjoying
75) persuade
76) to try
77) working
78) nonetheless
79) is
80) Physically
81) made
82) deformed
83) resemble
84) them
85) animated
86) with
87) make
88) appealing
89) enlarged
90) deformed
91) affluent
92) spread
93) which
94) that
95) deliver
96) destroyed
97) 동격의 접속사
98) production
99) its
100) differ
101) quickly
102) depends
103) it
104) sizable enough
105) found
106) flying
107) that
108) comes
109) what
110) how
111) estimating
112) needed
113) Give
114) fitting
115) if
116) in
117) that
118) that
119) explain
120) principle
121) evolve
122) long enough
123) was
124) refined
125) was turned
126) much
127) how
128) refine
129) bring
130) concluded
131) affects
132) what
133) and
134) them
135) arises
136) praying
137) told
138) shown
139) wandered
140) settle
141) to organize
142) themselves
143) 목적격 관계대명사 that/which
144) to work
145) By
146) called
147) reaches
148) its

149) During
150) themselves
151) which
152) depends
153) rapidly
154) because
155) break
156) the other
157) released
158) with
159) a
160) which
161) is converted
162) that
163) which
164) were given
165) containing
166) the other
167) which
168) were asked
169) expected
170) tended
171) that
172) affect
173) following
174) sensible
175) explains
176) it
177) adopt
178) shown
179) few
180) them
181) Faced
182) disappears
183) beneficial
184) been observed
185) sequences
186) reduced
187) Experienced
188) making
189) is increased
190) While
191) approached
192) that
193) demanding
194) used
195) taking
196) happening
197) if
198) continued
199) relaxing
200) disappeared

Prac 1 Answers

1) whom
2) that
3) to
4) equipment
5) falling
6) playing
7) repaired
8) native
9) watched
10) walk
11) to turn
12) sniffing
13) following
14) that
15) a grizzly bear
16) motivation
17) any
18) maintain
19) characterised
20) confident
21) demanding
22) cope
23) the most demanding task
24) thought
25) take
26) adopt
27) its
28) pushed
29) removed
30) work
31) producing
32) 목적격 관계대명사 that/which
33) physical
34) avoid
35) working
36) puts
37) sedentary
38) approach
39) same
40) the rubber-stamp approach; approaching every course, test, or learning task the same way
41) that
42) flexible
43) different
44) them
45) that
46) differently
47) what
48) how
49) improved
50) given
51) transport
52) it
53) opened
54) came
55) possible
56) Success
57) intended
58) rewarded
59) 당신이 잘하는 무언가
60) doing
61) enjoying
62) that
63) that
64) breathe
65) that
66) left
67) what
68) the
69) continued
70) was

71) was
72) that
73) Unlike
74) enjoying
75) persuade
76) to try
77) working
78) nonetheless
79) is
80) Physically
81) made
82) deformed
83) resemble
84) them
85) animated
86) with
87) make
88) appealing
89) enlarged
90) deformed
91) affluent
92) spread
93) which
94) that
95) deliver
96) destroyed
97) 동격의 접속사
98) production
99) its
100) differ
101) quickly
102) depends
103) it
104) sizable enough
105) found
106) flying
107) that
108) comes
109) what
110) how
111) estimating
112) needed
113) Give
114) fitting
115) if
116) in
117) that
118) that
119) explain
120) principle
121) evolve
122) long enough
123) was
124) refined
125) was turned
126) much
127) how
128) refine
129) bring
130) concluded
131) affects
132) what
133) and
134) them
135) arises
136) praying
137) told
138) shown
139) wandered
140) settle
141) to organize
142) themselves
143) 목적격 관계대명사 that/which
144) to work
145) By
146) called
147) reaches

148) its
149) During
150) themselves
151) which
152) depends
153) rapidly
154) because
155) break
156) the other
157) released
158) with
159) a
160) which
161) is converted
162) that
163) which
164) were given
165) containing
166) the other
167) which
168) were asked
169) expected
170) tended
171) that
172) affect
173) following
174) sensible
175) explains
176) it
177) adopt
178) shown
179) few
180) them
181) Faced
182) disappears
183) beneficial
184) been observed
185) sequences
186) reduced
187) Experienced
188) making
189) is increased
190) While
191) approached
192) that
193) demanding
194) used
195) taking
196) happening
197) if
198) continued
199) relaxing
200) disappeared

Answers

1) resident
2) attention
3) equipment
4) facilities
5) since
6) repaired?
7) appreciate
8) habitat.
9) sniffing
10) scent
11) issue
12) motivation
13) difficult
14) maintain
15) characterised
16) alertness.
17) demanding
18) peaks
19) observe
20) different.
21) technology,
22) livelihoods
23) producing
24) physical
25) chronic
26) Technology
27) education
28) low-tech
29) divorce
30) sedentary
31) starting
32) approach
33) funeral?
34) appropriate
35) occasions
36) Skillful
37) flexible
38) strategies
39) multiple-choice
40) economic
41) wage
42) improved.
43) given
44) transport
45) revolution
46) seaside
47) railways
48) possible
49) arrival
50) transport
51) tourism
52) intended
53) comfortable
54) rewarded
55) enjoying
56) breathe
57) superhuman
58) employment
59) locked
60) well-paying
61) shows
62) decrease
63) slightly
64) steadily
65) except
66) number
67) trousers
68) enjoying
69) career
70) wildlife
71) persuade
72) working

73) Eventually,
74) noticeable
75) projected
76) deformed
77) resemble
78) humanlike
79) deformed
80) animated
81) However,
82) appropriate
83) facial
84) appealing,
85) enlarged
86) philosophical
87) affluent,
88) competitive,
89) geographically
90) clients,
91) reasonable
92) essential
93) modernization
94) marketing
95) desire
96) diverse
97) biological
98) overcome
99) recovery
100) easier
101) lengthen
102) sizable
103) performance
104) perform
105) found
106) tougher
107) confidence
108) achieving
109) important
110) Over-optimism
111) estimating
112) experience
113) expected.
114) significant
115) available.
116) gear
117) longer
118) spare
119) discovers
120) from
121) do
122) Biologists
123) evolutionary
124) principle
125) evolve
126) run
127) which
128) thrive
129) pass
130) finished
131) started
132) idea
133) refined
134) perfected
135) reality
136) pictured
137) designs
138) process
139) idea
140) future
141) refine
142) perfect
143) vision
144) existence
145) concluded
146) affects
147) change
148) interpret
149) sympathies

150) conflict
151) different
152) outcome
153) viewpoint
154) shown
155) viewpoint
156) wandered
157) farming
158) settle
159) larger
160) communities
161) allowed
162) organize
163) efficiently
164) divide
165) dwellers
166) together
167) faster
168) share
169) more
170) same
171) processes
172) form
173) cools
174) reaches
175) trapped
176) lose
177) closer
178) combine
179) compounds
180) atoms
181) compounds
182) arrange
183) orderly
184) repeating
185) present
186) determine
187) form
188) crystals
189) rapidly
190) cools
191) cools
192) large
193) unaided
194) larger
195) rapidly
196) small
197) carbohydrates
198) Complex
199) carbohydrates
200) complex
201) compounds
202) break
203) trap
204) released
205) provide
206) simple
207) hold
208) from
209) breaks
210) quickly
211) converted
212) stored
213) mistaken
214) assumption
215) automatically
216) with
217) descriptions
218) received
219) containing
220) led
221) which
222) impressions
223) differences
224) formed
225) original
226) expected

227) interact
228) expectations
229) affect
230) impressions
231) behaviour
232) relationship
233) risky
234) safe
235) trustworthy
236) *social*
237) evolutionary
238) positive
239) prospects
240) survival
241) sensible
242) subtler
243) cues
244) trustworthiness
245) hassle
246) powerful
247) cue
248) demand
249) adopt
250) practices
251) shown
252) reproduce
253) memory
254) randomly
255) difference
256) reduced
257) advantage
258) familiar
259) patterns
260) previously
261) stored
262) Faced
263) unfamiliar
264) involves
265) familiar
266) domain
267) disappears
268) beneficial
269) familiar
270) structure
271) memory
272) observed
273) expertise
274) reproduce
275) sequences
276) notation
277) accurately
278) usual
279) sequences
280) ordered
281) randomly
282) Expertise
283) improves
284) memory
285) repeat
286) ordered
287) randomly
288) increased
289) familiar
290) approached
291) froze
292) throne
293) demanding
294) used
295) brandish
296) if
297) offered
298) offered
299) relaxing
300) kindness

Answer Keys

Prac 2 Answers

1) resident
2) attention
3) equipment
4) facilities
5) since
6) repaired?
7) appreciate
8) habitat.
9) sniffing
10) scent
11) issue
12) motivation
13) difficult
14) maintain
15) characterised
16) alertness.
17) demanding
18) peaks
19) observe
20) different.
21) technology,
22) livelihoods
23) producing
24) physical
25) chronic
26) Technology
27) education
28) low-tech
29) divorce
30) sedentary
31) starting
32) approach
33) funeral?
34) appropriate
35) occasions
36) Skillful
37) flexible
38) strategies
39) multiple-choice
40) economic
41) wage
42) improved.
43) given
44) transport
45) revolution
46) seaside
47) railways
48) possible
49) arrival
50) transport
51) tourism
52) intended
53) comfortable
54) rewarded
55) enjoying
56) breathe
57) superhuman
58) employment
59) locked
60) well-paying
61) shows
62) decrease
63) slightly
64) steadily
65) except
66) number
67) trousers
68) enjoying
69) career
70) wildlife
71) persuade
72) working
73) Eventually,
74) noticeable
75) projected
76) deformed
77) resemble
78) humanlike
79) deformed
80) animated
81) However,
82) appropriate
83) facial
84) appealing,
85) enlarged
86) philosophical
87) affluent,
88) competitive,
89) geographically
90) clients,
91) reasonable
92) essential
93) modernization
94) marketing
95) desire
96) diverse
97) biological
98) overcome
99) recovery
100) easier
101) lengthen
102) sizable
103) performance
104) perform
105) found
106) tougher
107) confidence
108) achieving
109) important
110) Over-optimism
111) estimating
112) experience
113) expected.
114) significant
115) available.
116) gear
117) longer
118) spare
119) discovers
120) from
121) do
122) Biologists
123) evolutionary
124) principle
125) evolve
126) run
127) which
128) thrive
129) pass
130) finished
131) started
132) idea
133) refined
134) perfected
135) reality
136) pictured
137) designs
138) process
139) idea
140) future
141) refine
142) perfect
143) vision
144) existence
145) concluded
146) affects
147) change
148) interpret
149) sympathies

150) conflict
151) different
152) outcome
153) viewpoint
154) shown
155) viewpoint
156) wandered
157) farming
158) settle
159) larger
160) communities
161) allowed
162) organize
163) efficiently
164) divide
165) dwellers
166) together
167) faster
168) share
169) more
170) same
171) processes
172) form
173) cools
174) reaches
175) trapped
176) lose
177) closer
178) combine
179) compounds
180) atoms
181) compounds
182) arrange
183) orderly
184) repeating
185) present
186) determine
187) form
188) crystals
189) rapidly
190) cools
191) cools
192) large
193) unaided
194) larger
195) rapidly
196) small
197) carbohydrates
198) Complex
199) carbohydrates
200) complex
201) compounds
202) break
203) trap
204) released
205) provide
206) simple
207) hold
208) from
209) breaks
210) quickly
211) converted
212) stored
213) mistaken
214) assumption
215) automatically
216) with
217) descriptions
218) received
219) containing
220) led
221) which
222) impressions
223) differences
224) formed
225) original
226) expected

227) interact
228) expectations
229) affect
230) impressions
231) behaviour
232) relationship
233) risky
234) safe
235) trustworthy
236) *social*
237) evolutionary
238) positive
239) prospects
240) survival
241) sensible
242) subtler
243) cues
244) trustworthiness
245) hassle
246) powerful
247) cue
248) demand
249) adopt
250) practices
251) shown
252) reproduce
253) memory
254) randomly
255) difference
256) reduced
257) advantage
258) familiar
259) patterns
260) previously
261) stored
262) Faced
263) unfamiliar
264) involves
265) familiar
266) domain
267) disappears
268) beneficial
269) familiar
270) structure
271) memory
272) observed
273) expertise
274) reproduce
275) sequences
276) notation
277) accurately
278) usual
279) sequences
280) ordered
281) randomly
282) Expertise
283) improves
284) memory
285) repeat
286) ordered
287) randomly
288) increased
289) familiar
290) approached
291) froze
292) throne
293) demanding
294) used
295) brandish
296) if
297) offered
298) offered
299) relaxing
300) kindness

Answer Keys

Quiz 1 Answers

1) ⑤
2) ②
3) ④
4) ⑤
5) ③
6) ④
7) ④
8) ②
9) ③
10) ④
11) ②
12) ④
13) ④
14) ⑤
15) ④
16) ④
17) ④
18) ⑤
19) ②
20) ④
21) ④
22) ⑤
23) ④
24) ③
25) ⑤
26) ④
27) ④
28) (C)-(B)-(A)-(D)
29) (A)-(C)-(D)-(B)
30) (B)-(A)-(D)-(C)-(E)
31) (C)-(E)-(B)-(A)-(D)
32) (C)-(A)-(D)-(B)
33) (A)-(B)-(D)-(C)
34) (D)-(B)-(A)-(C)
35) (C)-(B)-(A)
36) (D)-(A)-(C)-(B)
37) (A)-(C)-(B)
38) (C)-(A)-(B)
39) (D)-(A)-(B)-(C)
40) (B)-(A)-(C)
41) (A)-(C)-(B)
42) (D)-(C)-(A)-(B)
43) (C)-(B)-(D)-(A)
44) (C)-(A)-(B)
45) (C)-(A)-(B)
46) (B)-(E)-(D)-(A)-(C)
47) (C)-(B)-(A)-(D)
48) (C)-(A)-(D)-(B)
49) (C)-(A)-(B)-(E)-(D)

Quiz 2 Answers

1)
[정답] ⑤
[해설]
repairing ⇨ repaired

2)
[정답] ②
[해설]
what ⇨ that

3)

[정답] ②
[해설]
with ⇨ with them

4)
[정답] ④
[해설]
integration ⇨ divorce

5)
[정답] ②
[해설]
what ⇨ that

6)
[정답] ②
[해설]
industrious ⇨ industrial

7)
[정답] ②
[해설]
awarded ⇨ rewarded

8)
[정답] ④
[해설]
were ⇨ was

9)
[정답] ②
[해설]
trying ⇨ try

10)
[정답] ④
[해설]
making ⇨ make

11)
[정답] ①
[해설]
develop ⇨ to develop

12)
[정답] ⑤
[해설]
easier ⇨ tougher

13)
[정답] ③
[해설]
when ⇨ that

14)
[정답] ④
[해설]

collapse ⇨ thrive

15)
[정답] ③
[해설]
object ⇨ idea

16)
[정답] ⑤
[해설]
showing ⇨ shown

17)
[정답] ②
[해설]
organize ⇨ to organize

18)
[정답] ②
[해설]
gain ⇨ lose

19)
[정답] ①
[해설]
easy ⇨ difficult

20)
[정답] ③
[해설]
which ⇨ after which

21)
[정답] ②
[해설]
negative ⇨ positive

22)
[정답] ①
[해설]
replenish ⇨ reproduce

23)
[정답] ⑤
[해설]
took ⇨ taking

Quiz 3 **Answers**

1)
[정답] ⑤ ⓒ, ⓓ, ⓔ, ⓖ
[해설]
ⓒ damaging ⇨ damaged
ⓓ is ⇨ are
ⓔ were ⇨ have been
ⓖ repairing ⇨ repaired

2)
[정답] ③ ⓔ, ⓕ
[해설]
ⓔ pleasure ⇨ survival
ⓕ simulation ⇨ motivation

3)
[정답] ⑤ ⓑ, ⓒ, ⓓ, ⓔ
[해설]
ⓑ flexible ⇨ constant
ⓒ demanded ⇨ demanding
ⓓ with ⇨ with them
ⓔ you ⇨ yourself

4)
[정답] ⑤ ⓕ, ⓗ, ⓙ, ⓚ
[해설]
ⓕ mess ⇨ mass
ⓗ sick ⇨ seek
ⓙ integration ⇨ divorce
ⓚ rudimentary ⇨ sedentary

5)
[정답] ④ ⓑ, ⓒ, ⓓ, ⓗ
[해설]
ⓑ that ⇨ what
ⓒ what ⇨ that
ⓓ classes ⇨ class
ⓗ how ⇨ what

6)
[정답] ② ⓐ, ⓔ
[해설]
ⓐ retreated ⇨ improved
ⓔ coming ⇨ came

7)
[정답] ③ ⓐ, ⓑ, ⓓ, ⓖ
[해설]
ⓐ pretended ⇨ intended
ⓑ revolutionary ⇨ comfortable
ⓓ to do ⇨ doing
ⓖ which ⇨ that

8)
[정답] ⑤ ⓑ, ⓒ, ⓕ, ⓗ
[해설]
ⓑ birth ⇨ births
ⓒ were ⇨ was
ⓕ while ⇨ during
ⓗ those ⇨ that

9)
[정답] ③ ⓐ, ⓑ, ⓓ

[해설]
ⓐ to enjoy ⇨ enjoying
ⓑ trying ⇨ try
ⓓ excited ⇨ exciting

10)
[정답] ③ ⓑ, ⓒ, ⓖ
[해설]
ⓑ are ⇨ is
ⓒ Verbally ⇨ Physically
ⓖ resemble with ⇨ resemble

11)
[정답] ④ ⓙ, ⓜ, ⓞ
[해설]
ⓙ bought ⇨ wanted
ⓜ demand ⇨ production
ⓞ productions ⇨ needs

12)
[정답] ③ ⓑ, ⓕ, ⓙ
[해설]
ⓑ overwhelm ⇨ overcome
ⓕ flied ⇨ flying
ⓙ easier ⇨ tougher

13)
[정답] ⑤ ⓑ, ⓕ, ⓖ, ⓘ
[해설]
ⓑ Over-pessimism ⇨ Over-optimism
ⓕ when ⇨ that
ⓖ minimum ⇨ significant
ⓘ long ⇨ short

14)
[정답] ④ ⓓ, ⓗ
[해설]
ⓓ revolutionary ⇨ evolutionary
ⓗ collapse ⇨ thrive

15)
[정답] ④ ⓑ, ⓚ
[해설]
ⓑ finished ⇨ started
ⓚ excluded ⇨ concluded

16)
[정답] ③ ⓐ, ⓑ, ⓔ
[해설]
ⓐ affect ⇨ affects
ⓑ If you change ⇨ Change
ⓔ raises ⇨ arises

17)
[정답] ⑤ ⓐ, ⓒ, ⓕ, ⓗ
[해설]

ⓐ wondered ⇨ wandered
ⓒ smaller ⇨ larger
ⓕ During ⇨ While
ⓗ On the other hand ⇨ For example

18)
[정답] ④ ⓐ, ⓘ, ⓜ, ⓟ
[해설]
ⓐ progresses ⇨ processes
ⓘ order ⇨ orderly
ⓜ rapid ⇨ rapidly
ⓟ can ⇨ can't

19)
[정답] ③ ⓑ, ⓒ, ⓓ
[해설]
ⓑ release ⇨ trap
ⓒ relieved ⇨ released
ⓓ for ⇨ with

20)
[정답] ① ⓐ, ⓔ
[해설]
ⓐ organized ⇨ mistaken
ⓔ prescription ⇨ descriptions

21)
[정답] ③ ⓐ, ⓕ, ⓖ
[해설]
ⓐ physical ⇨ social
ⓕ meaningless ⇨ powerful
ⓖ adapt to ⇨ adopt

22)
[정답] ④ ⓑ, ⓗ, ⓜ, ⓝ
[해설]
ⓑ replenish ⇨ reproduce
ⓗ is disappeared ⇨ disappears
ⓜ less ⇨ much
ⓝ shorter ⇨ longer

23)
[정답] ⑤ ⓒ, ⓓ, ⓔ, ⓕ
[해설]
ⓒ which ⇨ that
ⓓ what ⇨ that
ⓔ words ⇨ word
ⓕ took ⇨ taking

Quiz 4 Answers

1)
[정답]
② favor ⇨ need
⑤ were ⇨ have been

⑥ are playing ⇨ playing

2)

[정답]

① inhabitant ⇨ habitat

③ what ⇨ that

⑥ simulation ⇨ motivation

3)

[정답]

② flexible ⇨ constant

③ demanded ⇨ demanding

④ with ⇨ with them

⑥ which ⇨ when

⑦ similar ⇨ different

4)

[정답]

② pushing ⇨ pushed

③ process ⇨ progress

④ love ⇨ love for

⑤ safe ⇨ dangerous

⑦ accept ⇨ avoid

⑧ sick ⇨ seek

⑨ worked ⇨ working

⑩ integration ⇨ divorce

⑪ rudimentary ⇨ sedentary

5)

[정답]

② that ⇨ what

⑤ inflexible ⇨ flexible

⑦ different ⇨ differently

6)

[정답]

③ industrious ⇨ industrial

7)

[정답]

⑦ which ⇨ that

⑪ that ⇨ what

8)

[정답]

① a ⇨ the

② birth ⇨ births

③ were ⇨ was

④ death ⇨ deaths

⑤ those ⇨ that

⑥ while ⇨ during

⑦ were ⇨ was

⑧ those ⇨ that

9)

[정답]

③ work ⇨ working

④ excited ⇨ exciting

10)

[정답]

③ Verbally ⇨ Physically

⑦ resemble with ⇨ resemble

⑩ used to ⇨ is used to

⑪ making ⇨ make

⑫ appealed ⇨ appealing

11)

[정답]

③ fluent ⇨ affluent

⑤ while ⇨ during

⑫ which ⇨ that

12)

[정답]

② overwhelm ⇨ overcome

③ discovery ⇨ recovery

④ shorten ⇨ lengthen

⑤ lengthen ⇨ shorten

⑥ flied ⇨ flying

⑦ worse ⇨ better

⑧ flied ⇨ flying

⑨ which ⇨ that

⑩ easier ⇨ tougher

13)

[정답]

③ that ⇨ what

⑦ minimum ⇨ significant

⑧ give ⇨ gear

⑨ long ⇨ short

14)

[정답]

① recovers ⇨ discovers

② what ⇨ that

③ from which ⇨ that

⑤ principal ⇨ principle

⑥ revolve ⇨ evolve

⑦ slowest ⇨ fastest

⑧ collapse ⇨ thrive

⑨ stop ⇨ pass on

15)

[정답]

① started ⇨ finished

② finished ⇨ started

④ after ⇨ before

⑤ philosophical ⇨ physical

⑦ progress ⇨ process

⑪ excluded ⇨ concluded

16)

[정답]
⑤ raises ⇨ arises

17)

[정답]
⑤ organize ⇨ to organize
⑦ doing ⇨ do
⑧ On the other hand ⇨ For example

18)

[정답]
① progresses ⇨ processes
② which called ⇨ called
③ arrives ⇨ reaches
④ gain ⇨ lose
⑤ farther ⇨ closer
⑥ entities ⇨ compounds
⑦ While ⇨ During
⑨ order ⇨ orderly
⑩ absent ⇨ present
⑪ that ⇨ which
⑫ deform ⇨ form
⑬ rapid ⇨ rapidly
⑭ why ⇨ because
⑮ large ⇨ small
⑯ can ⇨ can't

19)

[정답]
④ for ⇨ with
⑦ little ⇨ few

20)

[정답]
① organized ⇨ mistaken
② consumption ⇨ assumption
③ which ⇨ that
④ goes ⇨ go
⑤ prescription ⇨ descriptions
⑥ inscription ⇨ description
⑨ asked ⇨ were asked
⑫ transact ⇨ interact

21)

[정답]
③ negative ⇨ positive
④ sensitive ⇨ sensible
⑤ bolder ⇨ subtler
⑥ meaningless ⇨ powerful

22)

[정답]
① was shown ⇨ shown
② replenish ⇨ reproduce

③ little ⇨ few
④ increased ⇨ reduced
⑤ novel ⇨ familiar
⑥ familiar ⇨ unfamiliar
⑦ pattern ⇨ domain
⑧ is disappeared ⇨ disappears
⑨ observing ⇨ observed
⑩ produce ⇨ reproduce
⑪ rotation ⇨ notation
⑭ shorter ⇨ longer
⑮ more ⇨ less
⑯ reduced ⇨ increased

23)

[정답]
② approached to ⇨ approached
③ which ⇨ that
④ what ⇨ that
⑤ words ⇨ word
⑥ took ⇨ taking
⑦ that ⇨ what
⑧ With ⇨ As

Quiz 5 **Answers**

1) 필요로 하는 - in need of // 장비,설비 - equipment // 시설 - facilities // 즉각적인 - immediate
2) 천연의 - native // 서식지 - habitat // 향기 - scent // 경험 - experience // 생존 - survival // 동기 - motivation
3)
   (가) He stopped every once in a while to turn his head about, sniffing deeply
4) 특성화하다 - characterized // 정점 - peaks // 기민함 - alertness // 성취하다 - achieve // 자신감 넘치는 - confident
5)
   ⓐ
   think ⇨ thought
   observing ⇨ to observe
6)
   (가) if you schedule your most demanding tasks at times when you are best able to cope with them
7) 받아들이다 - adopt // 생계수단 - livelihoods // 장애 - disability // 만성의 - chronic // 질환 - disease // 이혼 - divorce // 물론 - Indeed // 앉아있는 경향의 - sedentary // 위험요소 - risk
8)
   ⓐ
   pushed aside ⇨ been pushed aside
   been removed ⇨ removed
   ⓑ
   produce ⇨ producing
   no love ⇨ no love for
9)
   (가) {At the same time, mass education and media

train humans to avoid low-tech physical work, to seek jobs working in the digital world

10) 접근하다 - approach // 연미복 - tuxedo // 장례식 - funeral // 수영복 - bathing suit // 종교의식,예배 - religious services // 숙련된 - Skillful // 유연한 - flexible // 전략 - strategies // 다지선다 시험 - multiple-choice tests // 논술형시험 - essay tests

11)

(가) And they not only know what to do, but they also know how to do it

12) 서서히 - Gradually // 휴식 시간 - time off // 산업혁명 - industrial revolution // 철도 - Railways // 세기 - century // 철도 - railway

13)

(가) As the social and economic situation of countries got better, wage levels and working conditions improved

(나) Later, the arrival of air transport opened up more of the world and led to tourism growth

14) 의도된 - intended // 경로 - path // 틀에 박힌 생활 - rut // 틀에 박힌 생활 - rut // 틀에 박힌 생활 - rut // 미끄러운 - slippery // 초인적인 - superhuman // 노력, 수고 - effort // 빠져나오다 - climb out // 효과적으로 - effectively // 갇힌,끼인 - stuck

15)
ⓐ
be well rewarded ⇨ (are) well rewarded
to be done it ⇨ for doing it
ⓑ
felt ⇨ feeling
ultimate ⇨ ultimately

16)

(가) And it's a situation that many working people worry they're in now

17) 감소하다 - decrease // ~동안 - throughout // 근소하게 - slightly // 증가하다 - increased // 지속적으로 - steadily // ~를 제외하고 - except

18) ~와 달리 - Unlike // 바지 - trousers // 모험적인 - adventurous // 활동 - activities // 직업, 경력 - career // 야생 - wildlife // 자동차 판매원 - car dealer // 그럼에도 불구하고 - nonetheless // 마침내 - Eventually

19)

(가) In order to persuade her to try a slightly safer activity, Lilian's dad bought her a car

20) 주목할 만한 - noticeable // 적합한 - appropriate // 표현 - expression

21)
ⓐ
to deform ⇨ deformed
resembled ⇨ to resemble

22)

(가) A general strategy that is used to make the animal characters more emotionally appealing, both to children and adults, is to give them enlarged and deformed childlike features

23) 철학적 - philosophical // 변화 - shift // 풍부한 - affluent // 경쟁적인 - competitive // 지리적으로 - geographically // 확산하다 - spread out // 마찬가지로

- equally // 필수적인, 중요한 - essential // 다양한 - diverse // 복잡한 - complex

24)

(가) This forced business to develop closer relations with buyers and clients, which in turn made business realize that it was not enough to produce a quality product at a reasonable price

(나) The modernization of society led to a marketing revolution that destroyed the view that production would create its own demand

25) 일반적으로 - Generally // 늘이다 - lengthen // 줄이다 - shorten // 연구 - Studies // 상당히 - significantly

26)
ⓐ
differ from ⇨ differ in
quick ⇨ quickly
overcoming ⇨ to overcome
depends of ⇨ depends on

27)

(가) This east-west difference in jet lag is sizable enough to have an impact on the performance of sports teams

(나) A more recent study of more than 46,000 Major League Baseball games found additional evidence that eastward travel is tougher than westward travel

28) 과도한 낙관주의 - Over-optimism // 기간 - time frame // 중요한 - significant

29)
ⓐ
to fit ⇨ to fitting
ⓑ
to try ⇨ in trying
a such task ⇨ such a task
between ⇨ in between

30)

(가) If you want the confidence that comes from achieving what you set out to do each day, then it's important to understand how long things are going to take

31) 발견하다, 깨닫다 - discovers // 생물학자 - Biologists // 진화 - evolutionary // 원칙 - principle // 진화하다 - evolve // 번성하다, 번창하다 - thrive // 유전자 - genes

32) 과정 - process

33)

(가) Long before the idea was turned into a physical reality, the mind had clearly pictured the finished product

34) 과정 - process

35)
ⓐ
working on harmony ⇨ working in harmony
bring ⇨ bring into
conclude ⇨ concluded

36)

(가) Long before the idea was turned into a physical reality, the mind had clearly pictured the finished product

37) 영향을 주다 - affects // 공감 - sympathies // 갈등 -

conflict // 일어나다 - arises // 결과 - outcome // 시각 - viewpoint

38)

(가) If we look at the events through another character's eyes, we will interpret them differently

39) 헤매다 - wandered // ~를 찾아서 - in search of // 정착하다 - settle down // 그 결과 - As a result // 작물 - crops // 거주인 - dwellers

40)

ⓐ

organizing ⇨ to organize

efficient ⇨ efficiently

41) 형성하다, 만들다 - form // 광물 - minerals // 갇힌 - trapped // 원자 - atoms // 결합하다 - combine // 화합물 - compounds

42) 형성하다, 만들다 - form // 광물 - minerals // 갇힌 - trapped // 원자 - atoms // 결합하다 - combine // 화합물 - compounds // 성분 - elements // 정의하다, 결정하다 - determine // 결정 - crystals // 빠르게 - rapidly // 개별적인 - individual

43)

(가) During this process, atoms of the different compounds arrange themselves into orderly, repeating patterns

(나) When magma cools slowly, the crystals that form are generally large enough to see with the unaided eye.

44) 탄수화물 - carbohydrates // 복합 탄수화물 - Complex carbohydrates // 쪼개지다, 분해되다 - break down // 영양소 - nutrients // 방출하다 - released // 연료 - fuel // 저장된 - stored

45)

(가) Because their structure is not complex, they are easy to break down and hold few nutrients for your body other than the sugars from which they are made.

46) 잘못된 - mistaken // 추정 - assumption // 자동적으로 - automatically // 포함하는 - containing // 토론 - discussion // 인상 - impressions // 소통하다, 상호작용하다 - interact

47)

(가) In one study, university students were given descriptions of a guest lecturer before he spoke to the group.

(나) This shows that different expectations not only affect the impressions we form but also our behavior and the relationship which is formed.

48) 위험한, 실패할 수 있는 - risky // 신뢰할 만한, 믿음직한 - trustworthy // 합리적인 - sensible // 설명하다 - explains // 영향, 영향력 - Influence // 자주 - frequently // 미묘한 - subtler // 단서 - cues // 신호를 주다 - signal

49)

ⓐ

which ⇨ that

on demand ⇨ in demand

50)

(가) From an evolutionary view, following the group is almost always positive for our prospects of survival.

51) 즉시 - immediately // 재현하다 - reproduce // 유리한 점, 이 - advantage // 익숙한 - familiar) patterns those <앞서서 // 포함하다 - involves // 범위, 영토, 영역 - domain // 사라지다 - disappears // 진행, 배열, 순서 - sequences // 악보 - musical notation // 정확하게 - accurately // 감소된 - reduced // 전문지식 - Expertise // 되풀이하다 - repeat // 범위, 범주 - range // 인지하다 - recognize

52)

ⓐ

able to ⇨ are able to

an only few ⇨ only a few

random ⇨ randomly

53)

(가) The beneficial effects of familiar structure on memory have been observed for many types of expertise, including music.

54) 경비병 - guards // 왕좌 - throne // 내리다 - get off // 휘두르다 - brandish // 즉시 - immediately

55)

(가) But he just grew bigger and bigger, eventually taking up the whole room